TILES & STYLES
JUGENDSTIL & SECESSION

Art Nouveau and Arts & Crafts Design in German and
Central European Decorative Tiles, 1895-1935

KEN FORSTER

Schiffer Publishing Ltd

4880 Lower Valley Road • Atglen, PA 19310

This book is dedicated to the memory of Eugene Reynolds –

"There's not a bonnie flower that springs
By fountain, shaw, or green;
There's not a bonnie bird that sings,
But minds me o' my Gene."
(With apologies to Robert Burns)

– and, in remembrance also of Andy Marton, honors the friendship and support of my brothers and sisters at the Dulles Triangles in Reston, Virginia.

CONTENTS

ACKNOWLEDGMENTS
and Credits

When I first embarked on the documentation of this subject – and the research required for the task – I did not realize how much I would learn from the composition of it. Though I had spent almost forty years studying, buying, selling, and collecting items of interest in the fields of Arts & Crafts design, Art Nouveau, Jugendstil, and Secession (in its various manifestations), I had not properly ordered in my own mind the similarities, contrasts, and differences of the four style categories, nor had I adequately recognized the specific influences transferred between them. Also, previously, I had not realized that – in spite of the fact that early pundits of late nineteenth and early twentieth century design stressed the revolutionary character of the new styles insisted upon by proponents in Britain and Continental Europe – the ogres of Historicism and Eclecticism were never satisfactorily banished.

Over the years, I extended my initial interest in the Arts and Crafts Movement and Franco-Belgian Art Nouveau to include the adoption and adaptation of aspects of these styles spreading under various names throughout Europe and even beyond. This resulted in a study of historical design of the period that was remarkably interesting, especially since enthusiasts and detractors expressed vehemently opposing opinions on matters of style. Whereas French and Belgian innovators considered what they knew of the English style to be conservative and staid, British Arts & Crafts proponents derided the "downright ludicrous," "loathsome," "degenerate" character of the design influence across the Channel. However, with the benefit of increased commercial experience over the years and having considered the opinions of customers,

collectors, dealers, other colleagues, and friends in Europe and the United States, I rationalized that the divergent characteristics separating the styles – as well as the principal similarities shared by them – are indeed evident, at least in the larger view. Artists, designers, and proponents of disparate backgrounds in diverse areas of Europe not only differed in their personal tastes, regional sensibilities, and particular traditions but also, with varying degrees of enthusiasm, enjoyed lively, sometimes unbridled imaginations or exercised preferences for disciplined, constructive simplicity.

At first with early contemporaries, including John Jesse, Dan Klein, and Adrian Tilbrook in Europe and Martin Eidelberg in the United States, I researched the development of the appropriate historical trends that produced the objects of applied art that were beginning to be collected from the 1960s on. Then, with a small cadre of enthusiasts in the United States, I shared a growing interest in acquiring a knowledge of and familiarity with a design and manufacture implicit in a sphere of interest nurtured later by tile collectors, dealers, and others from the 1980s into the twenty-first century. Finally, in the 1990s, my road led me to the burgeoning fascination – particularly in England, France, Belgium, and Germany – with the roles played by Arts & Crafts, Art Nouveau, Jugendstil, and Secession in the design of wall, floor, stove, and other tiles, dating from the end of the nineteenth century and afterward, in those countries and other areas of Europe.

My association with such collectors and dealers in Europe and South America as Gerhard Westermeier, Wolfgang König, Dirk Hämke, Heinz Baur, Mark Van Veen, Manfred Neumann, Dr. Dirk

Wegner, Joachim Hänold, Ulrich Hamburg, Ernst Wasic, Eleni Korani, Anna Bujovics, Ruth Werlange de Couto, Flavio Casale, Nicolas Malosetti, and Marcos Obelar benefited me greatly, along with the encouragement of colleagues, customers, and collecting friends, and to all of them I offer my lasting gratitude. Added to their contributions must be those made by the many dealers, whose eBay advertisements familarized me with a multitude of Jugendstil tiles, ascribed origins and posited attributions, and contained other essential information that was otherwise not often available.

Other support of my endeavor was rendered by friends too numerous to list here but special mention must be made of Wolfgang König, Rudolf and Ursula Weichselbaum, Dirk Hämke, Frank Radons, Robert Shores, and Dale Jones.

And Margo Preskill was always readily and genially at hand to solve any problems of a technical/operational nature that arose as a result of my limited computer skills in research.

Generous permission for the use of photographs of items not belonging to me was made by Federico Santi and John Gacher of the Zsolnay Tile Museum in Newport, Rhode Island, and by John Jesse, Mark Van Veen, Wolfgang König, Heinz Baur, Dr. Lothar Ern, and the Behnisch family. Otherwise, all tiles (and tile-related items) pictured here are from my collection – photographed by myself and by Dan Johnson – with significant additions from the collection of Dirk Hämke – photographed by him.

Above all, as always, I wish to compliment the invaluable assistance and kind counsel provided by my good friend Dr. David Taylor, without whose help much of this work would not have been accomplished.

INTRODUCTION

At the Vienna International Exhibition of 1873, it was noted that: "Of encaustic and coloured [*sic*] floor-tiles and glazed mural tiles the exhibits were comparatively few."[1]

During the next thirty-five to forty years, that assessment was radically remedied by the exhibits – awarded medals or receiving honorable mention – that represented the work of a number of European and American tile makers at national and international fairs and expositions. Improved production machinery and the invention of new pressing techniques allowed the everyday tile to become one of the first artistic wares that could be reproduced, in any quantity, with an at least partly industrial duplication of motifs and images. As relatively cheap objects of use, tiles – particularly in Western and Central Europe – found frequent application then as wall, floor, and stove decoration, furniture inlay, etc., which, with an attractive ornamentation and extensive palette, could overcome the notion of industrialization in the minds and eyes of observers. Today, the humble tile is noteworthy for having made the realm of art accessible to modern industrial technology and design, and vice versa. Indeed by the turn of the twentieth century,[2] it was already recognized as an important decorative item – both useful and inexpensive too – fulfilling many different purposes: embellishing the exterior façades of public buildings and interior walls in private homes; providing a durable and appealing floor covering; affording better hygiene in bathrooms, kitchens, and swimming pools, as well as for public drinking-water fountains; storing and disseminating heat; replacing expensive woodcarving as decoration in furniture; reflecting light; and serving various other functions in the everyday household.

All such tile usages of the nineteenth and twentieth centuries are worthy of examination in the history of environmental development and popular culture. Wall tiles – and, to a lesser extent, floor and stove tiles – merit special study as truly aesthetic representatives of an applied art that was to attain considerable stature after the introduction of industrialized manufacture in the Western world.

Of particular interest in a consideration of tile production through the ages are these industrially manufactured examples from the period extending from the last years of the nineteenth century up to the time immediately preceding the Second World War. It is to these very much neglected treasures – along with other tiles and plaques and other tile-related objects[3] of that time – that collectors and other tile enthusiasts and art historians have begun, recently, to pay so much more attention.

During that period, in Germany and Central Europe, the Jugendstil and Secession styles – as variant components of International Art Nouveau, yet reflecting a considerable debt to the influence of Arts & Crafts design – found their longest and, possibly, most exemplary expression in the production of decorative tiles. Of the different types of tiles manufactured then, ceramic wall, floor, and stove tiles (together with furniture tiles, tiles for other uses, decorative plaques, and wall plates) are of the most significance as representative of Jugendstil; thus, later, the German term "Jugendstilfliesen" (Youth Style tiles) to indicate, principally, those items made within the area of German/Austrian influence in the period 1895–1935, not only manufactured and decorated by industrial techniques but also handcrafted and/or hand-decorated.

This text, therefore, confines itself, principally, to:

i). definitions of Jugendstil and the Secessionist styles and comparisons/contrasts with Art Nouveau and Arts & Crafts design; and

ii). the manufacture/crafting of decorative tiles produced in Germany, Austria, Hungary, and Bohemia/Moravia/Czechoslovakia between c. 1895 and c. 1935.[4]

Since, apparently, the term "Jugendstilfliesen" – as it is generally used, today, by authors, critics, collectors, dealers, auction houses, and, particularly, eBay advertisers – seems to embrace many, if not all, decorative tiles of that time, of German origin (or Austrian, Hungarian, Bohemian/Moravian/Czechoslovakian, as well as Belgian, English, French, etc.), it will no doubt seem curious and, doubtlessly, contradictory to many persons introduced recently to this subject, that tile designs bearing no affinity to Art Nouveau (as originally defined by art historians) should fall, sometimes, under the heading of Jugendstil, as they, in fact, seem to do at present.

Indeed, today's eBay offerings in the category of Jugendstilfliesen, per se, sometimes, include not only English Victorian tiles, as well, in different styles but also Continental European tiles from much later periods (for instance, any time after the Second World War), along with modern reproductions of earlier designs.

Regrettably, considering the high aesthetic appeal of authentically Art Nouveau/Arts & Crafts/Jugendstil/Secessionist tiles and their significance in the applied art of the late nineteenth and early twentieth centuries, they have received – and still, up to this present time, receive – astonishingly limited attention in the scholastic and collecting fields, as compared to other decorative products of the time. Now, indeed, it is important that historians, students, and others should acknowledge that, just as the art of different times has been depicted on canvas, so different, often noteworthy, decorative styles have been readily adapted to tile design.

Prologue

(Tile Definitions, Usage, History, Manufacture, Style, Patterns & Motifs, Installation Design, Decorating Techniques)

Clay is an earthen substance that is plastic when wet. After firing in the form of tiles and bricks, it is an important – and ancient – everyday building material. With the addition of calcined flint, it produces an even harder ceramic, while the addition of grog (ground and pulverized, pre-fired clay, also known as chamotte) helps aerate the clay and prevents warping, speeds firing, and reduces shrinkage.

Ceramic tiles and ornamental bricks are often decorated in the same techniques as used in the craft of pottery. In addition to tile and brick work, sculpture in the medium of clay also plays an important role in the history of architectural ornamentation. But, of all architectural ceramic material intended to embellish homes as well as public and commercial buildings, tile is the most readily available, has a fascinating history, and is often of a scale and with an appearance that can be appreciated by small children as well as by adults with long experience in the building trade or interior-decoration field or as enthusiasts in art and the crafts.

Excluding ceramic roof tiles (German: Ziegel)[5], the different types of tiles by usage, are:

i). ceramic / encaustic ceramic floor tiles (Fliesen, Bodenfliesen, also often, in a more general use of the term, Mosaik) and tile pieces / tesserae used in combination to form patterns or pictures in mosaic floor installations (Mosaik, in a specific use of the term);

ii). cement / encaustic cement floor tiles (Zementfliesen);

iii). ceramic stove tiles (Kachel, Ofenkachel, Ofenfliesen);

iv). ceramic tiles for special uses (Fliesen, Platten, Kachel, Zierkachel), including
a). ceramic furniture tiles (also Möbelfliesen);
b). ceramic tiles for use as trivets, serving trays, etc.;
c). ceramic tiles for fireplace surrounds and chimneypieces, also
d). ceramic tiles for use in radiator covers;

v). "artistic" ceramic tiles (Fliesen, Kachel, Zierkachel).

vi). ceramic wall tiles (Fliesen[6], **Wandfliesen, Platten,** Wandplatten)[7] and tile pieces / tesserae used in combination to form patterns or pictures in mosaic wall installations (Mosaik, in a specific use of the term).

Roman "Dionysus" mosaic (ceramic/glass/stone) floor, c. 220AD, unearthed in Cologne in the 1940s.

Tiled roof of St. Stephen's Cathedral in Vienna.

CHAPTER ONE

FLOOR TILES

DEFINITION & USAGE

Ceramic floor tiles are usually composed of an earthenware body. Those for use in high-traffic, public areas might, instead, be made of stoneware – because of that material's higher density and better mechanical durability – and fired at a higher temperature.

HISTORY

The earliest floor tiles were made of colored clay and unglazed. Pavement floors of ceramic tiles began to appear in Europe by the thirteenth century and were increasingly used to embellish great churches, monasteries, and palaces. In medieval England, decorated pavements for both ecclesiastic and secular buildings were produced by artisans using mostly lead-glazed tiles, cut from slabs of reddish earthenware clay and impressed, by means of wooden stamps, with design indentations that were then filled with contrasting white clay. Alternatively, single-color tiles were formed from a base of uncolored clay covered by a layer of colored material, applied in a dry state or in slip on top of the basic shape, then pressed. Such tiles, in a variety of different single colors, could be laid next to each other, in a geometric arrangement, to form a simple, patterned floor-covering over a larger area. Or tiles in a variety of different colors, usually smaller in size and sometimes of polygonal shape – or tesserae of irregular shape – could be positioned together in the manner of a mosaic.

By 1840, in England, commercial production began to replace the handcrafting of encaustic floor tiles – with the use of molds – from plastic, wet clay.

MANUFACTURE

After a single firing at a temperature between 950° and 1150° C (1750° and 2100° F), floor tiles have a water-absorption rate of up to around 10%. They are of larger and smaller formats, usually between 3" (7.5 cm) and 10" (25.5 cm) square – and mostly around 4" (10 cm), 5.5" (14 cm), 6" (15 cm), 6.75" (17 cm)[8], and 8" (20 cm) square – with a thickness of up to about 0.75" (around 1.9 cm) or, sometimes, even 1" (2.5 cm). Floors made up of tiles of other shapes – mainly six- or eight-sided or rectangular – are also often laid. Smaller tiles – referred to as "fillers" (Einleger) in mosaic floors or otherwise used as border or edge tiles – are mostly between 1.5" and 2" (3.7 cm. or 5.0 cm) square and 0.4" (1 cm) thick.

In earlier times, the natural yellowish/gray tone of the body could be concealed with the addition of color to the clay mix.

The large-scale manufacture of encaustic tiles – in which the surface pattern results not from glaze but from the embedding of different colors of clay – was initiated in England from 1848.[9] Through

Details of tiled floors in Dresden.

V & B M floor tile, designed by Peter Behrens.

V & B M floor tile.

V & B M floor tile, designed by Peter Behrens.

the use of a metal stencil, different colored clays would be placed on top of an uncolored base layer, then subsequently pressed and fired to form a tile with a decorative surface. Alternatively, by the same method, different colored slips could be applied to an already formed biscuit-fired tile base.

In 1852 in Mettlach, Germany, at Villeroy & Boch (V & B M)[10], "a dry-press method ... (was invented) ... for the inlaying of colored designs with clay dust."[11] And, in the 1860s in England, experiments were conducted to create inlaid floor tiles by a similar process to that used in the manufacture of wall tiles and plain floor tiles there, prior to the issuing of a patent[12] to the press manufacturer William Boulton

and engineer Joseph Worthington for a machine capable of making dust-pressed, encaustic tiles with inlaid decoration of up to six (or even more) different colors.

For these, the patterned part of the tile was to be formed through the use of one or more metal plates, perforated to the required design. A sectional die, whose relief pattern corresponded to that of the plate, was used to compress the colored, powdered clay in the mold. Above that, more clay dust of a neutral color – to form the body or, rather, base of the tile – would be added to fill the frame of the shape and, when compacted, would result in the formation of a tile with decoration embedded in its face. Afterward, a single firing at around 1250° C (2300° F)

– fusing the different components – would result in a strong, functional product, long-lasting and hard-wearing.

In an encaustic floor tile, the pattern is incorporated into the body of the tile to a depth, usually, of not less than 0.13" (3 mm) so that the design remains as the tile is worn down in its function as a floor covering. It may be glazed or unglazed.

The dust-pressing process for the manufacture of floor tiles did not immediately do away with the plastic-clay method; indeed, both techniques continued in use for many years.

Ceramic, encaustic tiles can be laid outdoors in preference to their more vulnerable, cement counterparts.

STYLE

From the twelfth century, in England, up to the Reformation in the sixteenth century, floors of simple, inlaid tiles were installed in monasteries, abbeys, and other important religious institutions. From the time immediately preceding the Gothic Revival in the country in the nineteenth century, the lost art of encaustic-tile making was revisited, and later, in that century and in the early twentieth century, in churches and other large public buildings, polychrome floor coverings bore, mainly, designs that were reminiscent of medieval art or influenced by Roman or Moorish or Gothic styles. As previously, single-colored tiles were occasionally arranged in basic, ordered, geometric patterns, possibly including small mosaic tesserae.

Also, by then, patterns made up of four eight-sided tiles adjoining and surrounding a smaller, square tile, usually around 2" (5 cm) square, were popular features of large-area floors in churches, museums, etc. The small and, usually, thinner – about 0.4" (1 cm) – tiles were often used, too, as edge- and/or border- tiles.

As previously, single-colored tiles in several colors were occasionally arranged in basic, ordered, geometric patterns, possibly including small mosaic tesserae. Indeed, mosaic floors could be laid in very important buildings in designs requiring a predominance of such tiny tile pieces of varying surface shapes to form pictures and patterns of amazing complexity, separated by areas of floor tiles installed in more regular and, usually, simpler arrangements.

Villeroy & Boch supplied mosaic-tile floors[13] (more than fourteen thousand square feet / one thousand three hundred square meters) – installed in 1897–1899 with the approval of Kaiser Wilhelm II – at the newly completed Cathedral in Cologne.[14]

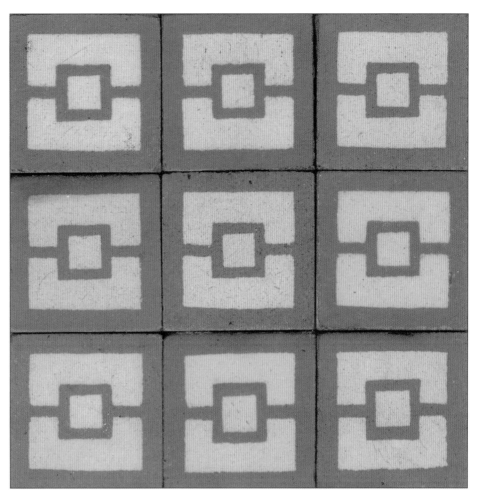

Nine separate V & B M floor (filler/border) tiles: each 2" (5cm) square.

Set of 4 Marienberg floor tiles: each approximately 6.9" (17.5cm) square.

V & B M floor tile.

PATTERNS & MOTIFS

Around the beginning of the twentieth century, in rare instances, in Germany, attempts at a more modern effect were made by such architects/designers as Henry Van de Velde and Peter Behrens. Behrens, particularly, designed floor tiles for Villeroy & Boch Mettlach incorporating spirals, concentric circles, or other devices, thus transposing the encaustic technique into the modern era with patterns of abstract geometry. Also, a few existent tiled floors in Germany and elsewhere evidence simple modernist – even Art Deco – design schemes; others, from later years before the Second World War, show the use of plain, colored tiles reliant on glaze effects – for instance, mottling – for their special appeal.

Details of the tiled floors in the chancel of Cologne Cathedral.

Four V & B M floor tiles, designed by Peter Behrens.

CHAPTER TWO
CEMENT FLOOR TILES

What has been said of ceramic floor tiles applies also, largely, to cement floor tiles, except that the latter are not fired but, instead, allowed to dry. They were usually made from a mixture of marble dust, cement, sand, and powdered stone; nowadays, a finely ground, dehydrated Portland cement is most often used with sand. After the addition of color pigments applied by means of a metal stencil, encaustic tiles with polychrome surface decoration are pressed, then dried.

During the nineteenth century and into the twentieth, cement tiles were used mainly as interior floor covering.

CHAPTER THREE

STOVE TILES

USAGE

For centuries, as a traditional form of heating, wood-burning stoves were manufactured and in common use in Northern and Central Europe. Among these were tall, tile-covered stoves with the ability to store and radiate heat, which, from about the middle of the nineteenth century, were industrially produced. Often placed against a wall, a tiled stove has accessible openings for the stoke-hole and flue, usually, at the rear.

M.O.&P.F. stove (rear).

Detail of M.O.&P.F. stove.

M.O.&P.F. small stove, c. 1910–1920: approximately 48" (120cm) tall.

HISTORY

The earliest tiled stoves were built using unglazed, disk-shaped, earthenware tiles; later, tiles of a more suitable, square or rectangular shape were introduced; and, finally – by the last quarter of the nineteenth century – color-glazed as well as decorated tiles with hollow backs. In time, stoves – in various sizes, shapes, and styles – became so grand that they were the visual focus even of elegantly formal rooms, and even more so, in palaces, etc., with the addition of such bold and colorful decoration as coats of arms and other heraldic devices.

Sometimes, tiled stoves would be contained in, and thus strengthened by, cast-iron framework.

The history of the stove-tile industry in Velten – the self-styled "Stove Town," with nearby sources of excellent clay for local use and for sale in nearby Berlin – dates from before 1830 and the first factory opened there in 1835. By 1878 – in addition to pottery workshops – there were twenty-two factories that, annually, produced tiles for around twenty-two thousand stoves, which number soon increased to thirty-six thousand; and, by 1905, tiles were supplied for a yearly manufacture of about one hundred thousand stoves for sale in the German capital city or for shipment (by rail or canal) elsewhere.

Already, by the 1850s, tiles glazed in enamel for so-called white "Berlin" stoves[15] were the main product of Velten and – because of their high chalk content and shrinkage ratio in manufacture – it was considered, then, that such tiles of comparable quality could not be produced of clays from other areas.

By 1865, twelve factories in Velten began producing tiles in a small variety of colors that would, later, be used extensively in stove-fitting after the start, in 1871, of the building boom in Berlin and elsewhere in Germany.

In competition – from around that time and into the twentieth century – the production of tiled stoves and stove tiles also grew well at the Meissen Stove and Porcelain Factory (M.O.&P.F.) in Meissen. Indeed, in 1888, there were six stove factories in Meissen and the surrounding area, with a seventh under construction that year.

MANUFACTURE

Stove tiles are manufactured, usually, in fairly thick relief – as much as two inches or more (around 5+ cm) – and in different sizes – with predominantly square formats of six, eight, or ten inches (around 15 to 25 cm) – and various colors. Sometimes with a decorated upper surface, they

Tiled stove, probably by the E. Fessler Stoves and Claywares Factory, at Laxenburg New Castle (Blauer Hof), in Laxenburg (Lower Austria). Photo courtesy of GNU Free Documentation License, Austria: Creative Commons Attribution 3.0; author Karl Gruber.

Tiled stove at Trausnitz Castle in Landshut (Bavaria). Photo courtesy of GNU Free Documentation License, Germany: Creative Commons Attribution 3.0 Unported; author High Contrast (Own Work).

Very early tiled stove (at the Victoria & Albert Museum, London) from Ravensburg (Baden-Württemberg). Photo courtesy of GNU Free Documentation License, Germany: Creative Commons Attribution, Share-Alike license; author: Andreas Praefcke.

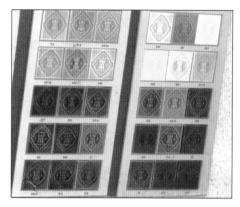

Two pages from SOMAG stove-tile glaze-sample catalog.

Cover of SOMAG stove-tile glaze-sample catalog.

SOMAG corner tile, cast: 16.5"h., 5.25"w., 3.75" deep (42 x 13.5 x 9.5cm).

usually incorporate deep hollows or ridges on the back as heat-retaining cavities. Used to clad stoves, furnaces, kilns, fireboxes, etc., that are lined with refractory brick or other ceramic material, such tiles can withstand relatively high temperatures but have low thermal conductivity, providing greater energy efficiency.

As in the case of wall tiles, manufacturers' catalogs, such as the one issued by the Saxony Stove and Wall Tile Factory (SOMAG) c. 1920, exhibit the variety of colored glazes offered.[16]

Though intended to fulfill a different purpose, they are pressed in a manner similar to wall tiles, as are, also, pediment tiles forming the often overlapping roof of the stove.

Some tiled stoves were ornamented, additionally, with very large, thick, and, usually, cast (molded) decoration, exhibiting a very high (partly, three-dimensional) relief more reminiscent of the ornate, architectural ceramics applied to building façades. These – even, sometimes, with a surface area of as much as 225 square inches (1,450 square centimeters) and with a maximum thickness of almost 6 inches (around 15 cm) – would be mounted on the front or sides of the stove or as corner pieces, and would usually, too, incorporate sizable cavities provided by the mold.

STYLE

Into the 1890s, eclectically imposing, tall, tiled stoves in traditional style – often featuring sculptural detail of human, animal, and floral forms, as well as other Historicist ornament, in white, brown, green, and some other primary colors – were produced in Velten and Meissen/ Dresden and other areas in Germany, as well as in Austria, Hungary, Bohemia, Moravia, and Silesia and other parts of Northern and Central Europe.

By about 1910, the manufacture of architectural ceramics was added to the programs of many of the stove factories in Velten as well as at other pottery workshops there.[17] Designs for these manufacturers were provided by a number of important architects of the time – among them, Alfred Grenander, Fritz Höger, John Martens, Erich Mendelsohn, Bruno Paul, Hans Poelzig, and Max Taut – for private and public buildings in Berlin, Leipzig, Hamburg, etc., including railway stations, town halls, post offices, churches, and villas with wintergardens.

Many such schemes incorporated provision for heating by decorative stoves of various kinds and in the style of the time up to the late 1930s.

PATTERNS & MOTIFS

By the turn of the century, in Germany, stoves were manufactured and marketed with Jugendstil decoration in floral, linear, and geometric schemes, with more modern designs and colors often determined by the customer or wholesaler or solicited from architects and artists. For instance, in c. 1903, in Saxony, many stoves were designed in the studio of architect Josef Feller, who also received commissions from stove manufacturers elsewhere. At the same time, stoves clad in tiles of Secessionist design were manufactured in similar numbers in Austria, Hungary, Bohemia, etc., as in Germany. In Austria particularly, tiled stoves were designed by such notable artists and architects as Herta Bucher, Josef Hoffmann, Bertold Löffler, Robert Obsieger, Dagobert Peche, Michael Powolny, Otto Prutscher, Emilie Schleiss-Simandl, Franz Schleiss, and Vally Wieselthier.

CHAPTER FOUR

TILES WITH SPECIAL USES

Other than its principal use as wall covering, the decorated ceramic tile was frequently used as furniture ornamentation or – occasionally, in combination with wood or metal – embellishment of household objects, accessories, and fixtures.[18]

FURNITURE TILES

In furniture manufacture, in the late nineteenth and early twentieth centuries, tiles occasionally replaced expensive hand-carving as the ornamental effect. For furniture companies not wishing – or not able – to establish their own expensive tile production, several tile manufacturers produced, for them, single tiles (and friezes) that were fired at the same temperatures as wall tiles but usually glazed on both sides and on the edges to prevent penetration of moisture and to give extra strength. With predominantly more naturalistic decoration, such tiles, slightly thinner usually than regular wall tiles, were produced, for instance, by the firms

Georg Schmider Zell United Ceramic Factories (SCHMIDER) – with tiles of a thickness of between 0.19" (4.8 mm) and 0.31" (7.9 mm) and on average 0.25" (6 mm) – and J. von Schwarz Majolica and Terra Cotta Factory (VON SCHWARZ) – between 0.25" (6.3 mm) and 0.44" (11.2 mm), and on average 0.4" (10 mm) – as well as by Villeroy & Boch in Dresden (V & B D) and Mettlach, for installation in sideboards, wall cupboards, tables, side chairs, hall stands, umbrella stands, and jardinieres.

V & B D special-use (possibly furniture decoration) tile: 0.25" (6.3mm) thick.

Von Schwarz special-use (possibly furniture decoration) tile, designed by Carl Sigmund Luber: 0.25" (6.3mm) thick.

Schmider special-use (possibly furniture decoration) tile: 0.25" (6.3mm) thick.

Mügeln wall tile, also possibly intended for kitchen-furniture decoration.

Unidentified special-use tile, possibly intended for (kitchen) furniture decoration: 0.19" (4.8mm) thick.

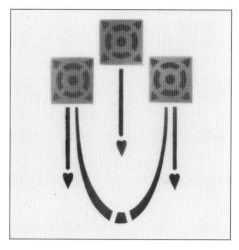

SOMAG wall tile, also possibly intended for kitchen-furniture decoration.

But for furniture that was less expensive and more utilitarian (in everyday usage), other companies, including the North German Earthenware Factory (NSTG), the Ludwig Wessel Porcelain and Earthenware Manufacturing Company (WESSEL), as well as Villeroy & Boch, produced and advertised regular wall tiles for use in kitchen cupboards, washstands – and other tables with splashbacks – flower boxes, planters, etc.

TILES FOR USE AS TRAYS, TRIVETS, ETC.

Von Schwarz, Schmider, and Villeroy & Boch, in particular, and the Wächtersbach Earthenware Factory (WÄCHTERSBACH), and other smaller companies also produced tiles for mounting in wood or metal by appropriate, neighboring businesses. Most of these were glazed on the front, back, and on the edges (if of square or rectangular format) or all around the circumference (if of circular form). In this way, makers of pewter, silverplate, and other metalwares as well as other manufacturers were able to offer such serviceable, yet decorative, items as serving trays and trivets to the public.[19]

Unmounted tiles – most often flat, without raised edges or galleries, and usually circular – were produced by the same pressing technique as others and

V & B D tray: 13.5" max. x 10.25" max. (34 x 26cm).

Two Von Schwarz trays: each 13.5" max. x 10.25" max. (34 x 26cm)

frequently decorated with printed or stenciled designs to be used as "table tiles or plates" (Tischplatten) for serving confections and other sweetmeats.

Also produced was a variety of other items where pressed tile surfaces were adapted in some way (for example, by simple reticulation or by the addition of ceramic elements) – including wall-light fittings (for architects, builders, wholesalers, and retailers) as well as kitchen ranges and other cooking/heating apparatus, menu-holders, and cake-stands (for private homes, restaurants and coffee shops).

Three unidentified trays: (top) 15.75" max. x 12" max. (40 x 30.5cm), (bottom left) 11.25" (28.5cm) diameter, (bottom right, with Orivit pewter mounting) 12.25" (31cm) diameter.

Unidentified tray: 15.5" max. x 11.5"
max. (39 x 29cm).

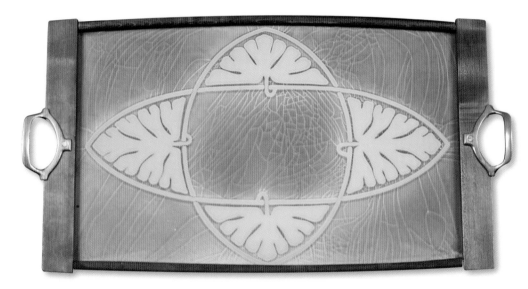

Wächtersbach tray, designed by
Christian Neureuther: 17.5" max. x
11" max. (44.45 x 27.94cm).

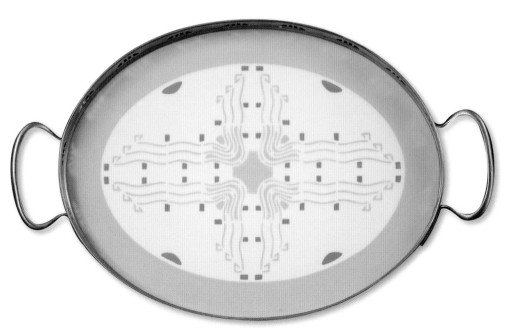

V & B D tray: 11.5" max. x 8.75" max.
(29 x 22cm).

Schmider special-use tiles, possibly intended for use as trivets: 0.25" (6.3mm) thick.

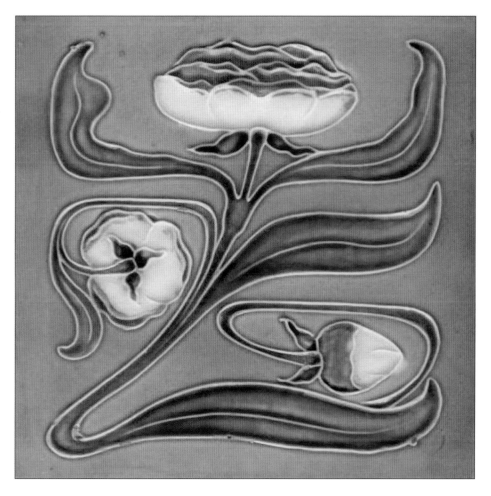

W. S. & S./Schiller hanging etagère or candle sconce: 13.5" high, 11" wide max., 2.63" deep (34 x 28 x 7cm)

FIREPLACE AND CHIMNEYPIECE TILES

In homes and other buildings – with fireplaces rather than stoves as the heating source – earthenware (and, sometimes, stoneware) wall tiles were often installed in a mantel or surround. Plain, single-color tiles, alone, could be used – at low cost – as usually, too, for hearths; or such tile placement might be interrupted by accent tiles (available at higher prices); also, single-color tiles with unusual glaze effects produced fairly affordable decoration; or, expensively, the installation might take the form of horizontal/vertical friezes, featuring creeping or climbing foliage. Sometimes, a picture frieze (of up to five or six tiles, or even more) could provide the horizontal accent, especially if it represented a landscape panorama.

TILED RADIATOR COVERS

Around 1860, a more modern central heating system – than any used previously – was first introduced, requiring the use of cast-iron radiators, and, very soon afterward, a demand was seen for presenting these devices in a more agreeably aesthetic manner both in public and commercial spaces and the home environment. Certainly by the time of the First World War, decorative tile-covers – many in openwork design – were already in use, as presented in domestic room-settings and other interior-decoration schemes by celebrated architects and designers and featured occasionally at national and international exhibitions in Germany in the last decade of the nineteenth century and first decade of the twentieth.

Detail of a Wienerberg horizontal frieze of wall tiles with possible alternative use as fireplace/chimneypiece decoration.

CHAPTER FIVE

ARTISTIC TILES AND PLAQUES

The designation indicating artistic, ceramic tiles (in German, most often, Zierkachel) – rather than decorative, ceramic tiles used in wall installation (most frequently referred to in German as: Fliesen, though, more specifically, as: Wandplatten) – indicates, mostly, attractively ornamental and aesthetically pleasing, flat plaques (of various sizes and in different dimensions) intended for display in the manner of pictures and photographs, hung on a wall or placed on stands or small easels on table-tops, mantelpieces, etc. They include, particularly, plaques by Max Läuger (at KANDERN and KARLSRUHE), Carl Sigmund Luber (at VON SCHWARZ), et al.

These are not to be confused with other similar kinds of wall ornamentation for similar display. "Wall plates" (Wandteller) are usually circular, concave, and with a foot ring; "reliefs" (Reliefs or Relieffliesen) are wall tiles or plaques with very high (almost three-dimensional) relief – as, for example, those made at the Majolica/ Ceramic Manufactory at Karlsruhe (KARLSRUHE) and the Ceramic Manufactory at Darmstadt (DARMSTADT).

Von Schwarz plaques, designed by Carl Sigmund Luber: (top) 10.75" x 6.38" (27 x 16cm), (bottom) 11" x 6.5" (28 x 16.5cm).

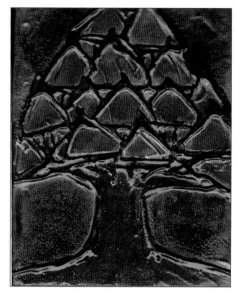

Three Max Läuger tiles/plaques, made at Kandern: (above) marked "ML 1902." 4.75" x 5.88" (12 x 14.9cm), (top right) 5.88" (14.9cm) square, (bottom right) 8" (20cm) sq.

Goldscheider plaque with unidentified designer/decorator monogram: 7.75" x 6" (19.5 x 15.2cm).

Karlsruhe plaque: 6.63" (17cm) square.

Karlsruhe plaque, designed by Hugo Ruf, c. 1937-1940: 11.25" x 10.75" (28.5 x 27cm).

Unmarked tile/plaque, designed/decorated by
Friedrich Hudler: 4.75" (12cm) square.

Unidentified plaque, possibly intended as furniture
decoration: 10" x 16.5" (25.5 x 42cm).

Unmarked plaque, possibly made at Eichwald:
5" x 10" (12.5 x 25.5cm).

The category of artistic tiles can also include wall tiles, whose ornamentation stems from the treatment of the glaze, alone, rather than surfaces decorated with colorful motifs of various kinds. Here, the "artistry" is the glaze effect achieved, for instance, through the use of metallic oxides (for crystalline/goldstone/aventurine clustering) or different and, sometimes, accidental firing techniques (such as reduction glazing); alternatively, it may be the intended or chance character of a flowing or streaky or speckled or blended or mottled glaze that is aesthetically appreciated.

Artistic tiles, plaques, reliefs, and wall plates were also produced in porcelain (and in various formats and sizes) by such companies as the Royal Porcelain Manufactory in Berlin (KPM), the Royal Saxony Porcelain Manufactory (MEISSEN), and the Hutschenreuther companies.

At times, the Rosenthal Porcelain Company, particularly – and, possibly, other firms in Germany, including Villeroy & Boch in Dänischburg (V & B DÄNISCHBURG), as well as Austria and Bohemia – manufactured plain, glazed, white tiles and other wall items for home decoration by professionals (private retail artists and teachers) and amateurs.

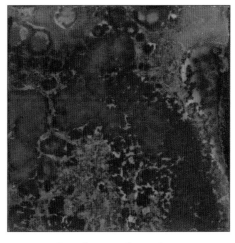

SOMAG tile with copper lustre decoration.

Unidentified special-use porcelain tile, marked "PW FW" (decorated with the Meissen "green dragon" motif): 0.25" (6.3mm) thick.

Tile/plaque, marked V & B Dänischburg and decorated by Friedrich Hudler: 4.75" (12cm) square.

CHAPTER SIX

WALL TILES

USAGE

Wall tiles[20] can be used both inside and on the exterior of buildings. As practical, hygienic, durable, robust, easy-care, comparatively inexpensive wall covering for public, commercial, and domestic buildings, they can also add an element of decorative, architectural enrichment, especially for homes, shops, restaurants, hotels, hospitals, etc. They are still used extensively, today, for bathrooms, swimming pools, therapeutic facilities, changing rooms, laboratories, etc. Also, with reflective surfaces – glossy or even with semi-high glaze – they can add luminosity in dim or dark environments or accentuate illumination, where required. And they can provide beauty as a visible expression of function, enhancing not only architectural façades but also, inside, decorating entry halls, corridors, kitchens, stairways, etc., in domestic interiors and sales halls and food courts in retail environments.

HISTORY

In Europe, the manufacture of wall tiles and other architectural ceramics developed from the local tradition of decorated floor tiles. By the beginning of the fourteenth century, commercial tile industries were established in a number of European countries, with tile works founded near their sources of raw materials.

By the end of the nineteenth century, tiles of many kinds had already been serving many functions for many years – wall tiles, in particular, in increasing numbers for both interior and exterior use. Of special, historical interest is the immense installation "Procession of Princes" (Fürstenzug) – still existent – by the Royal Saxony Porcelain Manufactory, in Meissen, that was mounted, in the first decade of the twentieth century,

Details of the Meissen "Procession of Princes" wall in Dresden, 1904-1907.`

on the outside wall of a building facing Augustusstrasse in Dresden Old Town.

MANUFACTURE

Most wall tiles for interior use are formed from an earthenware body; exterior wall tiles from a stoneware body. In preparation for manufacture, an amount of grog might be added to reduce the rate of shrinkage and make a stronger ceramic body.

Other than the production of tiles in high relief that were made by the casting

method with the use of molds, the manufacture of wall tiles – departing from traditional craftwork – became more and more industrialized, in time, as it benefited from mechanization and the introduction of time-saving decoration techniques. The dry process – for the mechanical compression of granulated/pulverized clay dust with low moisture content – to produce wall tiles and plain floor tiles was developed in England in the 1840s, after the adaptation of a button-technology patent[21] there in 1840. At first, the press was hand-operated with the help of a screw-type lever, then, later, the introduction of the hydraulic press replaced the necessity for manual labor. The easier, quicker, and cleaner production of thin, strong, and lighter-weight tiles was the intended result.

In the wet-clay process,[22] basic wall-tile forms were kept in drying rooms, then – prior to glaze firing – placed in a bisque kiln at around 900° C (1600° F).

The dust-pressed tile was bisque-fired at between 1100° and 1250° C (2000 and 2250° F) – most often around the lower temperature in that range – producing a hard-wearing, fine-grained ceramic body. After the application of uncolored or colored glazes, a final (glost) firing, mostly at a temperature of about 800–1000° C (1500°–1800° F), would result in a surface of even hardness.

With an approximate thickness of between 0.3" (7 mm) and 0.4" (10 mm),[23] wall tiles are most often produced in a square format of approximately 6" (15 cm),[24] though the dimensions can differ by up to 0.25" (6 mm) – depending on the maker – even in a maker's execution of the same tile design around that same time or even at a later date.

Other diverse sizes are also common, e.g. half tiles 6" x 3" (15 x 7.5 cm) and quarter tiles 3" (7.5 cm) square.

Smaller format tiles of about 4" (10 cm), 4.75" (12 cm), and 3" (7.5 cm) square or rectangular tiles as well as border and edge pieces and end tiles – of about 6" x

V & B M tile.

Offstein tile.

Osterath/Ostara tile.

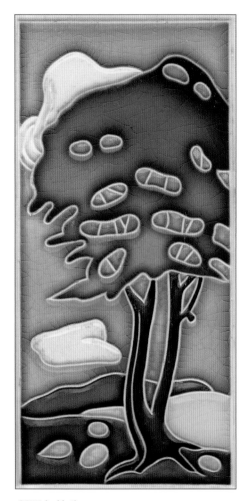

GWF half-tile.

NSTG half-tile.

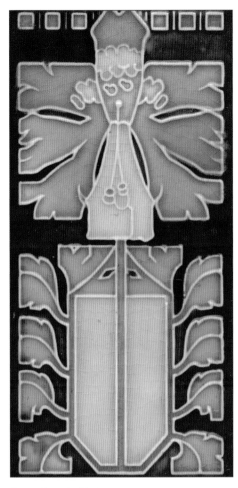

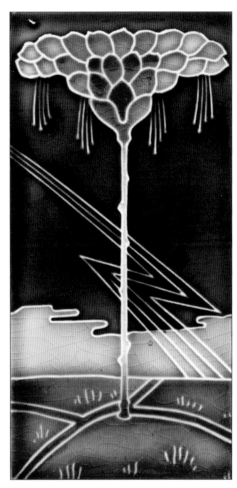

GWF half-tile.

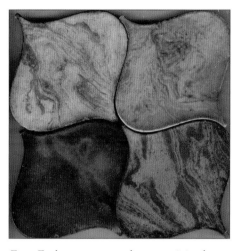

Boizenburg half-tile.

Osterath/Ostara half-tile.

Four Zsolnay tesserae, shown conjoined as a square measuring: 6" max. x 6" max. (15 x 15cm).

DTAG half-tile.

1" (15 x 2.5 cm), 6" x 2" (15 x 5 cm), or 6" x 4" (15 x 10 cm) are used in wall coverings (frequently, as accentuation, in wall coverings composed of one-color tiles); also, occasionally, in furniture. Smaller tiles, such as those 1.5" (3.8 cm) square, made by the Wessel, Zsolnay, and some other companies, were rarely produced. And only very occasionally were irregularly shaped wall tiles in various dimensions used in wall installations.

The pressing technique can serve several purposes other than forming a tile of prescribed dimensions as a plain article of use or as a functional object ready to receive decoration for the enhancement of a location or environment. In addition to preparing the obverse as an appropriate surface – possibly, for the easy application of design – it can also impress the reverse with a manufacturer's mark or signature. Impressing a simple pattern on the tile-back also aids in adhesion (bonding) and, consequently, the correct placement of the tile within an installation, assuring fault-less joints and, thereby, preventing pollu-tion or dampness from penetrating the mortar-bed or the reverse side of the tile. Moreover, in the absence of a specific maker's mark, etc., such a patterning of the tile-back – showing particularly dis-tinctive characteristics (raised or recessed ridges, squares, circles, etc.) – might be of help in later identification regarding maker, location, model number, etc.[25]

Exterior use demands glazed, stone-ware wall tiles – also glazed block tiles, corner tiles, grooved tiles, and other special forms, such as those incorporating housings for sanitary fittings, etc. – fired, mainly, at a temperature of about 1200°–1250° C (2200°–2300° F), to produce a strong, dense body. Containing clay, quartz, feldspar, and, possibly, other mineral ingredients (including kaolin), which have been sorted and prepared and mixed in various specific proportions, this formulation is largely frost resistant and impervious to moisture. With a maximum water absorption rate of under 3%, they are much less porous than earthenware wall tiles intended for interior installation. Their use in decorative façades, often in conjunction with brightly colored and richly molded terra cotta, was – and re-mains – cheaper than comparable work in stone masonry and easier to maintain against the polluting effects of soot, smoke, and grime.

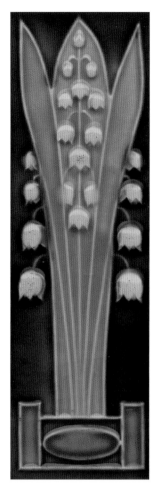

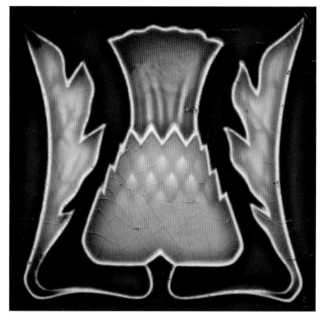

M.O.&P.F. tile: approximately 3" (7.6cm) square.

Boizenburg tile: approximately 6" x 1" (15 x 2.5cm).

(Left) M.O.&P.F. tile: approximately 6" x 2" (15 x 5cm).

From the beginning of the twentieth century – replacing previous glazing by hand – fully automatic glazing machines were operated for single-color tiles and for clear, colorless glazes covering decorated tiles. However, glaze application by hand in the production of some polychrome, decorative tiles continued through the middle of the 1930s. Also, up to 1940, glazes of lead or zinc oxide were used, mixed with other oxides (iron, copper, manganese, cobalt) to provide color.

STYLE IN WALL TILES

The early influences in Germany and Central Europe included the vast variety of English Victorian tiles, decorated in a number of techniques – including dust-pressed relief – and produced in many styles during the period of so much artistic innovation (in conflict/competition with so much revival eclecticism) after the Industrial Revolution in Britain. As practiced in England and in other neighboring countries, transfer-printed decoration continued in use in Germany, as did also Gothic patterns – these

particularly in floor-tile production – and Classical motifs. And the blue-and-white Delft painting of the Netherlands was greatly admired there and was used advantageously by the country's growing tile industry.

To these design elements was soon added, almost everywhere towards the end of the nineteenth century, the search for a new style to match and take advantage of the new mechanization. The attraction of the English Arts & Crafts style seemed to provide a solution and an opportunity, as did also, by the early 1890s, the precursory development in England of a style approximating the future Franco-Belgian Art Nouveau phenomenon that was detectable later in that decade.

By that time, in England, individual floral designs – often symmetrical and, at first, largely realistic – were already favored for the decoration of individual tiles or tiles that could be arranged in friezes and small panels. These featured most often in fireplace design as well as decorative wall coverings in domestic and public interiors. Soon, in France and Belgium, as late-nineteenth century design there began to yield, dramatically, to the extravagance of Art Nouveau, tile panels in the new style were introduced as adornment of building façades. Then, in Germany, particularly, and in Central Europe – as already in Great Britain – decorative wall-tile installations were to be found ornamenting rooms and passageways in homes and public architecture.

From the last years of the nineteenth century, plain tiles – of uniform dimensions and in a range of colors – comprised large wall coverings in houses and other buildings in Britain, France, Belgium, Germany, and some Northern and Central European countries, enclosing decorative friezes or interrupted by single-accent, polychrome tiles. But later, into the early 1930s, changing fashion began to demand plain-tiled wall areas accentuated simply either by arrangements of tiles of a different size or by thinner decorative strips or by relief border tiles in contrasting colors. Indeed, in the early years of the international Depression and particularly through the mid-1930s, not only were there fewer installations of decorative tile panels in new architecture, but also – where their use was required (for reasons of hygiene, cleanliness, and ease of maintenance, in hospitals, swimming baths, food shops, etc.) or continued, for other reasons – plain, single-color tiles, white or in lighter colors or tints or with special glaze effects, replaced the color-glazed, decorative, polychrome tiles of the earlier era.

It has been estimated that, in Germany, alone, there were about 8,000 designs used by manufacturers of wall tiles in the period 1895–1935,[26] most of

V & B M tiles, designed by (left) Otto Eckmann, (top right) Henry Van de Velde, (bottom right) Peter Behrens.

them originated by company personnel. A few are known to have been conceived by celebrated artists/architects of the Jugendstil or to have been inspired by – or adapted from – designs of theirs. Others might have been adapted from other sources.

Thus, though not so often incorporated into exterior architectural schemes, Jugendstil wall tiles were used widely – and, in many instances, are still to be observed today – in public buildings, business premises, sales rooms, etc., as well as houses and apartment buildings. The vast majority of them are, of course, of a single color (including some benefiting from glaze mixtures, techniques, etc., such as lustering, iridescence, speckling, and reduction-firing); others were executed with attractive multicolor decoration in a wide palette.

PATTERNS & MOTIFS

The very first tiles made and decorated by man showed simple patterns (often, in Europe, for example – from the mid-fourteenth century – in sgraffito technique), to be followed, later, by more ornate designs achieved by various methods including handpainting. In the nineteenth century, antique and medieval styles were copied by tile makers in Europe and produced along with tiles of Moorish and Persian inspiration.[27]

The first explicitly Art Nouveau tile patterns came to prominence, c. 1895, with tiles bearing naturalistic depictions of organic forms – flora and fauna – as self-contained, pictorial decoration. Recognizing the possibilities of this new stylistic orientation and the quickly growing appeal of curvilinear decoration in combination with the improved, industrial techniques in use at that time, tile makers, architects, artists, and designers were motivated to experiment and develop the application of the new style in this field.

DESIGN OF INSTALLATION

Covering an entire wall with an arrangement of relatively expensive, decorative tiles was not often contemplated in the interior decoration of public buildings – and, of course, even more rarely in domestic architecture. However, wall-size

ornamental murals – sometimes, possibly, of unique design – in some appropriate commercial locations were, in fact, composed around the turn of the century and afterward and ceiling-high columns in public buildings were, sometimes, clad entirely with pictorial or patterned tiles. Infrequently, a large tile picture – perhaps handpainted or, equally rarely, outlined in slip trailing – would adorn a salon or reception area in a hotel, railway station, or commercial building or might decorate an entrance hall in a museum, church, or other public space.

Usually, though, it was the lower section, only, of a wall, especially in foyers, hallways, corridors, etc., that was adorned up to chest height with regular tiles, each part of an overall, decorative, "wallpaper-type" pattern with symmetry in two directions (left/right, up/down).

V & B M tile.

Detail of tiled wall in Dresden.

V & B M tile, c. 1880: 7" (17.8cm) square.

Most commonly, such a wall scheme would consist of plain tiles interrupted by an ordered, inter-spaced scattering of accent tiles to break up the monotony. Often, a single tile, alone – featuring a central, self-contained motif, possibly surrounded by a distinctive framing edge – would sufficiently alleviate the monotony of a plain panel. Otherwise, an installation might be accentuated by a row of such tiles, all with the same self-contained motif, though without any evidence of framework, and without any added detail to suggest continuation, but instead giving an impression of completeness.

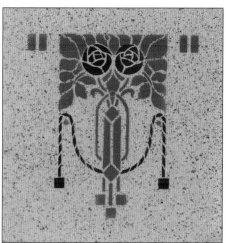

Complete, self-contained, single tiles, by (top left) Bankel, (bottom left) M.O.&P.F., (right) Osterath/Ostara.

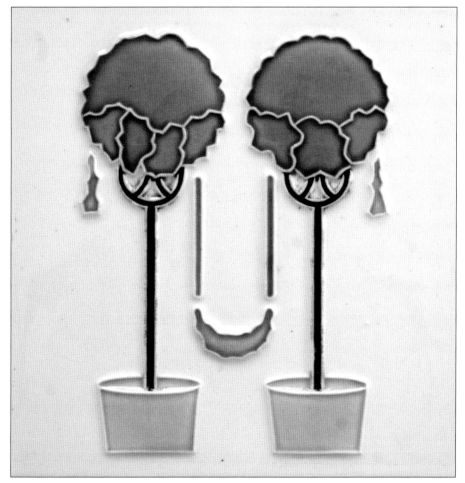

Complete, self-contained, self-framed, single tiles, by (left) Ernst Teichert, (top right) Offstein, (bottom right) M.O.&P.F.

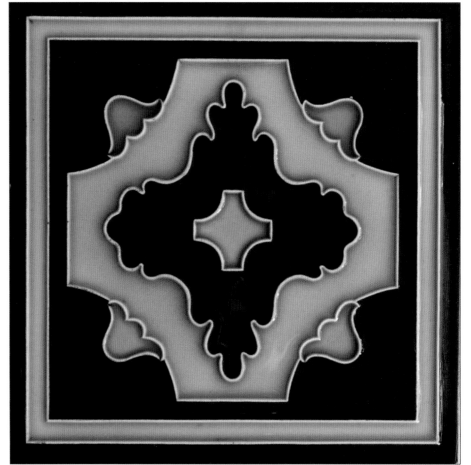

Or, sometimes, a pair of decorative tiles, forming a complete motif – horizontally or vertically – would relieve the single-color background.

Two V & B M tiles forming a complete image.

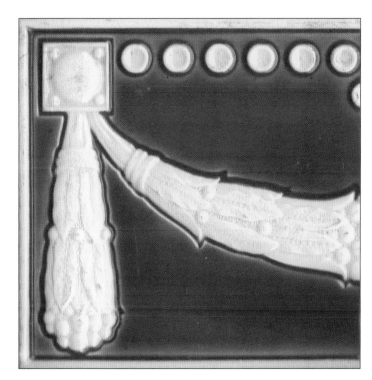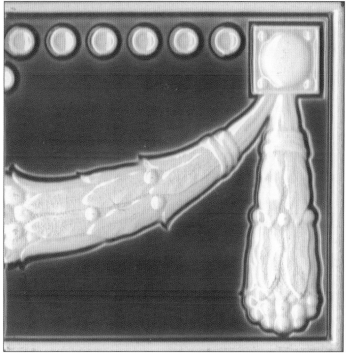

Two NSTG tiles forming a complete image.

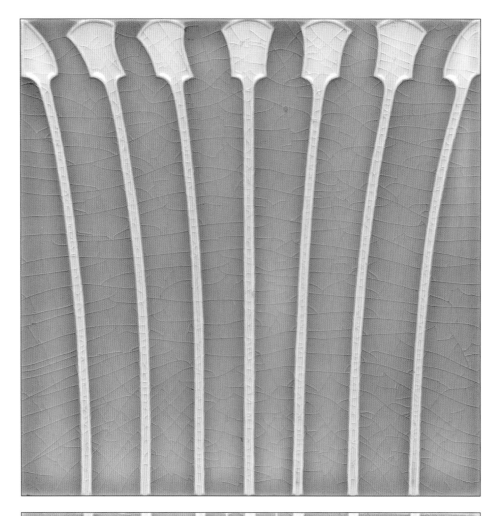

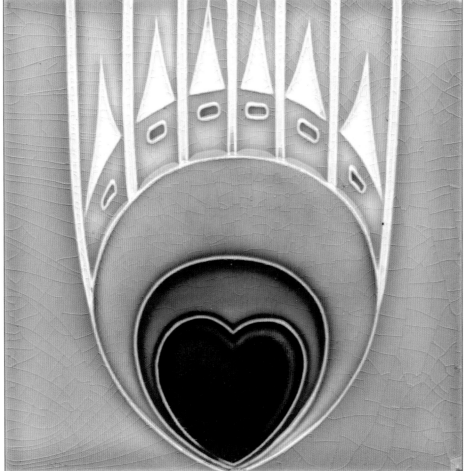

Two NSTG tiles forming a complete image.

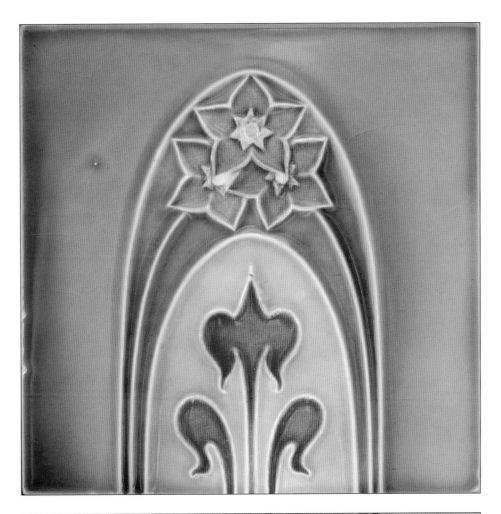

Two Mügeln tiles forming a complete image.

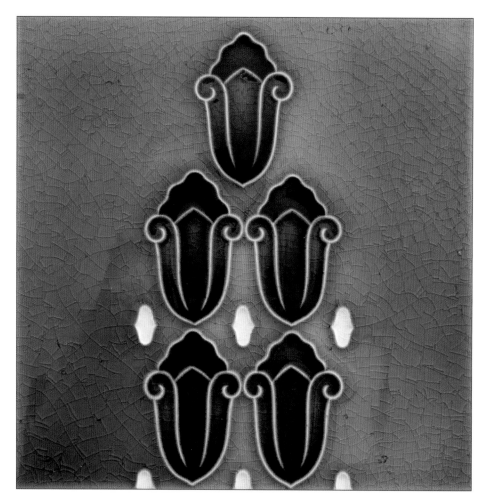

Two GWF tiles forming a complete image.

Or, adorned with a motif or pattern, which, itself, might allow the possibility of continuation, a single tile – or two or more tiles in sequence – might be repeated to form a vertical or, more commonly, horizontal frieze or dado, indicating a potentially endless ornamentation.

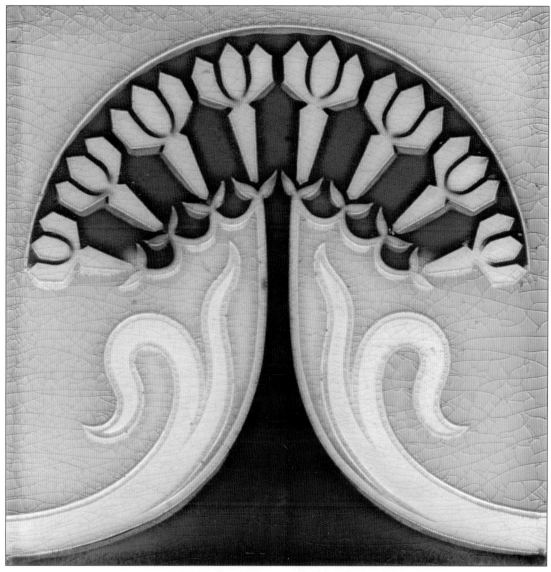

Three tiles, each with possibility of endless continuation, by (top) GWF, (bottom left) M.O.&P.F., (bottom right) GWF.

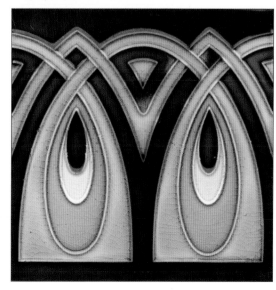

Consequently, the diversity of tile usage in installations was truly astonishing:

i). wall pictures or tableaux;

ii). single decorative accent tiles, positioned/repeated/scattered in an installation, producing singularly different effects;

iii). a horizontal or vertical running frieze composed of a number of distinctive, adjacent tiles, strikingly pictorial or colorfully patterned, continuing an ornate design against a background – or bordering or framing a background – of plain tiles;

iv). a decorative mosaic pattern, composed of small, polygonal, or irregularly shaped tiles or tesserae, and centered within a plain tile framework;

v). a handsome fireplace surround or its upper horizontal representation of, for example, a panoramic landscape or marine scene.

Tiles from friezes or pictures could also be suitable for use as single tiles. Naturalistically decorated tiles and others bearing curvilinear designs could be installed, symmetrically, with border or edge tiles of abstract/geometric design (such as wavy lines), in a manner so as to accentuate a rhythmic quality. Also, tiles in color variations could produce different effects. And small images – of flowers, buds, leaves, etc. – might be extended by the addition of tiles of complementary design – of stalks, tree trunks, etc.

In such wall schemes, the single-color tile panel surrounding the horizontal, decorative frieze, would be set above a bottom row of stronger plain tiles of greater thickness (of up to about 0.75" – 1.9 cm) at floor level. And near the top of such an installation, there might be a continuing stripe of whole (or, possibly, half) border tiles in a single color or, frequently, with simple decoration and complementary coloration, while, at the very top, a horizontal row of beveled-edge tiles (placed to make a smooth, gradual transition towards the wall) would preclude any abrupt surface differentiation.

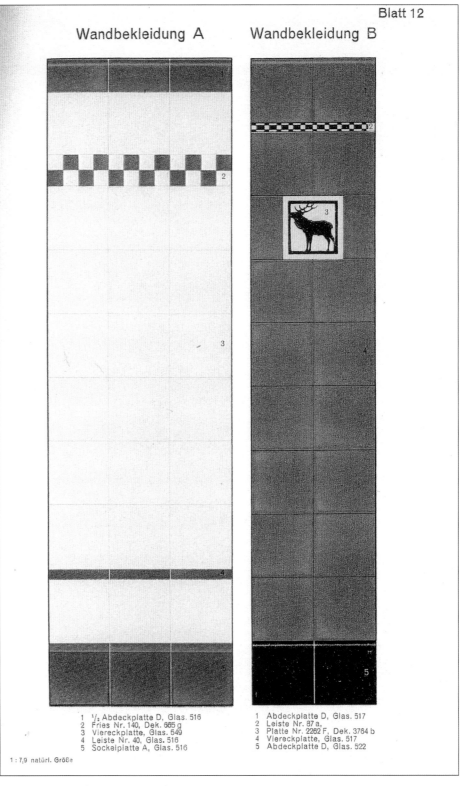

Page from undated M.O.&P.F. catalog: approximately 8" x 10.5" (20.32 x 26.67cm).

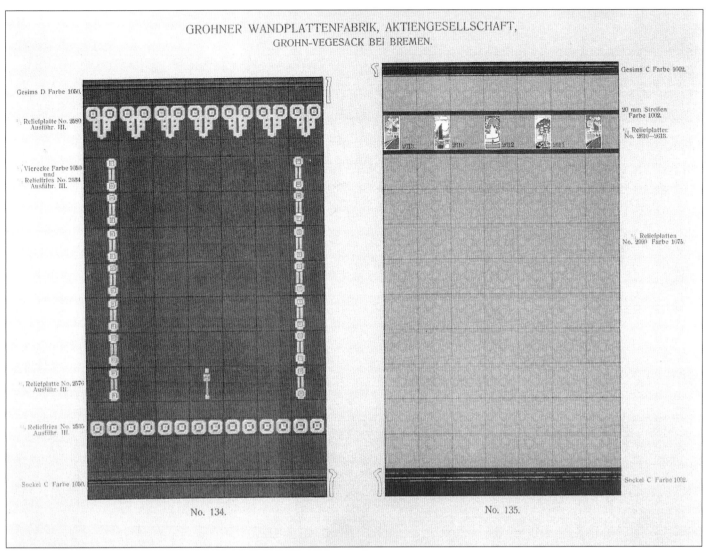

GROHNER WANDPLATTENFABRIK, AKTIENGESELLSCHAFT,
GROHN-VEGESACK BEI BREMEN.

No. 134. No. 135.

Page from undated GWF catalog:
approximately 8" x 10.5" (20.32 x 26.67cm).

NSTG tile. *Two Boizenburg tiles.*

Decorative friezes of tiles arranged in sequence – either horizontal or vertical – might be endless or complete or offer the possibility of extension through the insertion of additional tiles within the sequence. And a vertical frieze or picture strip consisting of up to five or six tiles – presenting not an endless but a complete image – might, often, be placed to close off a wall installation at the end of a hallway, whereas two such arrangements could form the side elements of a fireplace surround in harmonious conformity with the horizontal accompaniment.

Thus, the new tiles offered extensive possibilities of wall decoration with ornamental surfaces. Pictorial or patterned, they were produced, sometimes, with naturalistic design though, far more often – immediately before, then after, the turn of the century – with more stylized, conventionalized decoration. Abstracted ornament was more easy to install side by side – in friezes or borders, horizontally

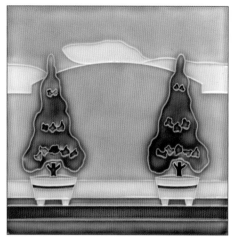

NSTG tiles.

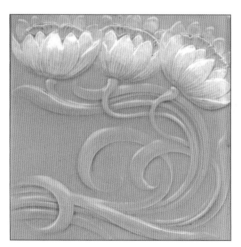

S. O. F. tiles.

NSTG tiles.

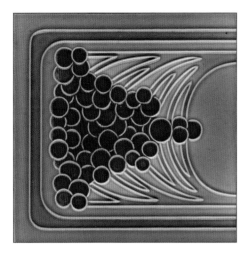

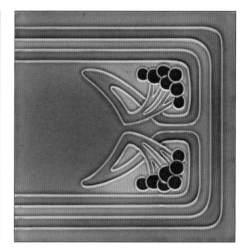

Ernst Teichert tiles.

or vertically – than the realistic/naturalistic portrayal of easily identifiable plant forms, since the latter, covering a surface of several tiles, required more careful selection and placement as adjoining or continuing decoration in order to represent natural growth correctly.

In fact, even from before the end of the nineteenth century, wall-tile installations would allow all kinds of possibility, limited, of course, by cost to the owner. Otherwise, few restrictions were put on the imagination of a designer or contractor other than those necessitated by the size and location of the wall space.

In a household or public installation, contractors could, possibly, use tiles by different manufacturers especially in an arrangement of full-size tiles by one maker in combination with other plain or decorative tiles – or especially friezes and half tiles – by another. It was necessary, however, that contractors be aware that, at different dates and without any intentional color variation, colors might differ, nevertheless, in the execution/adaptation/ replacement, of a specific design, especially with regard to brightness, intensity, and tone.

Ernst Teichert tiles.

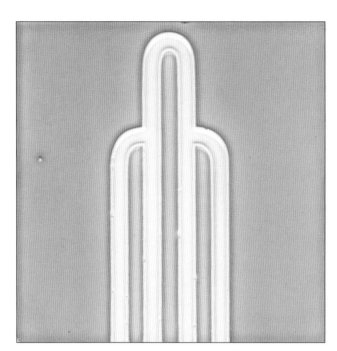

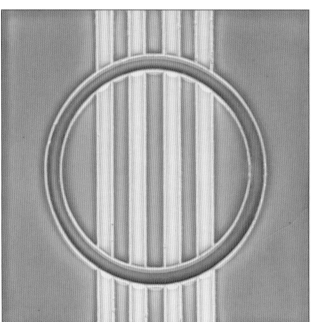

In one respect, a tile setter might require the advice of an owner or designer in the installation of a design, frieze, or even a single tile, particularly concerning the correct directional placement of naturalistic ornament schemes involving climbing and hanging plants, flowers, or fruits (for instance, bleeding heart blossoms, cherries, and dandelion puff balls).

DECORATING TECHNIQUES[28]

As with production techniques, the methods of tile decoration are very varied.

Like architectural ceramic elements produced almost exclusively in a single glaze color – for instance, gargoyles and other fantasy creatures in figural relief, masks, rosettes, columns, and water fountain spouts – decorative wall tiles with high-relief surfaces are most often produced from casts.

This differs from the production of tiles incorporating decoration in *low* or *high* relief (Flach- / Hochreliefdekor), which can be accomplished by adapting the design of the steel dies used in manufacture. Thereby, the pressing process can produce not only a flat shape of the required basic dimensions – for decorating in various ways – but can also stamp out the surface of a relief form, with the required hollows and/or raised areas. The design of the relief tile can then be enhanced by a covering of an opaque glaze that spreads and settles with different intensities at different depths for highlights and shadows, with the single-color glaze brighter on high points and darker in the deep-lying areas.

Handpainting a picture or other design on a flat-surface tile is a labor-intensive and, therefore, expensive procedure generally reserved for the production of a unique handwork.

Less expensive (though by no means cheap) and, therefore, also infrequently found in the area of decorative tilework, is a method known as *tube-lining* (Fadenschlicker) – or slip-trailing or, sometimes, squeeze-bag technique – to produce contours separating areas of different colors.[29] In this technique, delicate lines of colored slip are hand-applied (trailed/piped) over the surface of the tile (or vessel) to form the thread-like, ridged outlines of a pattern, delineating areas which can be, later, inlaid/filled-in with different, brushed-on colors.

M.O.&P.F. tile.

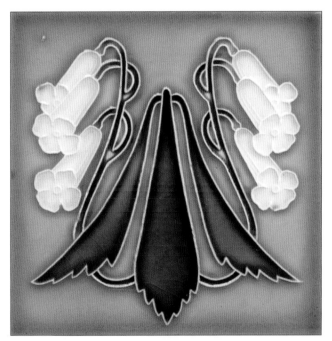

Bendorf tile.

GWF tile.

Three tiles with tube-lined decoration, (top left) Utzschneider, (bottom left and above) Kandern by Max Läuger.

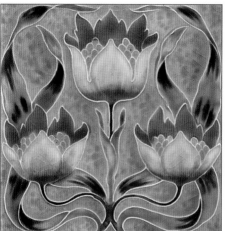

Examples of tiles with cuenca decoration, by (left) Servais, (top right) Utzschneider tile, (bottom right) unidentified special-use tile, 0.25" (6.3mm) thick.

This relatively high-cost method of decoration was used – though very seldom and by no means as often as by English or Belgian tile makers – by only a very few German wall-tile companies, including Lamberty, Servais & Cie. (SERVAIS), the Wessel Wall Tile Factory (WESSEL), Utzschneider & Cie. / Utzschneider & Co. (UTZSCHNEIDER), and the North German Earthenware Factory.

In simulation, however, machine-pressed, molded relief in a technique called *cuenca* (Fadenrelief) can be produced by means of dies – customized to the designs to be created – mounted in the press. Thereby, the obverse of the dust-pressed form bears the raised contours that facilitate the later decoration of the design. The cavities, separated by the ridges, can be filled-in without the colors bleeding or running into inappropriate areas of the design.

Examples of Von Schwarz plaques with cuenca
decoration, designed by Carl Sigmund Luber:
each 6.38" x 11" (16.2 x 27.9cm).

Von Schwarz plaque with cuenca decoration,
designed by Carl Sigmund Luber: 6.38" x 11"
(16.2 x 27.9cm).

Also, very infrequently, a *negative* pressing method could be employed, whereby an individually adapted die produces an image through areas of space and/or outlines sunken in the surface of the tile, resembling an incised/excised or "intaglio" effect, which is the reverse of raised-relief decoration. The use of negative-relief to produce this kind of design was a technique used extensively—though not exclusively—by the Georg Schmider company and only very rarely employed by other tile makers.

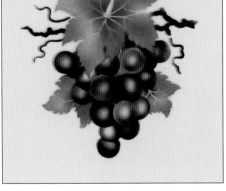

Examples of Schmider special-use tiles.

Examples of tiles with negative-relief decoration, by (top left) Zsolnay, (bottom left) Wessel, (above) Boizenburg: 5" (12.7cm) square.

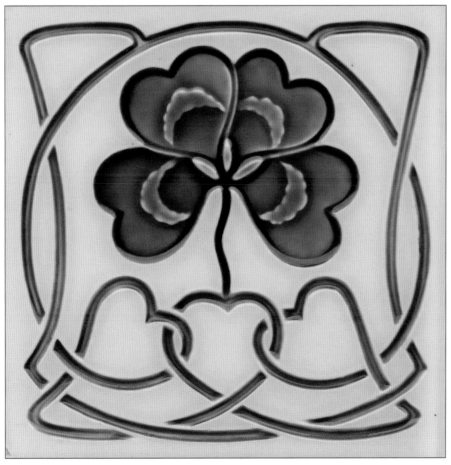

Alternatively – in an adaptation of an ancient technique called *cuerda seca* and with the use of a compound of iron oxide and a grease or wax substance – printed black lines on the flat, dust-pressed biscuit can serve as the design outline, often boldly delineating areas to be filled with enamel glazes of different colors.

From about the mid-1860s, color-glazed wall tiles were produced by the cuenca and cuerda seca methods in France and, soon thereafter, in greater quantity, in England and, later still, also in Belgium and Germany.

Much more commonly in European production, however, decorative tiles were produced by *transfer-printing*, first through the use of copper plates, which had been engraved or acid-etched, and, later, by screen-printing. In the second procedure, fine mesh material was used and several passes were necessary to allow the application of the correct amount of different colors on the tile. Screen-printing can be easily identified by the observation of a fine pointillist (pinpoint) structure of decoration. Later still – from c. 1880, for instance, in Germany – a chromolithographic method was used in the transfer-printing of tiles.

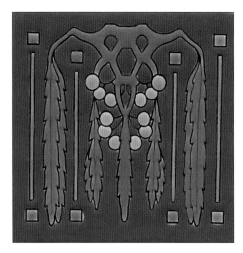

Examples of tiles with cuerda seca decoration, by (top left) M.O.&P.F., (bottom left) NSTG, (right) Zsolnay: 7.88" (20cm) square

Examples of tiles and half-tiles with printed decoration, by (top left) NSTG, (middle left) Wessel, (bottom left) Saxonia, (above) V & B D.

Again, alternatively, through the use of a thin, metal sheet perforated to designate the pattern, tiles might be decorated by *stenciling*. Color, in dry powder form, can be applied before pressing or, as slip engobes, painted on the biscuit form. Historically, as an inexpensive method of decoration, stenciling was used mainly, though not exclusively, for kitchen tiles.

By the late 1910s and increasingly in the 1920s and into the 1930s, transfer printing and stenciling became the more prevalent methods of European tile decoration, as also, in the 1920s/1930s, in the smaller production of tiles in an Art Deco or Modernist manner. However, German tile manufacturers' catalogs were still advertising the availability of some relief tiles with polychrome glazes, as previously, even into the 1930s. Also in continued production at that time were tiles in single plain – or mottled/speckled/rippled/streaked – colors and, more and more often than before, tiles with luster glazes from the Moorish tradition, produced by means of the reduction-firing of metal oxides in newly researched glaze combinations.

Examples of tiles with stenciled decoration, by (top) V & B D, (bottom left) Osterath/Ostara, (bottom right) Wessel.

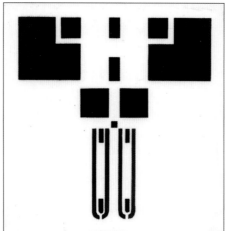

SECTION TWO

Art Nouveau and Arts & Crafts Design in German and Central European Ceramic Tiles, 1895–1935

HISTORICAL, SOCIAL, TECHNICAL, AND STYLISTIC BACKGROUND

The influences exerted internationally on late nineteenth century style in architecture and the applied arts were complex and disparate but, by and large, the upheavals effected in style – at the end of that century and the beginning of the next – were, in total, the result of a strong reaction to what had gone before.

Otherwise, it is difficult to point to an overriding, common denominator in the definitions of the English Arts and Crafts Movement, French/Belgian Art Nouveau, and Jugendstil/Secession, since those styles – though each arose from a similar dissatisfaction with the stylistic status quo and shared a number of the same influences – represented different, artistic developments, aesthetic aims, and considerations of the role of art and industry in public life, in often divergent ways and to varying degrees. Rooted, as they were, in rebellion against the jumble of Historicist revivals and imitation and presenting, in many instances, a conscious acceptance of the role in design of functionality and appropriateness for life, they were premonitions of a new beginning. As departures from the old, banal, and hackneyed, they were the awakening of progressive trends in the evolution of a modern style.

ENGLAND

In the 1840s, in the English tile industry, the adoption of the earlier-patented technique for pressing plastic, wet clay into forms by means of a screw mechanism was already leading to larger-scale, industrial production and, within a short time – by c. 1846[30] – the manufacture of wall tiles from compacted, dried, powdered clay was introduced in the country. In the next ten years, new decorating techniques were introduced along with the application of translucent glazes. In 1863/1864, yet another important, pertinent patent[31] was issued for the production of encaustic floor tiles by compressing clay dust.

Reflecting the progression of British art and design in the second half of the nineteenth century and the beginning of the twentieth, the tiles of the Victorian era reveal, at different times, the influences of a variety of stylistic treatments. In fact, "the tiles of the Victorian era are a microcosm of the art history of the period."[32]

Neo-Gothic design, characterized by the work of architect and designer Augustus Welby Northmore Pugin and his predilection for the encaustic technique in floor-tile manufacture and for the use of transfer printing in wall-tile decoration, remained influential in the second half of the nineteenth century. Other Historicist styles were also not ignored. But, already from the 1860s, several design-reform movements embarked on campaigns against the superfluity and indiscriminate use of ornamentation in design that had pervaded the contemporary scene.

In particular, the Arts and Crafts Movement began its promotion of radical social and artistic reform in reaction to the impoverished state of the decorative arts in the country and the conditions under which they were produced as a result of the Industrial Revolution. And other avenues were explored, as well, into the 1880s/1890s that, it was considered, might offer relief, if not escape, from the stultifying treatment of English socio-political themes and the often heavy-handed approach followed by Academicians. One of them, led by Edward William Godwin among others, was the Aesthetic Movement,[33] which,

through its banner of Art for Art's Sake, rejected the narrative emphasis and moral judgment in Victorian art in its resolve to raise aesthetic values in Britain. At the same time – in contrast to the Arts and Crafts Movement – it sought to promote and improve the industrial production of decorative objects; its adherents hoped to achieve this through reference to the artistic styles of cultures distanced in time and space from the British, nineteenth-century, urban, industrial environment.

Several themes overlapped in the predilections of the Aesthetes and the Arts & Crafts artists/designers, chief among them an interest in late Medieval / early Renaissance art. This preoccupation was also shared with the Pre-Raphaelites,[34] who were seeking to reform artistic sensibility through a determination to recapture the sincerity and simplicity of those earlier styles.

By the end of the century, many firms in England were mass-manufacturing, marketing, and exporting a large variety of Victorian tiles exhibiting Neo-Classical and Gothic Revival styles or the influences of Islamic and Japanese art, as well as the restrained, ordered designs of the Arts and Crafts enthusiasts and the introduction of initially proto-Art Nouveau, naturalistic features of decoration.

English tiles by various companies – especially Minton's China Works, Minton Hollins & Co., Maw & Co., and Doulton & Co. / Royal Doulton – were installed in a multitude of locations around the world, including: in London, the Palace of Westminster (also known as the Houses of Parliament) and the Victoria & Albert Museum; in the United States, at the Capitol Building, in Washington, DC; and in Australia, at St.

Stephens Cathedral and the Queen Victoria Building, in Sydney. Indeed, in the period from the 1840s through the end of the 1930s, they were exported in great quantities, particularly, to Australia, New Zealand, Canada, India, Africa, and the United States, for installation in various government buildings, cathedrals and churches, public and commercial buildings, and private homes, etc.

After the First World War and into the 1920s, the influence of Arts & Crafts design lingered along with the Art Nouveau aspects of English tile production – with an ever greater reliance on rectalinearity – until, finally, the decreasing home-use of colorful, decorated tiles, along with the increasingly influential fashion for unadorned surfaces, resulted in an emphasis on the production of single-color tiles with interesting, artistic glazes. In the 1930s, tilework retained its practical value as well as an aesthetic appeal, nevertheless, especially for use in large public spaces, including London's Underground stations.

SCOTLAND

What is known as Scottish Art Nouveau – often, also, called the Glasgow School – had little to do with the English Arts and Crafts Movement, other than its striving for renewal in art and life and its shared interest in restrained linearity. It was largely the combined result of such influential trends as "the Pre-Raphaelite School and [its] literary and symbolical tendencies, the refined line of Japan, the Celtic revival with its nationalistic urge, and the formal reaction which was a part of the age."[35] With its more restrained, sober, almost austere, structural clarity but, nevertheless, dynamic force, it shared the curvilinear emphasis and other excesses of the style then current in France and Belgium hardly at all. Also, the "muted secondary colours [sic] and airy tones" reinforced "the other-worldly aspects of the [Glasgow] style."[36]

The rationality of Charles Rennie Mackintosh's geometry, articulation of space, and exaggerated, soaring verticality was balanced by the expressive ornamentation and quasi-paganist, sexual symbolism in the work of other members of the Glasgow Four – Margaret and Frances Macdonald and James Herbert

MacNair – with their organic, biomorphic abstraction and the mystical poetry of their imagination.

It was those qualities and the distinctively sophisticated inclination shared by Mackintosh and his colleagues that, together with the stylistic tenets of the English Arts and Crafts promoters, had the greater influence on style and decoration in Germany and Austria and other countries in Central Europe.

With the publication of his work in the German monthly magazine *Dekorative Kunst* in 1898 and his participation in the Vienna Secession Exhibition of 1900, the evidence of the integration of architecture and design in Mackintosh's work struck an immediate, responsive chord with German and Austrian designers obsessed with their conception of the "Gesamtkunstwerk."[37] After other exhibits in Turin, Moscow, Budapest, Venice, Dresden, Munich, and Berlin, the appeal of the linear restraint exercised by him was widespread in much of Europe.

THE NETHERLANDS

Around the turn of the century, unlike the situation in neighboring Belgium and Germany, the Dutch economy did not benefit from the industrial production of floor tiles or colorfully glazed wall tiles. Instead, low production costs at that time allowed for a variety of designs in custom-designed, hand-decorated, tiled dados for interiors, as well as handpainted tile pictures and handmade Delftware that remained economically viable into the 1920s.

From the early 1880s – along with commemorative tiles and tile panels – handpainted, ornamental tiles and tile pictures (for framing) were sold by several Dutch potteries as reproductions of famous Dutch paintings. Others represented Classical motifs or displayed realistic landscapes, often including windmills and figures in traditional costumes. From the late 1880s, a few factories in the Netherlands enjoyed a larger-scale production of earthenware wall tiles that were, most often, plain or transfer-printed. By c. 1890, however, a selection of stenciled, dust-pressed wall tiles and tile panels was first produced in Nieuwe Kunst-stylized, geometric designs or with special glazes or, infrequently, with standard, floral, cuerda seca decoration

for functional use in dados or to cover walls in shops and house foyers and for fireplaces, etc.

Also in the 1890s and early 1900s, tile blanks were imported from Belgium and England for decoration, often, with stencil designs or, occasionally, by tube-lining. Relief tiles in the Art Nouveau manner and handpainted, artistic tiles were occasionally made – usually not for installation in wall decorations – by such art pottery companies as Rozenburg Den Haag, Zuid Holland, Goedewaagen, and De Distel, and a few smaller tile manufactories.

Firms with a larger production of color-glazed, industrial tiles for domestic installation included De Porceleyne Fles, De Sphinx v/h Petrus Regout & Co., M. O. S. A., Maastricht, and Jan Willem Mijnlieff's Holland factory.

At the turn of the century and for a few years afterward, a number of decorative tile panels and pictures – mainly without sculptural ornamentation – for railway stations, shops, hotels, and other public and private buildings were designed on a commission/freelance basis, by ceramists, architects, and painters, including Jac. van den Bosch, Adolf Le Comte, Lambertus (Bert) Nienhuis, Johannes Karel Leurs, Johannes Cornelis Heytze, C. A. Lion Cachet, W. Kromhout, and Jan Toorup.

In the years between the First and Second World Wars, the industrial production of plain, dust-pressed wall tiles in the Netherlands remained relatively small.

BELGIUM

In 1830, Belgium seceded from the Netherlands.

In the eighty years after the Belgian Revolution, the country developed into one of the most industrialized nations in the world, and, in the last half of the nineteenth century, re-established the native, moribund tile industry. The Boch family (later, proprietors of Boch La Louvière / Boch Frères Kéramis) introduced mechanical innovations that, from the 1850s, led to their eventual, economically successful production, by the dust-pressing process, of encaustic, ceramic floor tiles.

This filled a growing demand by architects and builders of public and commercial buildings, hospitals, schools, churches, public baths, etc., to supplement the use of cement floor tiles produced from the late 1840s. Cement floor tiles remained popular, however, especially after c. 1870, when they could first be produced industrially on an even larger scale by the dust-pressing technique. Though they were less durable than ceramic tiles, they were less expensively manufactured by a growing number of companies. After the introduction of mechanical and, later, hydraulic presses in the industry, cement floor tiles with polychrome patterns replaced the earlier single-color products, continuing to compete with ceramic floor tiles and floor mosaics into the 1930s.

From the late 1850s, following the intense interest in the country in Neo-Gothic and Neo-Renaissance decoration, the Boch family and, later, other competing ceramics companies began to add the manufacture of blue-and-white Delftware and the use of Islamic and Oriental motifs to the earlier emphasis on transfer-printed decoration.

In the last years of the century, a number of new factories were opened in Belgium and the Nord-Pas-de-Calais area of Northern France, to compete in the manufacturing and marketing of floor tiles, earthenware, and other ceramic products, with export orders from around the world. The SA Compagnie Générale des Produits Céramiques was established in 1881 as a floor-tile factory in Saint-Ghislain, adding wall tiles shortly after 1900. Henri Baudoux moved his production of enameled bricks and pavement tiles from Curreghem-Brussels to Hasselt and, within a couple of years – by 1895 – introduced the manufacture of wall tiles and panels there. One year later, in Belgium, there were six companies making floor tiles, including the factory at Saint-Ghislain, and three companies, including the one at Hasselt, that included wall tiles in their program of decorative ceramics. Though most of these and later, new companies adopted the dust-pressing technique, some manufacturers, including the SA Manufacture des Céramiques Décoratives – Majoliques de Hasselt, continued the use of the process for wet, plastic clay.

By the turn of the century and through the 1920s, Belgium was responsible for a large-scale production of color-glazed wall tiles and fireproof fireplace tiles – with, at first, conventionalized/abstract

and, later, more geometric decoration – matching the industries in Britain and Germany, as well as tile panels (mostly custom-made) for interior and exterior use and other architectural ceramic coverings and decorations.

Also, tile manufacturers delivered tile blanks to small decoration companies using ready-made glazes.

In 1914, there were over twenty-five factories in Belgium, producing wall tiles in Art Nouveau and other styles, with designs by in-house personnel or commissioned from architects, sculptors, painters, and graphic artists.

From around the early 1920s, with the diminishing appeal of complex, decorative, and, especially, expensive, custom, wall-tile façades and interior schemes in Belgium, as in France, gradual style changes began to develop in tile production there. At first, the surviving, less complex, ornate, Art Nouveau designs began to succumb to the growing popularity of Modernist decoration, with interiors decorated, more and more, in the 1930s, with mosaics of plain, colored tiles or artistic tiles dependent on glaze effects as wall and/ or floor installation. This brought to an end the period of the decorated tile in Belgium, which had begun with Boch Frères Kéramis and continued with the establishment of such companies as Hemixem (Manufactures Céramiques d'Hemixem, Gilliot Frères, in Hemiksen), and Helman/Le Glaive (Maison Helman, Céramiques d'Art, in Brussels, with factory in Berchem-Ste.-Agathe); later (in the period 1908–23), joined by Belga / De Dijla (Produits Céramiques de la Dyle SA / NV Ceramiekprodukten De Dijle), Morialmé (Société Générale des Produits Réfractaires et Céramiques de Morialmé), Bouffioulx (SA Faiencerie de Bouffioulx), Florennes (SA des Pavillons Florennes), and Herent (SA La Céramique de Herent).

Major influences on the Belgian tile industry included the work and design practices of native-born Victor Horta and Henry Van de Velde.[38] Horta was one of the earliest and most significant proponents of the Art Nouveau style in Belgium. Van de Velde – from the 1890s, active as an architect and designer – was admired as a style theorist and pragmatic innovator during his entire career starting in his home country.

The tile designer Joseph Roelants (1881–1962) worked for some years, and at different times, for Helman and Hemixem as did, earlier, the artist Jacques Madiol for Helman and Hasselt.

FRANCE

The Second Empire under Napoleon III marked two decades of prosperity and stable, authoritarian government in France. Industrial expansion brought the country to a position of power, second only to Great Britain in Europe prior to the Franco-Prussian War of 1870–1871. After the war – despite territorial losses – the country was soon able to move towards another period of economic progress.

By the early 1890s, French style was described as an eclectic confusion of Neo-Classicism with other remnants of the opulent style of the Second Empire, interest in Medieval art, and vestiges of the conflicting Renaissance, Romantic, and Gothic revivals in architecture and interior design. And young artists reacted against the separatism of academic art as well as the Historicist emphasis and the continuing insistence on drawing inspiration literally from Classic design sources in decorative art. They wished to sever all connections with the past in their search for a completely new style – particularly, in architecture, interior design, furniture, and the applied arts (glassware, jewelry, metalwork, pottery, textiles, posters, etc.) – and to take advantage of the new mechanization and other technical innovations introduced earlier. Many believed that the future should show a concern for the design of the everyday object, no matter how utilitarian. Not only were the barriers between the fine and applied arts to be overturned, but art was also to be made part of everyday life.

Nonetheless, the "styles current (in France) in the reigns of Louis XIV, Louis XV, and Louis XVI … [were] … absorbed into the framework of references of French Art Nouveau … [resulting in their] dominant presence in the decorative arts and architecture of the Exposition Universelle of 1900."[39]

Rejecting the rationality of the Industrial Age through the exploitation of themes of decadence and mysticism, Symbolism was another significant trend in French and Belgian art in the second half of the nineteenth century. As a visual language, employing the intensely personal and sometimes obscure or ambiguous references of myths and dreams, it was related to Gothic aspects of the late-Romantic tradition in the selection and use of images and motifs with esoteric connotations. Many of its themes of nostalgia and mysticism were carried over into the Art Nouveau style, which also advanced its use of curvilinear forms.

Building up to its apogee in the 1900 World's Fair in Paris, the growth of interest in Art Nouveau in France and Belgium, as a movement, nurtured dramatic changes, particularly, in architecture and the applied arts. Up through the turn of the century, the ceramic tile industry in France, with its long history, mirrored the developments made in the economic and cultural life of the nation.

In the 1850s, in France, encaustic, ceramic floor tiles were successfully manufactured by the wet-clay process in an attempt to compete with the more economically produced cement tiles. Soon, an interest in the production of decorative, architectural, ceramic designs in stoneware and earthenware (especially after the introduction, before the Franco-Prussian War, of metal construction in architecture) also joined the continued production of traditional, tin-glazed tiles.

Experimentation in ceramic bodies intensified along with the first instances, in the country, of the use of colored face bricks – both unglazed and glazed – and polychromatic ceramics in architectural decoration. The subsequent development of frost-resistant, ceramic bodies stimulated their later, very extensive use in architectural work, especially in Paris and other large cities.

Fire bricks and ceramic tiles were already used in fireplace installations prior to the production of the first dust-pressed wall tiles in the late 1860s and afterward by a few manufacturers. Among them were the faience/majolica company at Choisy-le-Roi, led by Hippolyte Boulenger – which exhibited some of the few examples of color-glazed wall tiles in 1873 in Vienna – and the Faiencerie de Gien. Both firms, later, from c. 1898, supplied tiles for Paris Métro stations.

Thus, by the 1870s, dust-pressed, ceramic, encaustic floor, stove, and wall tiles were available in the French market. Also, ceramist Eugène Collinot's 1864-reg-istered patent in respect of his "rediscovery" of the cuerda seca decorative technique was welcomed by French pottery companies, to be adopted, later, by a few competing tile makers after the end of the war with Prussia.

At the Paris Exhibition of 1878, the local exhibit included wall tiles covered in opaque tin-enamel or transparent, highly colorful glazes and produced in the cuenca and cuerda seca contour/outline techniques or by transfer printing or stenciling. The light and shade effects of varying thicknesses of glaze were seen there, too, not only in tiles made by the Boch factory in La Louvière, Belgium, and Villeroy & Boch in Luxemburg along with the English firms Minton China Works, Minton & Hollins, Craven, Dunnill & Co., and Maw & Co., but also those produced by Collinot and Boulenger. Théodore Deck showed painted tile murals along with tiles of Persian and Moorish inspiration. French ceramic, encaustic, and mosaic floor tiles compared well with Minton's English and Wienerberg's Austrian exhibits, the German "Mettlacher Platten," and floor tiles and paving bricks from the First Schattau Claywares Factory in Moravia. Indeed, visitors to the exhibit of French wall- and floor-tile manufacture were "surprised in regard to the great advance made by France since the Vienna exhibition, where it had just begun to devote more attention to this industry ... [and it was] ... extremely interesting ... especially ... to German clay workers, where the clay industry is likewise being led into the same condition."[40]

With the annexation of parts of Alsace-Lorraine by Germany, the Faiencerie de Sarreguemines (founded in 1785) – for some time previously, one of the largest ceramics concerns in France – was located in German territory for over thirty-five years and better known as Utzschneider & Co. (UTZSCHNEIDER). To continue serving the French market, the owners opened a new factory in Digoin, with a branch in Vitry-le-François – both in France – between 1876 and 1881, with the head office in Saargemünd (French name: Sarreguemines), in the Imperial Territory Alsace-Lorraine in Germany. By the early 1880s, all three works, with a total employment of over two thousand ceramics workers prior to the First World War, were producing all kinds of tiles: from c. 1890, dust-pressed in large-scale production and, by the mid-1890s, with Art Nouveau decoration in addition to earlier designs.

By the early 1870s, the Faiencerie de Longwy was producing tiles with printed or stenciled decoration and continued to do so for many years. In 1873, the company adopted Collinot's cuerda seca patent for the decoration of tiles in bright colors. Along with artistic tile panels for architectural interiors, these were produced with Classical, Isnik, Oriental, and other sophisticated designs for installation in furniture or for use as framed wall hangings, trivets, or serving trays.

In the 1890s, long-established tile factories – such as Fourmaintraux & Delassus in Desvres; Société Anonyme des Carreaux et Revêtements Céramiques du Nord in Orchies; and others in the Saint-Amand and Orchies areas of Nord-Pas-de-Calais – modernized their facilities for the introduction of dust-pressed tile manufacture.

Through the time of its closing in 1936, the Choisy-le-Roi factory, which discontinued faience manufacture by 1910, focused its production on tile work.

Other French potteries began the production of tiles as a sideline in the mid-to-late nineteenth century and new firms were founded specifically for architectural work, including tile manufacture.

Nevertheless, in spite of the significant tile-manufacture activity described, it would seem that industrially produced wall tiles with Art Nouveau decoration, as made in England, Belgium, and Germany, were not manufactured for as long a time by French ceramics companies for widespread use in domestic interiors in the country, excepting, of course – for reasons dictated by national status/location – by Utzschneider & Cie., in Saarguemines/Saargemünd.

Instead, France's more major contribution to the adornment of walls and façades around the turn of the century centered more on highly individual, monumental, sculptural, ceramic ornament, figural relief panels, and handcrafted, made-to-order tile friezes, with tiles in different shapes and dimensions. These were designed for public and commercial buildings in Paris and other large cities in the country. They were produced by such ceramics concerns as that founded by Émile Mueller – and continued by his son – as well as by ceramists

Charles Gréber and Alexandre Bigot. These and other manufacturers collaborated with avant-garde artists and architects, such as poster artist Jules Chéret, architect Hector Guimard, and designer François Jourdain.

Also, in 1901, the ceramists Alphonse Gentil and Eugène François Bourdet opened Gentil, Bourdet et Cie., in Billancourt (Paris), for the production of stoneware goods (including ornaments and figures), ceramics for construction, and other furnishings in enamel, pâte-de-verre, and marble. Prior to the First World War, collaborating with architects, they executed important commissions for tiled flooring and "special" mosaics (for floors, walls, etc.), in sophisticated, colorful, Art Nouveau and other styles, for installation in major commercial buildings, thermal spas, apartment houses and mansions, as well as several Paris Métro stations and the Bibliothèque Nationale. Their mosaics were "special" due to architectural schemes involving the intricate installation of unusually shaped tiles, with the use of cement in complementary colors – or, more significantly, contrasting colors emphatically outlining designs in a cloisonné manner – to form large, pictorial tableaux or panels of elegant, complex patterning. Between 1904 and 1925, the company received gold-medal and Grand-Prix awards at expositions in Arras, Brussels, Ghent, Liège, London, Paris, Saragossa, and Turin.

GERMANY

After Prussia's victory over France in the war of 1870–1871 and the subsequent unification of the German states in 1871, there followed a period of large investment of capital, entrepreneurship, and manpower in industry and commerce that was to mark the foundation of the new German nation. These years of rapid industrial expansion and economic boom in the country came to be known as the "Gründerzeit."[41] Furthermore, through aggressive imperialism in the period 1884–1918, the German Empire was assembled with the inclusion of new colonies in Africa – East, South West, and West Africa – and the Pacific – German New Guinea, German Samoa, Nauru (in Micronesia), the Northern Solomon Islands, and the Marshall, Mariana, and Caroline Islands.

The new prosperity brought with it a continuation of the earlier eclecticism and Historicism in architecture and design. With further development, existent revival styles – from Gothic and Renaissance through Baroque and Romantic – were promoted as the true expression of German nationhood. For over twenty years, there was little evidence of innovation in architecture, furniture, and the crafts in spite of the new processes and technologies (especially in regard to steel) resulting from the ongoing industrialization. This was also in spite of the access to knowledge and training at universities and the growing number of so-called arts and crafts schools and other technical and applied arts schools in the country (and elsewhere in Europe) from the late 1860s.

From around the 1820s, floor tiles, made of cement, were produced in Germany and – installed in various ways in single colors or polychrome arrangements – remained popular, throughout the remainder of the nineteenth century, due to low cost and competitive pricing. The usage of cement floor tiles in the country by such manufacturers as Otto Kauffmann (KAUFFMANN) of the Dresden area and Matthias Grathes (GRATHES) of Dusseldorf (afterward, Osterath) was widespread during the Gründerzeit and continued into the Jugendstil era.

In the 1830s, the first use of ceramic floor tiles was in colorful, mosaic patterns formed by the installation, in combination, of small tiles in geometric shapes, which were made, expensively, by hand.

In the mid-1840s, the first serious experimentation in the mass-manufacture of single-color floor tiles was made at Septfontaines, in Luxemburg, by Jean François Boch, using plastic, wet clay and, in 1846, using clay dust. His work was continued by his son Eugen Boch at the Villeroy and Boch Earthenware Factory in Mettlach-on-the-Saar and, soon, larger-scale, floor-tile production began there. At first, for a short time, single-color, dust-pressed floor tiles were made on a limited industrial basis – by means of hand-operated (and lever-assisted) screw presses – and then, from 1852, the first encaustic floor tiles, too, after the introduction of hydraulic presses,[43] around the same time there, allowing greater mass production. These multi-colored, dust-pressed, encaustic floor tiles, first made at this Mettlach

location – with metal stencils reproducing designs – came to be known as "Mettlacher Platten."[44]

Nevertheless, for a few years, tile production remained a sideline in Mettlach, subsidiary to Villeroy & Boch's main business of household china and decorative ceramic wares. Around 1856 in Dresden, however, new premises were established to continue and expand this floor-tile program and add to it the manufacture of terra cotta ornamentation and other architectural ceramics. And later, in 1869, a separate Villeroy & Boch Earthenware and Floor Tile Factory was opened in Mettlach at a time when other firms were beginning to enter the market.

Between 1878 and the end of the century, major competition for Villeroy & Boch's floor-tile manufacture came from Lamberty, Servais & Cie. (SERVAIS) in Ehrang; Hess & Co. (HESS) in Marienberg; Matthias Grathes in Osterath; Ransbach Floor Tile Factory (RANSBACH) in Ransbach; and Clayworks Industry in Klingenberg-on-the-Main (KLINGENBERG). By the end of the first decade of the twentieth century, there were over fifteen manufacturers of multicolored ceramic floor tiles in the country, competing successfully with makers of cement floor tiles, which, though cheaper to produce, were less hard-wearing.

The first German stove tiles were produced c. 1857 by master potter Carl Teichert in Meissen under a patent filed two years earlier by Gottfried Heinrich Melzer. At the 1873 Universal Exposition in Vienna, where several hundred tiled stoves were displayed by manufacturers from a number of different countries, the German stoves were considered to be the best in construction and decoration.[45] In Germany, the market in tiled stoves was dominated in the last third of the nineteenth century and into the twentieth by the Velten factories (VELTEN) and the Carl Teichert (TEICHERT) company.

After the start of floor- and stove-tile production in Germany, the larger industrial manufacture of ceramic wall tiles began, and with a much more extensive range of style, involving a greater variety of technique.

In the 1860s, the manufacture of, at first, plain and, then, decorated wall tiles, from wet clay was added by the Villeroy & Boch facilities in Mettlach and Dresden;

V & B D tile

and from 1875, they were using the dust-pressing technique there.[46] The company's Earthenware and Floor Tile Factory was one of the first factories in Europe to specialize in tile manufacture, adding the production of plain and, later, color-glazed wall tiles to that of floor tiles; by 1906, they employed about one thousand three hundred workers.

Between the late 1870s and the mid-1880s, Villeroy & Boch's competitors in the wall-tile market were Utzschneider in Saargemünd (Sarreguemines); Wessel in Bonn; Witteburg (WITTEBURG) in Farge; and the North German Earthenware Factory in Grohn.

In 1891 – following on Villeroy & Boch's example – the production of color-glazed wall tiles began at the Meissen Stove and Porcelain Factory, formerly Carl Teichert, Meissen. From then on, wall-tile manufacture continued to grow ever more rapidly in Germany – with tiles becoming cheaper because of competition between older and newer firms and new manufacturing techniques – to meet the growing demand from architects and builders for tile installation in not just public buildings, businesses, salesrooms, shops, railway stations, restaurants, coffee houses, etc., but also apartment houses and villas.

By the beginning of the twentieth century (and lasting well into the new century), Villeroy & Boch, under the direction of René von Boch, along with the Teichert companies continued the leadership with extensive ranges of tile designs.

By the time of René's death, there were nine Villeroy & Boch factories in Germany and Luxemburg, with more than eight thousand employees. Then, there were also, already, over twenty other factories in Germany with a total or partial production of colorful wall tiles. Consequently, at that time and afterward – during a period when there was so much ambivalent opinion regarding the fundamental contrast of handwork production and industrial mass-manufacturing techniques in German art/design circles – the aesthetically designed tile enjoyed a noticeable and continuing popularity as an industrial product, which was both decorative and useful, as well as being relatively inexpensive.

In 1903/1904, in western Prussia, Kaiser Wilhelm II established the modern Royal Majolica Workshops / (later) Majolica Workshop Cadinen (K.M.W.) at the Hohenzollern estate at Cadinen (Elblag), near Elbing, for the production of plaques, tiles, and other wall decorations, as well as terra cotta, architectural and other ceramic work.

By 1911/1912, there were almost thirty major firms with forty factories within Germany serving the German domestic tile market – the principal companies being Villeroy & Boch, with factories in Mettlach, Merzig, Dresden, Lübeck-Dänischburg, and Schramberg (V & B S); the three Teichert factories in Meissen; the North German Earthenware Factory, with three facilities in and around Bremen; and smaller companies with more than one manufacturing plant, including Servais, Wessel, and the Dusseldorf Claywares

V & B M tiles.

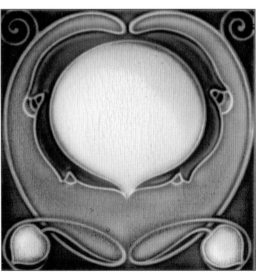

*Villeroy & Boch Mettlach floor-tile sample
sheet: 3.38" x 5.5" (8.59 x 13.97cm)*

*Villeroy & Boch Mettlach and Dresden 1910
catalog cover: 8" x 11" (20.32 x 27.9cm)*

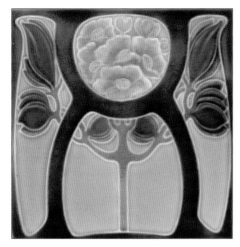

V & B D tile.

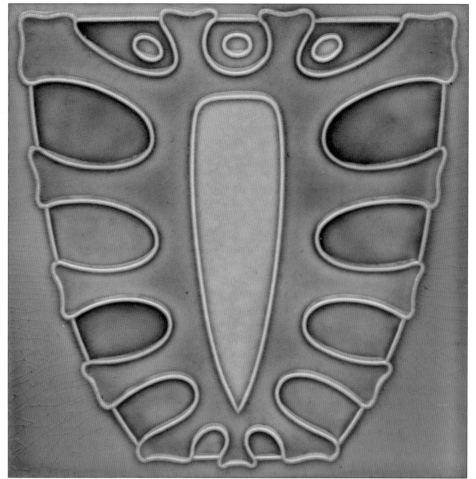

Ernst Teichert tile.

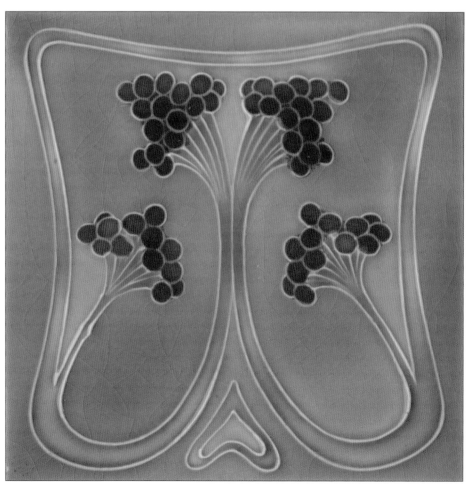

Utzschneider tile.

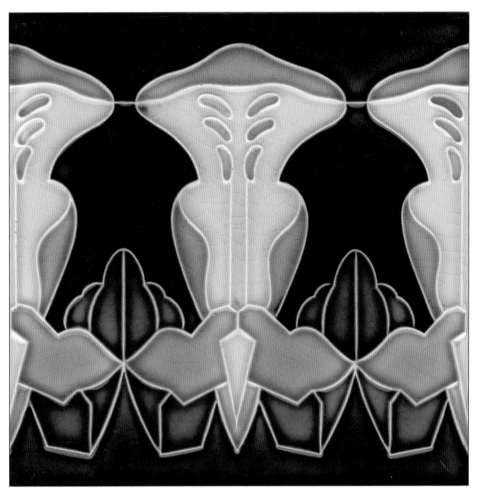

M.O.&P.F. tile.

S.O.F. tile.

Servais tile.

Utzschneider tile.

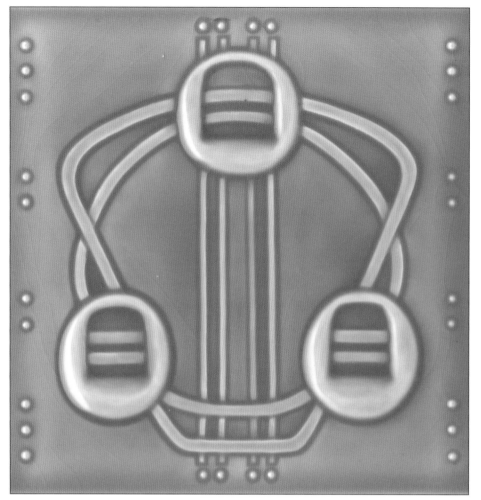

Wessel tile.

Factory (DTAG). Added to these was Utzschneider located at Saargemünd (Sarreguemines), at that time, in the Imperial Territory Alsace-Lorraine.

Through that time and even after the end of the war, some German tile companies also enjoyed a vigorous export trade in South America, Africa, Asia, and – in spite of tariffs and taxes, at various times – other countries in Europe.

In c. 1910–1911, Villeroy & Boch supplied floor tiles for the First Class Smoking Room of the ocean liner RMS *Titanic*[47] and, in the mid-1920s – along with the Rakonitz Tile and Stove Factory (RAKO) in Czechoslovakia – wall tiles for installation in the Holland Tunnel (opened in 1927) linking New York and New Jersey.

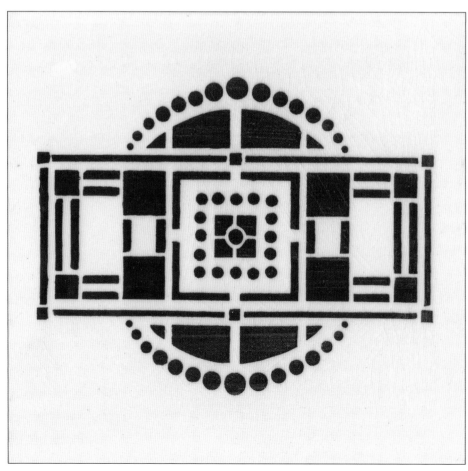

DTAG tile.

AUSTRIA, HUNGARY, BOHEMIA WITH MORAVIA & CZECH/ AUSTRIAN SILESIA[48]

With the Kingdom of Hungary already under total Austrian rule for almost a hundred years, the Congress of Vienna of 1814–1815 confirmed Austria – then heading a new Confederation of German States – as the dominant power in continental Europe.

Some fifty years later – in the Austrian-Hungarian Compromise of 1866/1867 – a constitutional Dual Monarchy was formed uniting the crowns of Austria and the Kingdom of Hungary and acknowledging the Austrian Empire as the Austro-Hungarian Empire, with Hungary as a recognized partner. Though granted limited self-rule then, Hungary continued to strive for full autonomy through the turn of the century.

In Vienna, capital of the illustrious Habsburg Empire, the second half of the nineteenth century saw the significant rise of a prosperous middle class and the growth of the city's reputation as a center for fine art as well as music and theater. The great boulevard – the Ringstrasse – was built to enclose the city on three sides with the River Danube bordering it on the fourth; the street was lined with grand buildings, as in other areas, exhibiting a revival of retrograde architectural styles, including Gothic, Renaissance, and Classical – at least until the reaction to Historicism and academic authority began to lead to a more modern and functional aesthetic.

At the same time, in Hungary, from the late 1860s and especially after the union of the two towns Buda and Pest to form the new metropolis of Budapest in 1873, the "formerly backward Hungarian economy became relatively modern and industrialized by the turn of the twentieth century, although agriculture remained dominant until 1890." [49]

In Bohemia, Moravia,[50] and Silesia, in the more populated regions where German and Austrian presence was entrenched, the influences of Viennese style and German innovation slowly infiltrated and were gradually acknowledged in matters of fine art, decorative art, and architecture, but the theory and practice of new design awakened the greatest interest only in the larger urban areas.

Rako tile.

Wienerberg tile.

Zsolnay tile.

At first – drawing much also from Franco/Belgian Art Nouveau, the English Arts & Crafts style, and German Jugend-stil – Secession, in Central Europe, differed in Austria, Hungary, and Bohemia/Mora-via (Czechoslovakia). In Austria, the in-spiration was floral and geometric; the Hungarian style was composed of a mix of Art Nouveau, vernacular culture, and nationalism; the Czech combination of Art Nouveau and other stylistic influ-ences (for instance, the familiarity of Neo-Renaissance form in architecture) reflected elements of Romanticism. In addition, both Secessionist styles in Hun-gary and Bohemia/Moravia, along with the active continuation of local influences, betrayed a strong interest in Eastern art.

At the end of the First World War, the Austro-Hungarian Empire was dissolved with the establishment of the federal republic of Austria (about one-quarter the size of the former dual monarchy) and a separate, smaller, totally independent nation of Hungary. Bohemia, Moravia, and Austrian/Czech Silesia formed the new, democratic republic of Czechoslovakia (now, Czech Republic) along with what had been Upper Hungary (now, Slovakia) and Carpathian Ruthenia. Also, at that time, an eastern region of what had been the Prussian Province of Silesia was returned to Poland. And what remained then of the Prussian Province became the "German" provinces of Lower Silesia and Upper Silesia, later, between 1938 and 1945, merged as the German Province of Silesia.[51]

CHAPTER TWO

THE STYLES

ARTS & CRAFTS DESIGN

In Britain, the Industrial Revolution fostered sterility in design, shoddiness in manufacture, and appalling working and living conditions for the masses employed on production lines there. Quantity was increased to the detriment of quality. Utilitarian ceramic wares and tiles were easily and cheaply mass-produced for a growing population by such methods as press molding and transfer printing.

Reaction to this ugly materialism and the recognition that reform was essential in British life and art were the "raison d'être" of the Arts and Crafts Movement. Starting in the 1860s, William Morris and the other British reformers hoped to achieve their social aims through the arts: reversing the degradation of life in the cities caused by industrialization and repairing the damage to the environment. To negate the harmful effects of mass-production on the urban populace, they wished to replace mindless, monotonous labor with creative craftsmanship, in which design was fully integrated with execution, whilst respecting local traditions. This was to result, they conjectured, not only in a rejection of indiscriminate reproduction and intermingling of unrelated revival styles of decoration but also in the creation of a supposedly affordable product proudly and joyfully made, and a pleasure to own.

In this reaction and in its attitude to Historicism and eclecticism in English architecture and style, "the Arts and Crafts Movement of the nineteenth century compounded many different aspects of the design, modes of production and politics of its time."[52] The terms "honest work" and "fitness for life," advocated by William Morris and others of the Movement's enthusiasts, were the basis of the handicraft revival they promoted. Many of the simple but refined features of the Movement's aesthetics were soon adopted by many designers of decorative products made by conventional industrial methods and processes. Eventually in Britain and – at an even earlier stage in the Movement's progress there – the United States, the Movement's social ideals and its political aims in respect of labor and capitalism were superseded, inevitably, by considerations of style and economic practicality in manufacture and decoration.

In the decorative arts, the Arts & Crafts style, growing out of "a communal aesthetic" – including different approaches and intentions, but unified by a recognition that "the principles of decoration needed reform"[53] – was based on a vocabulary of generally simple, sober, and, often, symmetrical and rectilinear designs. Its aesthetic appeal derived almost always – then and now – from a fundamentally straightforward, conservative restraint in furniture construction and, often, solely from visible aspects of the method of construction of chairs, tables, and cased pieces, while refined simplicity and functionality were the hallmarks of many of the most successful household objects it fostered.

The earliest Arts and Crafts pottery and tiles exhibit a largely realistic portrayal of natural forms but, later, decorative motifs, often in bold outlines, are "abstracted in a more rigid, almost mathematical way."[54] By the 1890s, however, conventionalization that was neither too realistic nor too abstract was desired and encouraged. Also denotive was ordered composition, frequently with symmetry and sometimes with strong vertical emphasis, in essentially two-dimensional surface designs occasionally constrained within a framework of border areas. Such motifs as flora and fauna and vegetal phenomena were often transmuted into flat, organic shapes that provided pattern forms, as well as – often, static – decorative features. Colors were, at first, frequently muted and matt glazes common along with Eastern and other artistic glazes – flowing, reduction, crystalline, etc.

Manufacturers of the time were aware of the Movement's critical concern with the division between art and industry caused by the Industrial Revolution. Pottery and tile makers, in particular, attempted, in the last third of the nineteenth century and afterward, to bring about some degree of reconciliation by attracting leading artists and designers from other areas of decorative art to their medium of ceramics and involving them in the design and production of vessels and other objects, and industrially produced tiles.

Previously, in the 1860s, British tile companies had continued their reliance on the popular Delftware. To this had been added the large-scale manufacture of printed tiles in series based on historical, literary, biblical, and other themes; such series were printed in blue, black, brown, or polychrome. Around the 1870s, they were joined by patterned and pictorial tiles with flat, simplified motifs from, at first, slightly and, later, more strongly abstracted, natural forms that were in harmony with the flat surface. Soon, colorfully painted, pictorial tiles were introduced that portrayed floral, animal, bird, and fish motifs, along with topographical scenes and rural themes – British countryside and farmyard activities, in particular – that evoked a mood of quietude. These grew in popularity with romantic, sentimental, and picturesque images – illustrating nursery rhymes, fairy tales, idylls, familiar verse and stories, and British pastimes – and others of pseudo-Medieval, Persian, and Japanese inspiration.

Many of the scenes and pictures were surrounded by a decorative, even geometric, framework within the tile's boundaries. Flowers, floral groups, and vegetal motifs were adapted to the requirements of a pattern for a square tile.

Other images were often featured in quartered-pattern grounds and other unusual placements, though always with a consideration of symmetry, balance, and containment. A single, regular, six-inch square tile could often feature several separate, enclosed designs or conjoined, independent segments or sections, each representing a different image.

Beginning in 1880, "over 1,000 new patterns ... (were) ... introduced in ... (a) ... sixteen year period"[55] by Mintons China Works, alone. In the design portfolios and sample sheets of this and other major British tile concerns in the last decades of the nineteenth century and into the twentieth century, Arts & Crafts imagery and presentation existed along with earlier, traditional tile styles and subject matter, while the often-fussy detail and moralistic content of Victorian art also tended to continue unabated throughout the Queen's reign.

However, by the early 1890s, the appeal of transfer printing in the industry began to wane, to be replaced by the ever-increasing popularity of molded-relief tiles, which had begun in the previous decade. These, in high or low relief and in monochrome or a variety of different colors, were covered in the translucent glazes that were to become the mainstay of Art Nouveau tile decoration. Accompanying these new facets of tile design and production was a strong interest in the cuenca technique, along with occasional incursions into the practices of sgraffito, slip-painting, and tube-lining and the beginning evidence of the more fluid linearity and rhythmic movement in representation that prefigured the evolution of Art Nouveau.

Tiles decorated in an Arts & Crafts vein were produced by the English companies well into the twentieth century, alongside those with Art Nouveau treatment, which had increased in popularity during the last five years of the nineteenth century. During the period of major tile production in Britain – c. 1870–1910 – the ranks of principal designers included Walter Crane, Lewis Foreman Day, William J. Neatby, Edward William Godwin, William Wise, John Moyr Smith, Charles Frances Annesley Voysey, Herbert Wilson Foster, Christopher Dresser, William Stephen Coleman, William de Morgan, Leon Victor Solon, and John Chambers.

As a result of the Arts and Crafts Movement, British High Victorian architecture and decoration came to embrace – though without an acknowledgment of economic viability – the development of a democratic art that had roots in vernacular style. And, in this achievement, it "was the principal agent in making folk art into a major component in fin-de-siècle culture all over the world," as well as "a vehicle for the expression of an overtly national culture after 1890."[56] For, through the association of local domestic traditions and rural motifs with Arts & Crafts design features and Art Nouveau influence, many countries – including Germany and the countries of Central Europe – developed their own distinctive turn-of-the-century styles that contributed to the establishment of modern, often independent, national identities.

The influence of the English Arts & Crafts style was, eventually, spread wide, too, in some other European countries, particularly, from about 1890 in Belgium, and, soon after in Germany and Northern Europe, as well as the United States. Before, around, and after the turn of the century, the work of Morris, Crane, Voysey, and Ashbee – alongside that of architects and designers Mackay Hugh Baillie Scott (in England) and Mackintosh (in Scotland), especially – was featured in international periodicals and expositions. In Germany and Austria, not only was the artistic influence of the Arts and Crafts Movement strongly identified, but also, even, to some degree, was the social effects of the Movement, which were first seen in the period 1895–1910, particularly, with the development, in Germany, of the national concepts of "homeland protection" (Heimatschutz) and "homeland style" (Heimatstilstil und -kunst).[57]

ART NOUVEAU[58]
The Franco-Belgian Style

Professing to reject what was, in the late nineteenth century in France and Belgium, antique, historical, imitative, and commonplace in art and style, Art Nouveau, beginning around the mid-1890s, was a reactionary, complex, and, often, flamboyant style – based on committed concepts of the new and largely original in decorative design – that pervaded architecture and all visual arts there. Its strength lay in its diversity and frequent ambiguity.

Concerned with evolutionary and dynamic growth, fantasy, and symbolism, the Franco/Belgian style was preoccupied with nature and natural forms in images and patterns that were, at first, naturalistic but, soon, conventionalized, often to subordinate the natural to the ornamental and emphasize curvilinear qualities. For many Art Nouveau designers, for whom conventionalization was the most significant aspect of style, nature represented a vehicle for design – rather than a model for formal imitation – through which they could evoke the power, vitality, and static tension of organic phenomena. And, indeed, French and Belgian Art Nouveau, from very early on, allowed nature to play mainly a secondary and supportive role to that of ornamentation and decoration. The structure of plants, along with blossoms and fruits, represented in full maturity or in cross-section, and leaves, buds, stamens, and other elemental parts of flowers, in ornate detail or sketched in outline, offered the artist/designer optimal, personal freedom of design.

Of special appeal were the energy of line and sinuous energetic force in spiraling smoke and swirling hair, as well as the undulating movement of swaying grasses, waving slender stems, bending stalks, drooping leaves, climbing and creeping tendrils, and the writhing motion of organic forms, entwining or unraveling, as found in natural growth – in fact, "a sinuous, tensile abstraction of natural form, that constantly looked as though it were about to burst out of some invisible force that held it under constraint."[59]

Due to the remaining strong influence of Symbolism in French and Belgian art, examples of flowers, fruits, and other plants with symbolical associations recur in Art Nouveau decoration, along with metamorphosis and organic evolution. Among the most popular were the poppy, with its connotations of sleep and dream – also prevalent in Decadent Art due to its narcotic association – and the waterlily, representing both beauty and danger as well as having a connection with mysticism. Other flowers invested with deeper significance by the Symbolists included the rose, anemone, honesty plant, and bleeding heart, together with plants and trees long considered to have special, natural, organic power. Along with them, animals, too, and insects, and birds (especially swans) were treated not merely as functional images in decoration, but also helped in setting an appropriate atmosphere in moody landscapes, suggestive of melancholy and, sometimes, with allegorical significance. Also, inherited by Art Nouveau artists and designers from the Symbolists – with their offer of "a more subversive world of introspection, desire, and uncertainty"[60] – were metaphysically and poetically representative motifs – princesses and castles, dragons and other monsters, mermaids, ghastly apparitions, etc. – from the world of fairy-tale, myth, and legend.

The human form, especially that of an almost-idealized, beautiful woman (she of the swirling hair), extravagantly dressed and with extraordinary jewelry, was also used – not only in fine art but in poster art and book illustration, of course, as well,[61] and in the design of furniture and the applied arts – to represent organic growth. Human and animal forms were portrayed in conjunction with floral ornament, shells, or flames or fused together in a hybridization of seductive, mysterious, and, sometimes, grotesque beauty. In painting, sculpture, and such applied arts as glass design and ceramics, "organic form could be made to elide from plant to human" with bodies "melting … into their landscape surround" in an attitude of "metaphysical metamorphosis."[62]

Not only did Art Nouveau draw inspiration from nature and – with its use of indigenous motifs from French and Belgian rural, artistic heritage – vernacular traditions, it also benefited from distant, foreign design sources. Artists and designers influenced, particularly, by the abstract quality of Japanese woodblock prints, recognized that an emphasis on flat areas of color added power and vitality to linear decoration. Asymmetrical composition was favored in both two- and three-dimensional design, especially since it accentuated the removal of the restraints so evident in the art of Neo-Classicism and other previous revival styles. However, within a consideration of symmetry and asymmetry, ornament was not only seen as an extraneous application to a three-dimensional object (furniture, silverware, ceramics, etc.), but it was also preferred that the form should have the appearance of having developed almost organically from the material.

As is evident in architectural ceramics of the time, including wall tiles with flat,

two-dimensional decoration or with aspects of sculptural relief, artistic design in France and Belgium was often influenced, as well, by the production techniques employed in industry and craft in the period from the mid-1890s almost up to the outbreak of hostilities in Europe.

In Art Nouveau's progress into the twentieth century, ornamentation remained insistently vital to style, but conventionalization, more and more, implied abstraction, as the depiction of organic forms moved ever further from naturalism until reduced to essentials. In a relatively short space of time, its gratuitous opulence began to reach satiety and yield to simpler, more sober, and more modern design. Even before the First World War, attention was diverted towards a form of expression demanding clarity and transparency and, particularly in France and Belgium after the war, a new departure point for design and decoration was found in the application of constructivist and cubistic ideas in art.

The International Style

For about ten to fifteen years in France and Belgium, Art Nouveau truly pervaded all design, invading all fields, particularly, those of architecture and applied art. Through handwork or with the aid of industrial mechanization, its influence was immediately apparent in the crafting/manufacture of furniture, ceramics, glass, jewelry, and metalwork, in book illustration, and in the production of posters and textiles. In addition, the Art Nouveau style (as, later, its variants in Germany, Austria, Central Europe, and elsewhere, as well) was easily and often adapted to sculptural, architectural faience, terra cotta decoration, and tile design.

Spreading beyond the borders of France and Belgium, Art Nouveau began to diversify as the twentieth century approached, taking different directions as its popularity grew in other European countries and the United States of America. Paralleling aspects of the English Arts and Crafts Movement, it broadened its appeal, while transforming some of its fundamental focus. In this transmutation, it also absorbed influences from different national styles in Europe. In Germany, for instance, the traditional depiction of rural scenes was of particu-

lar local relevance as a stylistic source, as was also folk art in Hungary and Bohemia/Moravia.

In spite of its professed anti-Historicist bias, Art Nouveau did not totally reject historical precedent in France and Belgium, nor in any of the other centers/areas, where it diversified and was adapted to local needs. "History was not to be copied ... [but] it was there to be manipulated, reinterpreted, and, where other models provided better solutions, rejected."[63] In architecture, particularly, this alternative use of history was to be seen, for instance, in buildings everywhere in such styles as Neo-Classicism, Neo-Gothic, and Neo-Renaissance that showed elements of Art Nouveau adaptation in their basic forms and/or whose façades were enhanced with Art Nouveau ornament.

Regions of influence were able to adapt or broaden the focus of the Art Nouveau style to suit a particular purpose that was more in accordance with local temperament, aspiration, and taste. To different degrees, artists of major international stature also stamped their distinctly personal signatures over the more general, stylistic features of Art Nouveau. These included Antoni Gaudi (in Spain), Charles Rennie Mackintosh (in Scotland), Louis Sullivan and Louis Comfort Tiffany (in the United States), Victor Horta (in Belgium), Belgian-born Henry Van de Velde (in Germany), Josef Hoffmann and Koloman Moser (in Austria), Carlo Bugatti (in Italy), Hector Guimard and the Nancy School, with the Gallé and Majorelle companies (in France), and the Czech Alfons Mucha (in France, also, and Bohemia/Moravia).

In addition, the argument of handicraft versus industrial mass-production, which was debated so vigorously at the turn of the century, played a role not only in the development of the English Arts and Crafts Movement but also in the characterization of Art Nouveau, wherever it extended its reach.

Because, in its various international manifestations, Art Nouveau often seems to be "marked by dichotomies and contradictions,"[64] it is advisable to differentiate the homogeneous, Franco/Belgian phenomenon from other late nineteenth-century and early twentieth-century, stylistic components of what might be called "International Art Nouveau." Other countries – or, more correctly, cities, regions, and centers in other countries – adapted Art Nouveau in accordance with national/local temperament and pragmatism or, in the case of Glasgow, introduced, almost simultaneously, a new style related to both Art Nouveau and Arts & Crafts design, with similarities of sophisticated design and reactionary spirit.

England

Other than "New Art," there is no specific term identifying English Art Nouveau. Nevertheless, significant examples existing in English art, architecture, and the applied arts of the time discount a total rejection of the style in England (and other areas of Great Britain); the architectural façade of Everard's Printworks Building of 1909 is a case in point, as is also the English tile industry, above all. But, by and large, English critics were, from the first, disdainful of the Franco/Belgian phenomenon and later denied that there was any such influence of the style on the English arts and crafts.

All the same, though Art Nouveau, in the main, was not to play a strong role in English design for industry, the English art movements of the last third of the nineteenth century, in many ways, anticipated the fin-de-siècle style in France and Belgium. In fact, between 1880 and 1895, particularly, the precursory, Art Nouveau aspects in some examples of English art and the production of furniture and decorative, everyday objects signaled an important connection between English Arts & Crafts design and the future Franco/Belgian Art Nouveau style.[65]

Particularly apparent, early on, in English tile decoration, were the qualities of softness and pliancy of line apparent in plant-influenced decoration. Such characteristics were exhibited by the mid-1890s in work by Crane, Foreman Day, Neatby, and other commissioned and in-house designers of the major tile manufactories of the time.

In British art history, reference is made, oftentimes, to these "precursory" or "proto"-Art Nouveau examples in English art, design, and manufacture towards the end of the nineteenth century, but, up to recently, hardly at all to the convincing evidence of the continuation of Art Nouveau-style decoration in the English tile industry well into the twentieth century

For at that time, in fact, the new design approach in tile work led soon to the more mature Art Nouveau products manufactured in the early twentieth century by T. & R. Boote, Ltd.; W. & E. Corn Brothers; Doulton & Co. / Royal Doulton; H. & R. Johnson Ltd.; Maw & Co.; Alfred Meakin & Co.; Minton's China Works; Minton Hollins & Co.; H. Richards Tile Co.; Pilkingtons Tile & Pottery Co. Ltd.; Sherwin & Cotton; and several other firms. In particular, Neatby at Doulton's designed tiles with a strong resonance of Art Nouveau for Harrods Department Store in London and the 1905 interior refitting of shipbuilder Joseph L. Thompson's mansion in Sunderland, as well as the afore-mentioned, architectural façade of a heightened, Art Nouveau character for Edward Everard's Printing Works in Bristol.

In other British industries, however, manufacturers were guided in matters of style by current taste and critical opinion, which reflected local critics' largely derisory attitude towards French and Belgian Art Nouveau as a transitory, degenerate, foreign affectation devoid of substance and realistic representation – at those times when it was even given a second thought. Architect, sculptor, and glass artist John Richard Clayton described it as nothing more than "a fungoid growth" and Walter Crane as "a phase rather than a craze," while C. F. A. Voysey called it "a debauch of sensuous feeling" and Alfred Gilbert said it was "absolute nonsense" – comments representative of opinions expressed by artists/designers regarded as key forerunners/initiators/innovators of, or participants in, the Art Nouveau movement.[66] Moreover, Lewis Day considered that Art Nouveau "shows symptoms … of pronounced disease. It is more than morbid; there is a suspicion about it of something downright loathsome."[67] And, at the very least, at that time in the realm of the decorative arts, British artists' observation of the natural world did, indeed, differ markedly from that defined as the principal source and base of the Franco/Belgian style, being far more concerned, as they were, with an accurate, faithful portrayal of nature.

In the end – apart from its significant role in tile manufacture in England – Art Nouveau appeared, pragmatically, only in individual and occasional, commercial production in some parts of Britain.

Scotland

As already noted, Art Nouveau in Scotland is frequently referred to as "Glasgow School," in regard to architecture and products originating in that area of the western part of the country or, otherwise, sometimes, as "Glasgow School-type," when the more appropriate, generic term, Scottish Art Nouveau, is not also applied to the style of works produced elsewhere in Scotland (for instance, in the capital city Edinburgh).

During the last few years of the nineteenth century and the first decade of the twentieth, design as practiced by the Glasgow School – including asymmetry and geometric ornament and abstraction, as well as floral-inspired, decorative motifs and attenuated, figurative, even androgynous forms – challenged convention as a restrained, linear, and angular alternative to Franco-Belgium Art Nouveau style, with economy of means replacing opulent, Franco/Belgian ornamentation.

Germany, Austria, Bohemia/Moravia (Czechoslovakia) & Hungary

Here, in particular, the stylistic mix of the generic forms of Art Nouveau, with the addition of local ingredients, was composed, in different degrees, of influences from France/Belgium, England, and Scotland. Most notable as variants of the Franco/Belgian style were the German "Jugendstil" (or "Youth Style"), the Austrian "Secession," the Bohemian/Moravian (later, Czechoslovakian) "Secese" or "Moderna," and the Hungarian "Szecesszio."

USA

In considerations of the decorative arts of the late nineteenth and early twentieth centuries in the United States, scattered manifestations of "American Art Nouveau" are sometimes regarded as components of the American Arts & Crafts style. Otherwise, "the American public … were distinctly ambivalent towards Art Nouveau [itself], with its connotations of permissiveness, degeneracy, and, perhaps, social revolution."[68]

Art Nouveau, however, is very much present, certainly from the mid-1890s, in the work directed by Louis Comfort Tiffany, including his "favrile" glass in fluid forms and intense color, leaded glass lamps and windows, enamels, pottery, jewelry, and metalwares. Also, by that time, stylistic qualities of an Art Nouveau nature, including organic ornament, were already evident in the designs of architect Louis Henri Sullivan and his draftsman

George Grant Elmslie, as they were, also, as early as 1890, in the "Broom Corn" silver design, for Tiffany & Co., by the German-born and, later, celebrated French Art Nouveau designer Edouard Colonna.

Apart from designs for American furniture, glass, pottery, metalwork, and jewelry adapted from European models, others in an Art Nouveau vein originated from the imaginations and hands of native-born artists. In ceramics, for instance, designers/sculptors Artus Van Briggle and Anna Marie Bookprinter Valentien – both strongly under the influence of Rodin, while in Paris and, afterward, on home ground – created vessels incorporating figural forms emerging from or extending along the item's surface that were reminiscent of works by French ceramists. Aspects of Art Nouveau are also evident in the work of George E. Ohr, Adelaide Alsop Robineau, and such pottery producers as the Rookwood Pottery Co., Newcomb College Pottery, Grueby Faience Co., and American Terra Cotta Tile and Ceramic Co. (Teco). A number of American makers of art glass and leaded (or painted) glass lamps attempted to emulate the design of Tiffany's creations, including the Handel Lamp Co., Pairpoint Manufacturing Co., and Quezal Art Glass & Decorating Co. Other names associated with the style, in the United States, were those of furniture designer Charles Rohlfs and illustrator and poster artist Will Bradley.

Elsewhere in Europe
The Italian version of Art Nouveau was known as "Stile Liberty," "Stile Floreale," or "Dolce Stil Nuovo," and the Spanish as "Modernista" or "Modernisme." In the Netherlands, "Nieuwe Kunst," and, in the Scandinavian countries, other variations of the style owed a debt, to different extents, to the Franco/Belgian model.

Various other names[69] were given to variant forms of Art Nouveau or were applied in other countries to aspects of the Art Nouveau style apparent in decoration in the applied arts, graphic art, book illustration, typography, etc., or relating to aesthetic composition in the fine arts.

Occasionally, aspects of International Art Nouveau and the Arts and Crafts Movement – "two distinct traditions" – amalgamated in variants of an aesthetic that embraced

"national overtones" yet, also, shared a common "universal modern identity."[70]

At first, Art Nouveau's pursuit of decoration as the basis of style was much admired in Continental Europe and its emphatic concern with curvilinear design and conventionalized natural form, together with its luxuriously ornamental quality, inspired imitation by painters, architects, graphic artists, and craftsmen there. But some aspects of the Franco/Belgian style, such as its emphasis on decoration based on flowers and plants, together with the shock value of its ornate opulence, began quickly to lose their appeal.

Even in the last few years before the turn of the century, a number of architects, designers, artists, and craftsmen, particularly in Germany, Austria, the Netherlands, Scandinavia, and other areas of Continental Europe, recognized that Art Nouveau did not relate to their concern with clarity and functionality in the design of buildings and houses, furniture and everyday objects, etc. In their determination to reform architecture and embellish, anew, the total domestic environment, they wished, above all, to create modern, beautiful, and unified living and working spaces through a synthesis of the applied arts that would include all areas of life at every level of society. And for them, everyday life required an ornamentation more intrinsically and functionally satisfying than that offered by Franco/Belgian Art Nouveau. Their concept of the Gesamtkunstwerk required practical construction and decoration through rational, efficient design to create a consonant, harmonious whole, preferably, through machine production.

Influenced by Mackintosh and the Glasgow artists, as well as by stylistic achievements of the English Arts and Crafts promoters, Joseph Maria Olbrich, Henry Van de Velde, Peter Behrens, Josef Hoffmann, Koloman Moser, Jan Kotera, and others among their contemporaries, for instance, began to embrace a more sober aesthetic of restrained decoration contrasting with the excesses of the style in France and Belgium. In design concepts based more on the single, stylistically unique, tense line within decoration, they introduced forms that were to become more and more stringently abstract after c. 1905, as the orientation moved in a direction towards geometric abstraction – with only distant reminiscences of nature – and, finally, "complete artifice."[71]

Also, exemplary of the synthesis of opposite values in a quest for the beautiful within the broader, anti-Historicist Art Nouveau movement was the "apparently contradictory, eclectic use of Historicist styles,"[72] evident in the German and Central European variants.

As emergent, divergent forms, Jugendstil in Germany and Secession in Central Europe thus very soon began to challenge and transform Art Nouveau, as it was first introduced, in a manner that was to affirm modernity yet appeal to the different national temperaments. Intent on reforming design and rejecting existing criteria, the alternative preoccupation – determined as much by economic consideration (particularly in Germany) as by artistic principle – foreshadowed the beginning, internationally, of "modern" architecture and design and – in its elementary and, sometimes, even brutal, utilitarian simplification – had a lasting effect on twentieth century industrial design.

JUGENDSTIL[73]

It was from the literary and artistic journal *Jugend,* founded in 1896, that Jugendstil took its name. This was at a time when a number of artists and designers in Germany – as elsewhere – wishing to discard previous historical styles and academic traditions, were beginning to turn to applied arts and architecture and adopt forms derived from nature and fantasy. Among those whose names were soon to become inextricably associated with this modern dynamic image of energy and who transformed the new style into an intensely personal and spiritual artistic language were Hermann Obrist, August Endell,[74] Otto Eckmann, and Hans Christiansen.

Hermann Obrist's work in textile design, particularly, emphasized conventionalized treatment of vegetal and organic imagery. First apparent in his tapestry *The Whiplash* (*Der Peitschenhieb*) of 1895, with its undulating rhythms, his exploitation of line and color for expressive purposes led to his becoming acknowledged as a foremost Jugendstil exponent. In this seminal work, in which the cyclamen stalks are depicted as ferociously sinuous curves, the treatment assaults the eye and mind.

Just as expressive – and even more provocatively immoderate – was Endell's iconic design, in 1896–1897, for the exterior façade of the Atelier Elvira studio that included a large stucco ornament depicting a highly stylized, red and yellow dragon creature emerging from a turbulent, wave-like element. Other decoration in his design of the interior featured similarly strange – and disturbing – organic imagery.

A strong, personal reaction is also achieved by Otto Eckmann's important tapestry *Five Swans* (*Fünf Schwäne*) but this is one of quietude. The work is a sensitive evocation of calmness, though, perhaps at the same time, with a disquieting hint of anxious yearning for permanent, spiritual contentment. Reflecting the influence of Japanese prints while also revealing Eckmann's simplistic approach to design, the long, rectangular composition presents a stylized scene of swans in an orderly procession following the course of a winding stream within an idyllic forest. As an expressive composition, like his other tapestries *Forest Pond* (*Waldteich*) and *Advent of Spring* (*Fruhlings Einzug*) of the same period – c. 1895–1898 – its Jugendstil conception of an image of

joyful or wistful or enigmatic beauty was both more straightforward in its relaxed Arts & Crafts symmetry and less affected in its symbolist imagery than French/ Belgian Art Nouveau. Many other designers and craftsmen would soon try to emulate its poetic naturalism.

With an early interest in Japanese art and British Arts & Crafts design, together with his familiarity with French Art Nouveau (after spending so much time in Paris around the turn of the century), Hans Christiansen was an outstanding and versatile decorative artist with a special regard for material and technique. Working in a variety of media, he used naturalistic and abstract styling integrated with figurative and mythical designs in a unique way, as witnessed by his tapestries *Guardian Angel* (*Schutzengel*) and *Frau Musica*, to develop individual and innovative decoration. Other work shows an economy of design and superb construction of the surface ornament that avoids the opulence and self-indulgent exaggeration of so much French-Belgian

Art Nouveau of that time in favor of a more simplistic, subjective Jugendstil individualism.

In the late 1890s, a number of popular German art and design magazines featured this design genre – expressively decorative subject-matter – prominently in their editions. Among them, *Deutsche Kunst und Dekoration* promoted frequent design competitions in such media as tile, stoves, wallpaper, carpets, interior design, bedroom furniture, wardrobes, chairs, desks, pianos, table lamps, plant stands, table runners, cushions, jewelry, window glazing, posters, book illustration, and amateur photography.

Most of the illustrations in this and other magazines of this time exhibited conventionalized Art Nouveau motifs, as well as naturalistic scenes (often with an intimation of nostalgia), though, very soon, several of the designs were more abstract, prefiguring an important change in the contemporary conception of the Youth Style variation on the Franco/ Belgian theme.

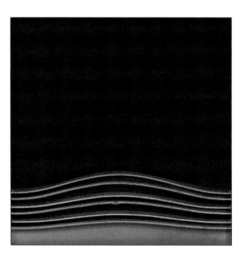  

Horizontal frieze of three M.O.&P.F. wall tiles.

Horizontal frieze of three NSTG wall tiles.

From around the beginning of the twentieth century, the important, Belgian-born architect, designer, theorist, and teacher Henry Van de Velde, who was, later, to be celebrated as a forerunner of functionalism and modernism, was instrumental in improving and promoting German design. Originally, in the early to mid-1890s, the influence of Franco/Belgian Art Nouveau showed strongly in his design of furniture and objects, with his use, for instance, of organic, intertwining lines to create a stylized interpretation of natural, particularly floral, form. Nevertheless, the rhythmic lines in his design avoided the more sensual qualities of Art Nouveau and the curvilinear aspect was more abstract and, in general, less dependent on plant structure. In the late 1890s, his growing interest in the English Arts and Crafts Movement led him to redirect his efforts as a designer of interiors, household goods, and jewelry. His stated wish[75] was to replace the "old symbolic elements, which have lost their effectiveness," with a universal aesthetic "in which ornament has no life of its own but depends on the forms and lines of the object itself, from which it receives its proper organic place." Relying on his concept of the union of form and function, his complex and comprehensive work, though having little in common with geometric modernity, was more constructional than decorative. The convincingly rational principles of his teachings, his sparing design, and his belief that "line is power" – exemplified by the assertively and innovatively linear quality of his work – already resonated with other architects, artists, designers, and craftsmen in Germany in the earliest years of the twentieth century. In his book *Vom Neuen Stil*,[76] he demanded a complete change in the practice of architecture and craft to reflect a concern for the norms of rational construction and the laws of a new ornamentation proceeding from the line.

Joseph Maria Olbrich in Austria, after assisting in the transformation of the Historicist legacy in architecture and design in Central Europe and before taking up residency in Germany in 1899, began to subject his work to new parameters concerning decoration and pattern. At first, owing much to Mackintosh and Baillie Scott, he often combined architectonic designs with organic motifs, showing his affinities with the Arts and

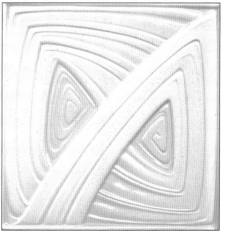 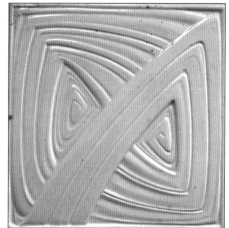

V & B M tiles, designed by Henry Van der Velde.

Crafts Movement, Art Nouveau, and Secession. Later, he continued to refuse to allow decoration to obscure the functional aspects of his design in his use of simple, geometric details and harmonious forms at Darmstadt, Germany.

Peter Behrens was also a pioneer in the field of modern, objective, industrial architecture and design. From his earliest commissions for furniture, silverware, dinnerware, glassware, and jewelry around 1898/1899, he made use of a style that

was restrained in shape and ornament, and largely based on both linear and geometric considerations. Previously, his work in book illustration and typography had owed much to the burgeoning interest in Art Nouveau in Germany, but, with the approaching turn of the century, his seminal work began to exhibit the evocative possibilities of pure visual elements, such as line and plane, in a more sober, austere design, moving away from the early Jugendstil exuberance of other artists. For

V & B M tiles, designed by Peter Behrens.

his Darmstadt house, completed by 1901, his silverware design was based on a subtle decoration of avant-garde, geometric, linear patterns, and his dinnerware exhibited the same on hexagonal, octagonal, and flat circular forms. He was already developing then an elegant, functional style, incorporating linear emphasis and spatial form that prefigured modernism. After moving to Dusseldorf in 1903, his work continued to reflect this rational, simpler idiom.

Like Behrens, Richard Riemerschmid embarked early on a course of design that would lead eventually to extreme economy of form and decoration. By the late 1890s, a dissatisfaction with typical Art Nouveau devices – such as the rhythmic suggestion of undulation in delicate designs derived from plant forms and the common motif of interlacing stalks and leaves – led him to a rejection of decoration based on ornamental, organic imagery. He replaced this with a more straightforward aesthetic dependent on the relatively geometric and modernist discipline of pure line, with function and construction often determining design in his work in furniture and other media, though, often, with the use of traditional forms and techniques.

Accordingly, in Germany, Jugendstil – characterized from the beginning by the adaptation of elements of Franco/Belgian and British influences – soon added the aesthetic principles of Van de Velde, Olbrich, Behrens, Riemerschmid, et al, and considerations of appropriateness and inventive freedom in ornament. Architects, painters, and sculptors turned their attention to the applied arts, at the same time rejecting handcraftsmanship as the ideal (in contrast to the views of their English Arts and Crafts forbears) and encouraging practicality and the use of machinery to produce affordable furniture and household decoration and decorative, functional objects.

With the work of Olbrich and Behrens, in particular, represented at the Artists' Colony[77] there, the exhibition at Darmstadt in 1901 marked a distinct turning point in German design with the introduction of a modern idiom arising from the use of more plain, geometric forms with relatively minimal decoration.

By the time of the founding of the German Work Federation (Deutscher Werkbund) in 1907 – and, arguably, with the approbation of its members – the floral decoration in Jugendstil had begun to concede stylistic dominance to a stronger rectilinear emphasis and the translucent beauty of geometry in asymmetrical composition. With a membership of twelve artists, craftsmen, architects, designers, and industrialists, the Federation – though owing something to the principles and priorities of the English Arts and Crafts Movement – wished to promote good German design and craftsmanship in mass-produced goods and architecture by establishing close relations between industry and designers. An equal aim was to elevate the overall level of taste in Germany by improving the design, quality, and appropriateness of products in everyday German life (including, for instance, well-conceived tilework decoration in interior design and stoneware/terra cotta use in exterior architecture). With Van de Velde, Olbrich, Behrens, and Riemerschmid, along with Bruno Paul, as driving forces within the membership, the preference for the more restrained, rational, less expressive side of Jugendstil design was to gain greater acceptance amongst other design professionals and product manufacturers as a more worthy and fitting, modern style in German national culture. After all, the importance of the more celebrated German artists and designers was to be seen not only in their own production and their promotion of their own work, but, also, in the effect their creativeness had on the anonymous designs and products on the wide, national, public market.

The aim of improving standards of design and production for the benefit of a greater public was a feature first aspired to by the promoters and enthusiasts of the English Arts and Crafts Movement, who, from the 1860s, though unsuccessfully, sought aesthetic penetration of all areas of life. Unlike them, however, designers in Germany during the Jugendstil era, such as Van de Velde, Behrens, and Riemerschmid, did not, fundamentally, abjure industrial manufacture but, on the contrary, by and large, expressly encouraged serial production and were, thereby, successful in promoting their own demand for affordable and tasteful practicality.

Thus, though the artistic forms arising in France and Belgium in the mid-1890s constitute the stylistic upheaval of Art Nouveau, Jugendstil can be defined – within the broader outlines of International Art Nouveau – as an evolving, progressive force in the development of modern twentieth-century design. However, avoiding oversimplification in dating the changes of emphasis as well as dubious assumptions regarding the diverse artistic inspirations that are characteristic of Jugendstil, it has been recognized that all aspects of the style existed side by side, for a while, in the continuing history of the applied arts in everyday life in Germany in the early twentieth century. In the case of Jugendstil tile production, that was so almost up to the time of the Second World War, as evidenced by tile companies' sample books of the period into the 1930s as well as surviving homes and buildings after the Second World War and before postwar remodeling.

AUSTRIAN SECESSION

In Austria, the name of the Secessionist style was taken from the founding of the Vienna Secession in 1897 by a group of progressive architects, artists, and designers, including Joseph Maria Olbrich, Josef Hoffmann, and Gustav Klimt. Opposed to Historicism and the conservatism of academic art and supporting the concept of the Gesamtkunstwerk as a synthesis of the arts, the aims of the Vienna Secession were the promotion of a modern aesthetic in architecture, art, and the visual arts, improvement of standards of decorative design, and the revival of craft. Its mouthpiece *Ver Sacrum* was published from 1898 through 1903, but, though concerned with art and graphic design, was not particularly influential in the applied arts of that period. The words carved above the entrance to the Vienna Secession building were "To every age, its art / To art, its freedom," embodying the wish to break with the past and the academic constraint associated with it.

Earlier, in Austria, two architects/designers, Otto Wagner especially – and Adolf Loos, had begun to prepare the way for a new stylistic direction governed by a rational and practical aesthetic and the significance of function in the technical construction of furniture and everyday objects.

Wagner – a radical theorist and teacher, though not a founding member of the Vienna Secession – was a proponent of the concept of form resulting from function and material, and, by the mid-1890s,

Detail of the façade of the Secession Building.

Detail of the façade of the Majolika House. Photo courtesy of GNU Free Documentation License, Version 1.2: Creative Commons Attribution 3.0 Unported; author: Gallery Donau Reiskoffer.

promoted change in architecture and design towards a revolutionary rectilinearity and economy of ornament. In practice, however, he diverted from this path when he approved his student Aloys Ludwig's design[78] for the façade of his Majolica House (c. 1898) in Vienna that called for an overall installation of Wienerberg (WIENERBERG) glazed ceramic tiles – with Secessionist decoration – flowing into floral shapes as they extend higher up the wall.

In also emphasizing functionality, Moravian-born Loos, working in Vienna and Prague, went beyond Wagner's ethos in repudiating all superfluous ornament.

More influential on the architects and designers associated with the Vienna Secession was the sophisticated appeal of the Glasgow School's design. Predicated on geometric ornament, dynamic abstraction, and sparing, rational use of space, as well as expressive conventionalization of floral forms and stylization of figural forms, its appeal to members of the Secession was immediate from the time of the first publication of Charles Rennie Mackintosh's work in the German magazine *Dekorative Kunst* in 1898. In

1900, to great acclaim, Mackintosh was invited to exhibit at the Secession building in Vienna.

Also of interest to the members of the Secession was the example of the English Arts and Crafts Movement and its emphasis on handicraft, together with the stylistic influence of Ashbee, Voysey, and Baillie Scott, as well as Richard Norman Shaw.

As was the case in Germany, where the Artists' Colony in Darmstadt pointed the way to a more constructivist, functional aesthetic, Vienna spearheaded a slow and gradual direction towards a restrained, sober, linear design, concerned with structural clarity, which gained strength as the obsession with the excessive, curvilinear, floral ornament of Franco/Belgian Art Nouveau flourished and then began to wither. Austria's Secession was "specifically Viennese,"[79] emphasizing simplicity of design and featuring abstracted motifs from nature in a restrained, elegant linearity.

Though preoccupied in the main with geometric patterns, it was, nevertheless, a pluralistic style combining innovation with tradition and fantasy. And, as with

Jugendstil in Germany, Secession in Austria was to "assimilate some fundamental characteristics" of Biedermeier.[80]

The Vienna Workshops (Wiener Werkstätte) organization was founded in 1903 as a production cooperative for craft and design with a Secessionist aesthetic in an industrial society, in which handicraft was dying. Its first products, evidencing a close relationship with the two-dimensional quality and geometric abstraction of Scottish Art Nouveau, emphasized handcraftsmanship – in contrast to the contemporaneous achievements of the avant-garde artists in Germany – but did not altogether reject machine production. Josef Hoffmann's tile designs, often suggesting three-dimensional qualities, were more geometric than those of Koloman Moser, whose work was more abstract and graphic. Many other Vienna Workshops tile designs – particularly those incorporating stylized plant motifs (before an almost complete obliteration of the original floral inspiration of Art Nouveau there) – were represented sparingly within a limiting framework, with a flat, geometric decoration composed of constructive

Wienerberg tiles.

elements. With this conception of linear, reductive, and almost constructivist design, Hoffmann, Moser, and their colleagues – in their determination to overhaul contemporary Viennese design, particularly of household objects, through an emphasis on function and the unification of ornament and structural form – were, possibly, as instrumental in prefiguring a new cosmopolitan style in Austria in the new twentieth century as were Van de Velde, Behrens, and Riemerschmid in Germany. Indeed, though becoming more eclectic in time, the distinctive, elegant work of the Vienna Workshops stretched the boundaries of the decorative arts in Europe.

HUNGARIAN SECESSION

The Hungarian Secessionist style, known locally as "Szecesszio," was very strongly connected in the last years of the nineteenth century to the country's search for an independent identity and cultural independence from Austria.

With the spread of the Art Nouveau idiom from Paris to Budapest, young architects and designers – wishing to reject Historicism in favor of a new and, possibly, more specifically Hungarian system of ornament – viewed it as a step towards an internationalism that might announce a modern age. At the same time, they welcomed the opportunity for the exercise of national vitality in a combination of the new influence with vernacular sources in Hungarian applied arts. This coincided with the millennial celebration in 1896 – a festival commemorating the migration of the first Hungarian tribes to the area in 896 AD – that was designed to emphasize a cultural and commercial separation from Austria.

Thus, an integration of the influences of Franco/Belgian Art Nouveau, Austrian Secession, and the English Arts and Crafts Movement appealed to art and design enthusiasts in Budapest because of their search for new forms in a modernized aesthetic, on the one hand, and interest in the revival of craft techniques, on the other. Along with the German tendency towards

sentiment and nostalgia, the Hungarian variant form of Art Nouveau shared with Jugendstil the imagery of fantasy and Symbolism. Nevertheless, a distinctive, local style was achieved with the implementation of a unique design vocabulary of peculiarly vernacular and urbane motifs and patterns that had roots in the nation's strikingly decorative, indigenous folk art (including, particularly, embroideries and other textiles) and peasant traditions, combined with resonances of Persian and Indian architecture, ornament, and design from the history of the ancient Magyar homelands.

Wishing to reject the influences of eclectic and Historicist design, a number of designers and architects in Budapest, along with some manufacturers, began, at first tentatively, to incorporate the new European stylistic advances into their work. From around 1898, Art Nouveau influence infiltrated artistic production, more and more, at the Zsolnay factory (ZSOLNAY), directed, already by then for over thirty years, by Vilmos Zsolnay. It was Vilmos Zsolnay, who approved the

Two Zsolnay plaques: (left) celebrating the Hungarian Millenial, 8.13" x 8.5" (20.7 x 21.6cm), (right) 12" x 13.25" (30.5cm. x 33.7cm).

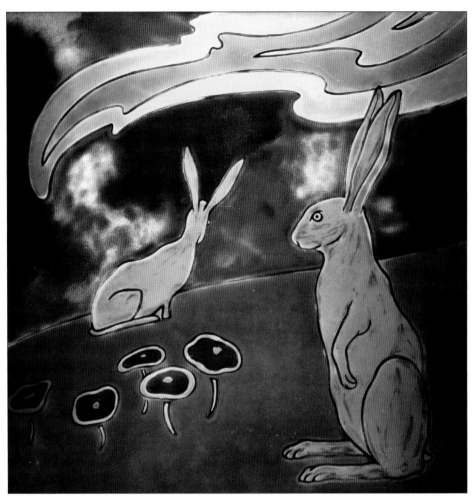

reproduction of Scheerhart's iconic image as his company's contribution to the millenial celebration.[81]

Though some designers shunned the self-conscious, national character sought by their compatriots, others – like their contemporaries elsewhere – enjoyed the pronounced stylization of native flora and fauna together with other motifs frequently derived from Hungarian tradition. On the other hand, whilst the constructivist, variant form of Jugendstil found expression, particularly, in the production of industrially manufactured tiles in Germany and Bohemia/Moravia (Czechoslovakia), it was far less apparent in Hungary, as in Austria.

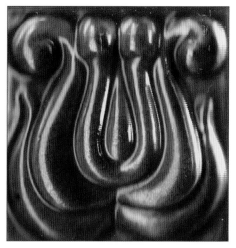

Three Zsolnay tiles: (right) 1.5" (3.8cm) square, 0.75" (1.9cm) deep.

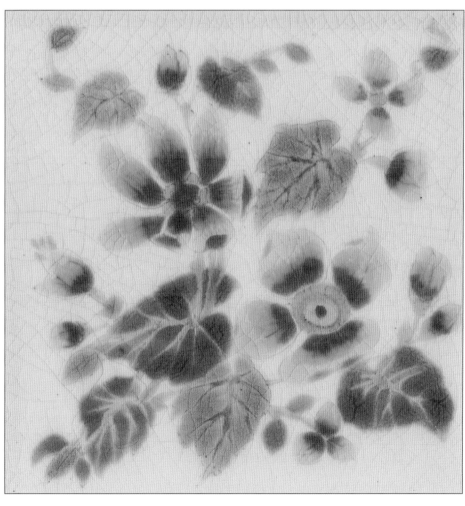

BOHEMIAN/MORAVIAN (CZECHOSLOVAKIAN) SECESSION

Until shortly after the turn of the century, the influence of the floral, Franco/Belgian Art Nouveau style was prevalent in the Austrian crown lands Bohemia and Moravia (both, now, together with Czech/Austrian Silesia, part of the Czech Republic). It was reflected in the decorative design of interiors in Prague and other urban areas, as well as in objects produced by craftspeople and factories there. Together with their own growing freedom in the use of historical precedent and symbolical association – and with the encouragement of the Imperial/Royal School of Arts & Crafts in Prague – Czech designers enthusiastically embraced the curvilinear representation of sinuous ornament, fantasy forms, and the "dynamism and metamorphism that fused figures and foliage ... into an integrated flowing whole."[82]

But there were already, in the early years of the new century, the seeds of change in the "orientation of Czech Art Nouveau ... [with a] gradual departure from French patterns ... and from 1905, as in several other centres [sic] geomet-

ricization began to emerge as the basis for stylistic abstraction."[83]

The peculiarly Czech version of International Art Nouveau, under the name "Moderna" or, more often, "Secese" – manifesting a combination of the cosmopolitan and the vernacular – represented an escape from previous ornamental styles, as in Germany, Austria, and Hungary, in a deliberate attempt to define an independent and distinctively Czech style, which, nevertheless, shared initially the essential tenets of Art Nouveau combined with aspects of Arts & Crafts design.

To some degree, this stylistic development in Bohemia can be seen, in many ways, as mirroring the career of its most prominent architect, designer, and teacher, Moravian-born Jan Kotera. In the mid-1890s, Kotera studied under Otto Wagner in Vienna, was appointed professor at the School of Arts and Crafts in Prague in 1898, and professor of the Academy of Fine Art there in 1910. Designing in all branches of applied art, including wall tiles, and initially influenced

by the Secessionist style, he indulged, at the same time, an interest in the Czech folk-art tradition and insisted on everyday practicality. More and more, especially after 1906, he emphasized functionality, structural clarity of form, and "the simplest spatial and plastic articulation."[84]

His efforts, and those of other local architects, designers, and builders, resulted in the treasury of Art Nouveau style in Prague architecture – still gloriously visible today in beautiful buildings, constructed and decorated around the turn of the nineteenth century to meet the demands of a modern era and also functional, even nowadays, in public use. Architectural form at the time was basically Neo-Renaissance in style but – with a superb, vegetal and figural, stucco ornament – conceived with a lighter, freer approach. A wealth of Secessionist decoration embellishes not only the exterior of buildings, but also the interior, with entrance halls exhibiting fascinating images and patterns of colorful ceramic tiling.

Eichwald plaque: 14.5" x 4.38" (36.8cm. x 11.1cm)

W. S. & S./Schiller tile.

Rako tiles.

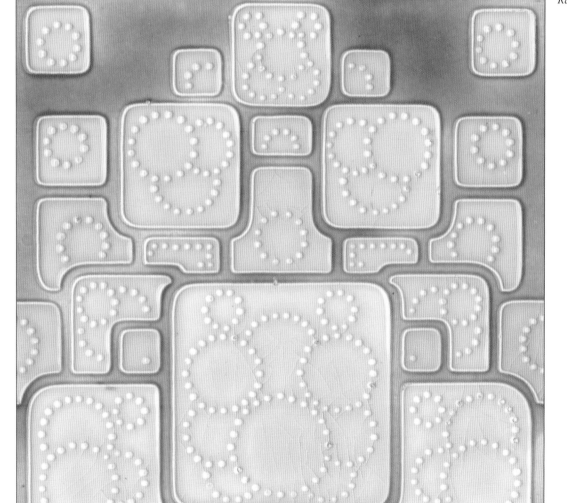

CHAPTER THREE

THE TILES

GERMAN JUGENDSTIL TILES

Jugendstil, in its maturity, described a stylistic direction that was determined by the desire of its architects, artists, designers, and craftsmen to create a synthesis of the arts that would include all areas of everyday life at most levels of society. And the more avant-garde designers, from before the turn of the century in Germany, considered wall coverings in domestic (and public) interiors to be part of this Gesamtkunstwerk, making "the modern house a combined work of art and a practical construction of simple and dignified beauty."[85] By the late 1890s, it was, therefore, likely through wall decorations in vestibules, hallways, and stairwells, etc. – and also kitchens and bathrooms – that Jugendstil was able to find an entry into German homes and other buildings due to the affordability, practicality, technical production process, and aesthetic appeal of locally produced, ceramic tiles. Consequently, the humble wall tile at that time gained the capacity to reform the aesthetics of home construction and decoration in the country.

This was made possible when, in the 1890s, the German tile industry – having earlier benefited greatly from English mechanized processes – also drew inspiration from a number of significant sources. Amongst these were the teachings of British design theorist Christopher Dresser and the development, in England, of the Arts and Crafts Movement with its bold, flat, polychrome, as well as monotone, patterns. At the same time, notice was also taken in German design and manufacturing circles of the proto-Art Nouveau aspects of style – with nature-based decoration – introduced in the English tile industry by Crane, Day, Solon, Neatby, and other commissioned and in-house designers.

V & B D tile.

V & B M tile.

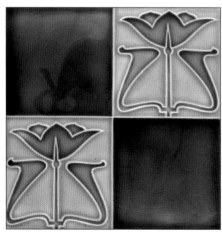

Wessel tile.

Wessel tile.

Another important influence on the Jugendstil tile was the stylistic preference in German decorative art for vernacular imagery due to the nation's continuing preoccupation with the simple life and folk traditions. Nostalgia for an earlier, supposedly happier and purer time in a peaceful homeland was reflected in the well-known appeal of designs representing bucolic idylls and rural scenes.

Though Jugendstil in Germany, as a variant component of International Art Nouveau, was to offer a reaction to earlier styles and revivals, manufacturers continued to rely on the commercial popularity of favorite familiar themes. Accordingly, they also were cognizant of the German public's admiration for the appropriateness of neo-Gothic patterning and the attachment to Biedermeier ornamentation, with its swags, garlands, fruit baskets, and overflowing cornucopia. The rationality of Biedermeier design and, particularly, its two-dimensional patterns continued to appeal to the sentimental and orderly aspects of the German temperament, as well as to nationalistic inclinations and preferences, elsewhere.

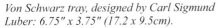

Von Schwarz tray, designed by Carl Sigmund Luber: 6.75" x 3.75" (17.2 x 9.5cm).

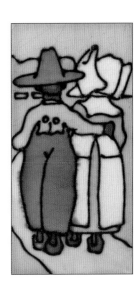

Boizenburg half-tiles.

Boizenburg tile.

V & B M tile.

V & B D special-use tile.

In fact, Jugendstil owed much to the Historicism of the Gründerzeit, reverberating with vestiges of Neo-Classicism and resonances of late-Romanticism, while the appeal of the Dutch style of Delft blue-and-white printing was also a factor remaining from the previous eclecticism. These aspects of design were carried forward in the late 1890s as a positive influence.

NSTG tile.

DTAG tile.

V & B D tile.

Von Schwarz plaque, designed by Carl Sigmund Luber: 6.25" x 4.38" (15.9 x 11.1cm).

V & B M tile.

Bendorf tile.

Wessel tile.

V & B M tile.

GWF tile.

Biedermeier style – though apparently in conflict with the excesses of the new foreign enthusiasm – could, nevertheless, join with the neo-Gothic restraint, the neo-Classical historical interest, the late-Romantic vernacular motifs, the nostalgia and mysticism implicit in Symbolism, and the richness of floral decoration and dynamism of the curved line apparent in the first influences of Art Nouveau to foreshadow the true identity and originality of the mature Jugendstil.

DTAG tile.

Ernst Teichert tile.

S. O. F. tile.

GWF tiles.

Wessel tiles.

With the burgeoning interest of German designers/manufacturers in the stylistic development in neighboring France and Belgium, the effect of Art Nouveau's nature-inspired ornamentation was noticeable in German design and manufacture. From the time that Jugendstil-decorated tiles first became available, flower and plant representation predominated. Spring flowers, such as tulips, snowdrops, anemones, and lily of the valley, were frequent choices as naturalistic – and, later, conventionalized – motifs. Roses, pansies, carnations, poppies, sweet pea, bleeding heart, and waterlilies were popular, as well, together with bindweed and other vines, wildflowers of the field, trees, ivy, etc., and decorative plants. Many of these were endowed with a symbolical value.

Servais tile.

Schmider special-use tile.

V & B S tile or, possibly, special-use tile, signed "JB," possibly designed by Jean Beck.

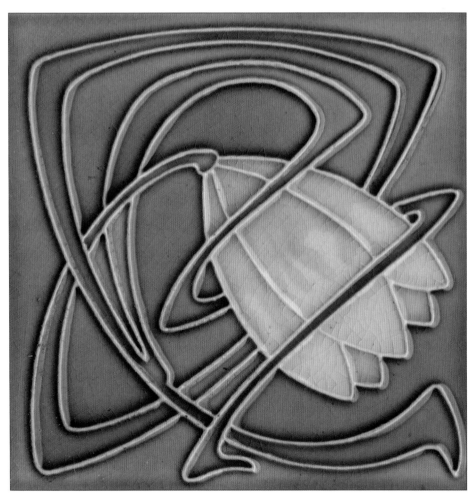

Servais tile.

Witteburg tile.

Schmider special-use tile.

Indeed, from the beginning of the Jugendstil/Secessionist era in the German and Central European markets, the more purely Art Nouveau-inspired, expressive, floral designs represented beauty and hope in a darkening and threatening age, while the idyllic realm of fairy tale, with princesses and knights, contributed a marvelous expression of deep-rooted longing for an imaginary era. Picture books were the source of images of beautiful women – with perfect faces framed by shining hair and jeweled headdresses – wearing long, flowing robes, their bodily forms at once dangerous and fascinating, ethereal and demonic, and their attitudes and expressions, though sensual, both melancholic and introspective. Myths and legends provided dragons and other fantasy creatures.

Two Von Schwarz plaques, designed by Carl Sigmund Luber: (top) 18" x 6.75" (45.72 x 17.15cm), (bottom) 11.75" x 6" (29.85 x 15cm).

S. O. F. tile.

S. O. F. tile.

S. O. F. tile.

NSTG tile.

S. O. F. tile.

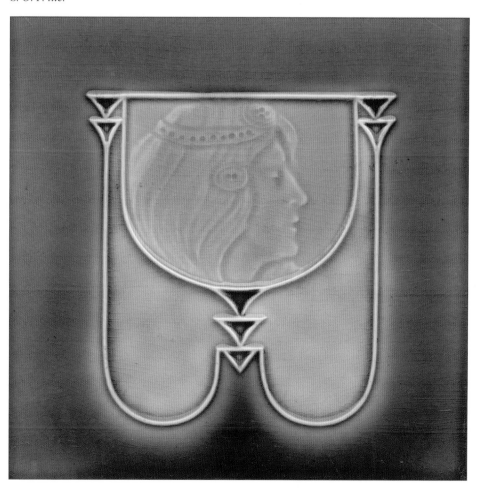

Ernst Teichert tile.

Peasant scenes at harvest time, costumed people with boats in front of bridges and windmills, and galleons on swelling seas nostalgically reflected a peaceful, undamaged world, as did lake scenes with shimmering dragonflies and majestic swans gliding amongst reeds, snow-white in deep blue water. Along with hauntingly uninhabited, pristine landscapes, peacocks on tree branches, parrots, storks, cranes, geese, kingfishers, owls, crows, and birds of paradise, as well as butterflies and other creatures, appealed to the German temperament, while castles, chapels, churches, ruins, and other charming scenery, in bright sunlight or by moonlight, were also suggestive of mystical contentment.

GWF tile.

Boizenburg half-tile.

GWF tile.

GWF half-tile.

Boizenburg tile.

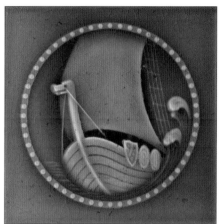

NSTG tile.

NSTG tile.

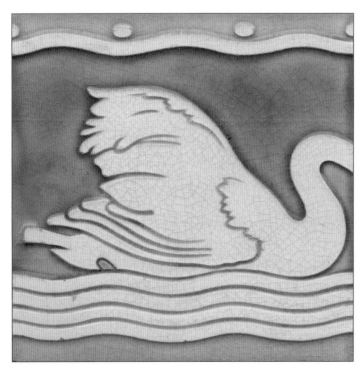

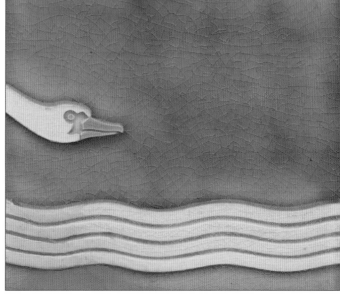

GWF tiles.

Boizenburg tiles.

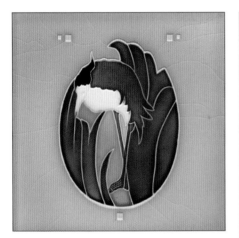

Boizenburg tile.

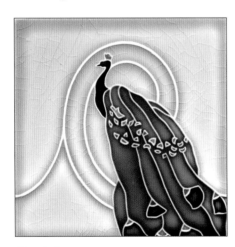

Wessel tile.

M.O.&P.F. tile.

V & B D tile.

Wessel tile.

GWF tile.

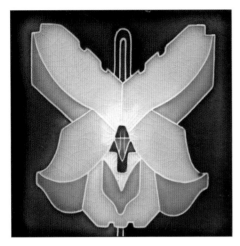

DTAG tile.

Schmider special-use tile.

Ernst Teichert tile.

These competed for attention with underwater worlds with mermen and mermaids, corals, seahorses, crabs, and fish, and other images that featured snails, squirrels, hares, deer, gazelles, bears, monkeys, elephants, and enchanted horses.

During this early period of expressive imagery, designs for the Jugendstil tile could be translated from other artistic media. Others originated from the carpeting or wallpaper industries as well as advertising art and, especially, book illustration, as propagated by such publications as *Jugend* (first published in 1896 in Munich), *Pan* (in 1895 in Berlin), *Deutsche Kunst und Dekoration* (in 1897 in Darmstadt), and *Dekorative Kunst* (in 1898 in Munich), which supported the idea of the exchange of design between different art media. More designs were to be found in the areas of graphic art and interior decoration publicized by *Dekorative Vorbilder* and *Innendekoration* (both started in 1889, the first in Stuttgart and the second in Darmstadt), with motifs adapted to suit the medium of tile as a flexible art form.

V & B M tile.

V & B M tile.

Ernst Teichert tile.

V & B S tile, designed by Ludwig Hohlwein: 4.88" (12.4cm) square.

M.O.&P.F. tile.

Wessel tile.

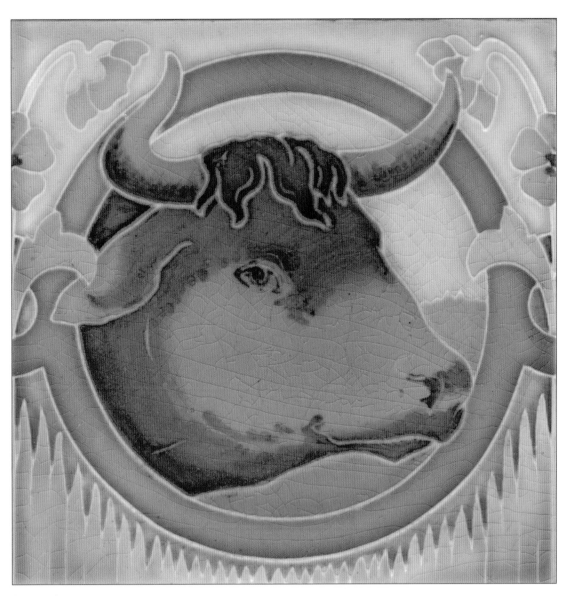

Servais tile.

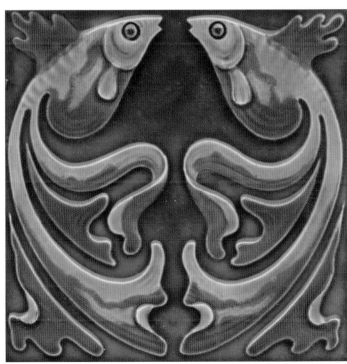

V & B M tile.

Boizenburg tile.

S. O. F. tile, designed by Margarethe Von
Brauchitsch.

S. O. F. tile, designed by Gertrud Kilz.

S. O. F. tile, designed by Anna Gasteiger.

Tile design was featured regularly in German publications. Also, competitions in the category of wall-tile design and other media – particularly in the years immediately preceding the turn of the century – were promoted by *Deutsche Kunst und Dekoration*, which announced the names of prizewinners and recipients of honorable mention and illustrated the so-honored selections in its monthly editions. In the results (announced in January 1899) of "Adjudication of Competition XII" (Wettbewerb-Entscheidung XII) – a wall-tile design competition first publicized in its October 1898 issue – the magazine explained that entries had to have been submitted, half-size, for a design incorporating four tiles (each 16 cm. square) in two colors, only, and composing a total image intended for a decorative wall installation. The schemes submitted (comprising the four tiles) were to be complete in themselves, but were also to be suitable for innumerable repetitions in an installation. Additionally, all four tiles could be identical to each other but with the capacity, through positioning in the overall square format requested, of composing together a uniquely complete image, with each tile representing a quarter of that image.

Of the eighty-two designs received, many were immediately rejected for such reasons as:

i).   not being in conformity with the regulations and requirements as outlined in the instructions;
ii). unsuitability of the entry for application to tile decoration, specifically, rather than, say, dinnerware; and
iii). contributors' lack of technical appreciation of tile production.

The prizes offered in three rankings totaled 105 DM. All entries remained the possession of the contributors. Two Greens (Zwei Grün) by Frau Anna Gasteiger (of Schloss Deutenhofen, near Dachau) was awarded the first prize of 60 DM and her Fashion (Mode), one of three third prizes of 15 DM .[86]

Deutsche Kunst und Dekoration, without charge, willingly arranged sales, on the designers' behalf, to companies (or agencies) desirous of purchasing designs.[87]

From the late 1890s, the early, expressive aspect of Jugendstil, represented, for instance, in the work of Hans Christiansen (at that time) and in much of the work of Albin Müller (up to c. 1908), continued as a dominant force in German design for a number of years. In tile design, flowers and plants with strong curvilinear emphasis, but nevertheless usually recognizable as distinct species, contributed an immediate appeal provided by an abundance of different shapes, colors, tints, and shades in attractive images to brighten and enliven any environment in German public and private life.

Von Schwarz tray, possibly inspired by the work of Hans Christiansen, designed by Carl Sigmund Luber: 12" x 4.38" (30.48 x 11.13cm).

V & B M tile.

Tile or, possibly, special-use tile, in the manner of Hans Christiansen, thought to have been produced at one of the Villeroy & Boch locations in Germany.

GWF tile.

V & B D tile.

V & B D tile.

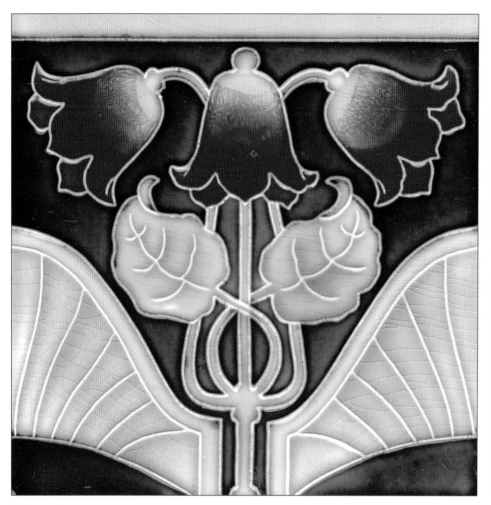

Offstein tile.

M.O.&P.F tile.

V & B D tile.

The variety of the flora and fauna depicted in these tiles – soon including schemes that suggested, rather than imitated in detail, natural growth – was extensive, with every part of the plant or flower explored and depicted. Designs presented not only the whole or principal image of the specific plant and the blossom itself – at all stages of growth and maturity – but also the individual petal, stamen (with filament and anther), leaf, stalk, seedpod, etc. Emulating the fluid and pliant quality of English proto-Art Nouveau floral decoration – restrained by a degree of Arts & Crafts discipline – but, at times, approaching the extravagance of the unbridled ornamentation of the Franco-Belgian prototype, German manufacturers competed among themselves for a major stake in the local and export markets at the turn of the century.

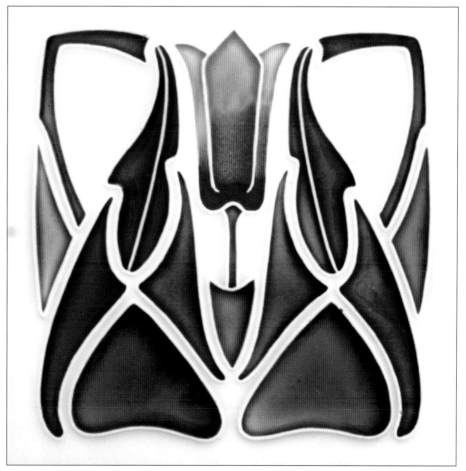

DTAG tile.

NSTG tile.

V & B D tile.

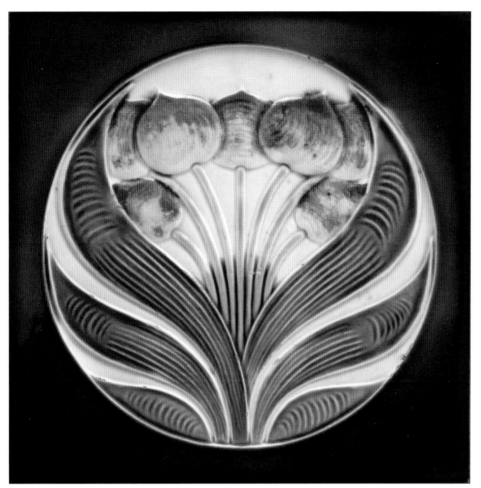

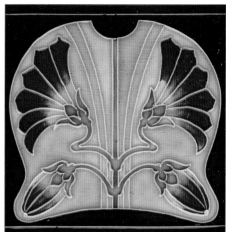

Offstein tile.

Mügeln tile.

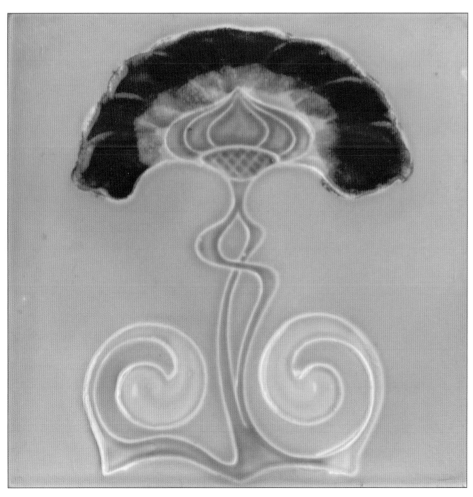

Schmider special-use tile.

S. O. F. tile.

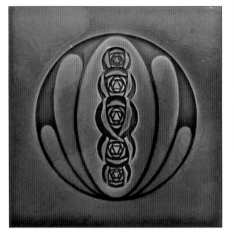

NSTG tile.

M.O.&P.F. tile.

Already by then, however, avant-garde architects, artists, and designers in the country had made a pragmatic approach towards a simpler, rectilinear, more functional, rationalist, and, even, modern design. As a consequence, abstract elements very soon began to be added to tile design, leading to stylization that was more divorced from floral inspiration. The trend toward simplification and a greater degree of sobriety in decoration started to grow in opposition to the previous excess, as the not-so-gradual progression of the varying degrees of abstraction contributed to a reduction in the popularity of the previous, typically French and Belgian, variety of style. Thus, in the first years of the new century, the stricter, more constructivist form entered the arena of industrially manufactured wall tiles.

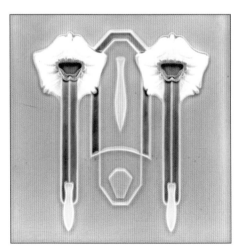

Mügeln tile.

Servais tile.

V & B D tile.

Mügeln tile.

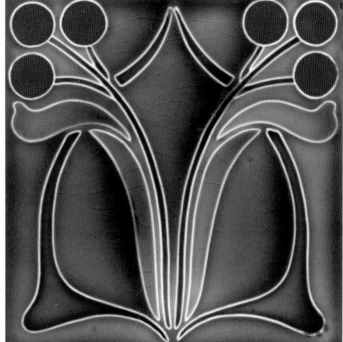

DTAG tile.

V & B M tile.

This alternative, fledgling aesthetic, conforming, even, with some of the tenets of the Arts and Crafts Movement, could be suitably applied by architecture and industry and appealed to the more sober spirit in the German character. Consequently, the previous individualistic, ornate designs of Art Nouveau submitted more and more to the simplicity and restraint of linear ornament and abstract stylization. Within a short time around the beginning of the twentieth century, this new stylization became as popular as the former conventionalization.

Boizenburg tile.

S. O. F. tile.

Offstein tile.

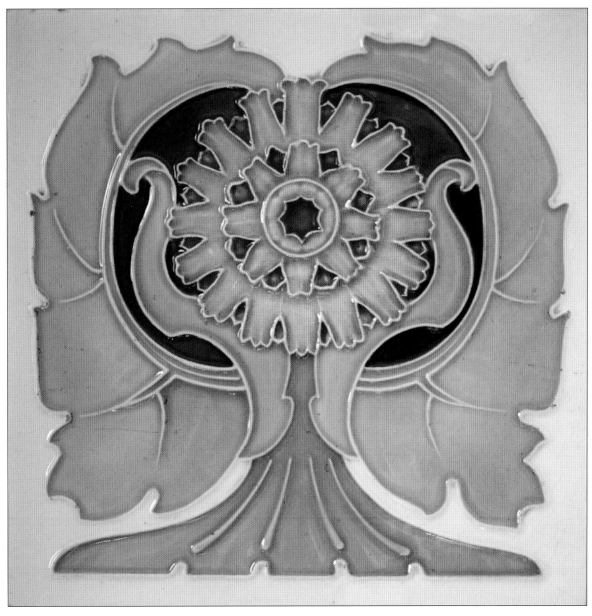

SOMAG tile.

NSTG tile.

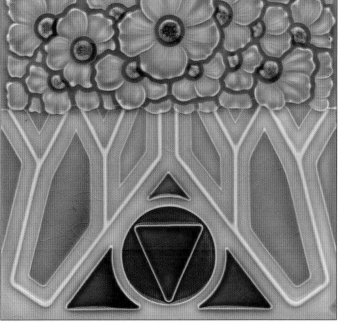

NSTG tile.

This more revolutionary, variant form of Jugendstil decoration grew in influence and popularity, bringing about, first of all, a more rational manipulation of space, perspective, and symmetry, as well as some interesting combinations of the floral and linear elements of German contemporary design. For instance, sometimes, organic stems and leaves in Jugendstil ornament were depicted in a curvilinear manner but with blossoms represented geometrically, and vice versa; at other times, blossoms would be enclosed in geometric forms. Thus, in addition to the diminished continuance of the more typical, conventionalized, floral Art Nouveau decoration, the depiction of blossoms soon began to yield to abstract ornamentation, with shapes progressing from round to square and with lines and rectilinear motifs merely suggestive of natural forms.

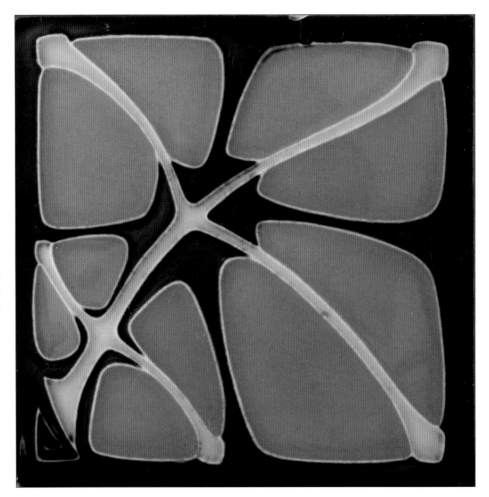

Servais tile.

Utzschneider tile.

V & B M tile.

Ernst Teichert tile.

Witteburg tile.

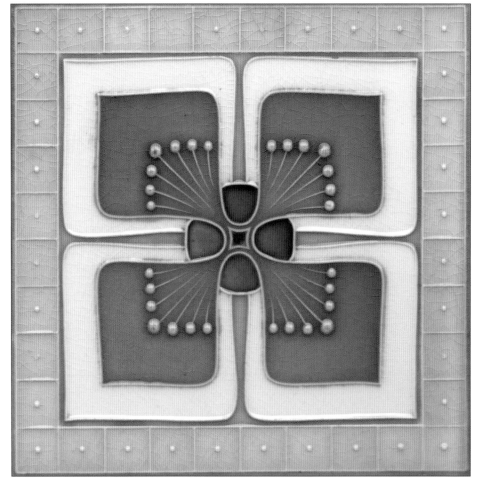

Boizenburg tile.

Boizenburg tile.

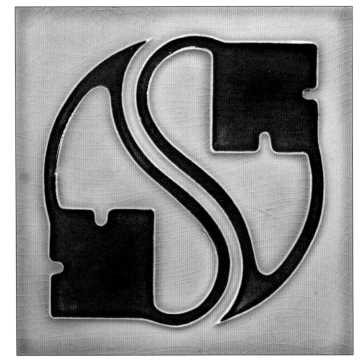

DTAG tile.

Osterath/Ostara tile.

DTAG tile.

Ernst Teichert tile.

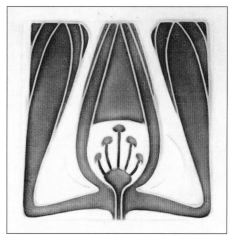

Utzschneider tile.

Soon, however, this stylization increasingly became even more abstract, until, within a short time, the floral element of the imagery became almost totally unrecognizable within the abstraction. Indeed, some Jugendstil design represents structural shapes or details that are stripped of reference to any specific, natural phenomena, sometimes even recalling "organic forms without imitating anything in Nature."[88]

Wessel tile.

SOMAG tile.

Offstein tile.

Linear ornamentation and abstract decoration, without any hint of natural form, were more and more appreciated in artistic and manufacturing circles, as also were geometric schemes involving such devices as squares, interlocking triangles, circles, half-circles, ovals, spirals, chevrons, and random lines. These were found to be no less captivating in the clarity and simplicity of abstraction than the conventionalization of natural, organic forms. Therefore, by c. 1905, the constructivist, variant form of Jugendstil – exhibiting an assortment of linear, rectilinear, geometric, symmetrical, and asymmetrical ornament – found noteworthy expression in the production of industrially manufactured tiles in Germany.

Nevertheless, both the floral abstraction and the geometric abstraction continued to be illustrated in manufacturers' catalogs and promotional material for many years, alongside the conventionalized floral treatment of the earlier tiles.

Witteburg tile.

Boizenburg tile.

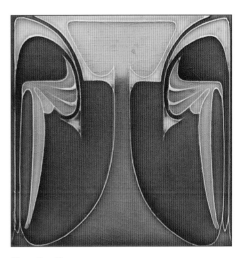

Servais tile.

Servais tile.

V & B M tile.

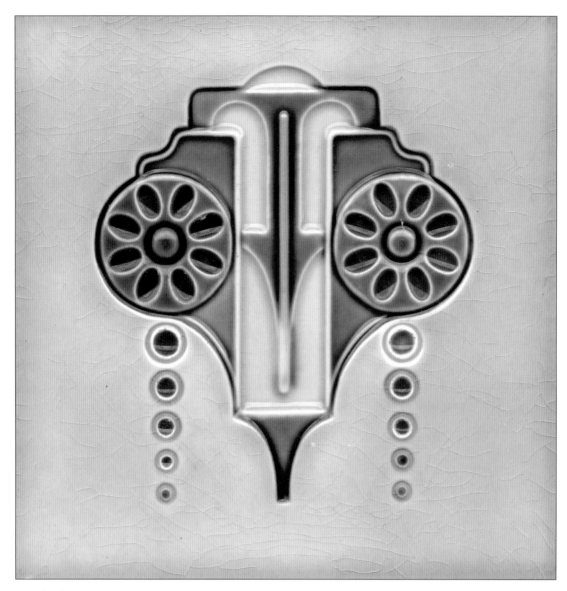

Mügeln tile.

Servais tile.

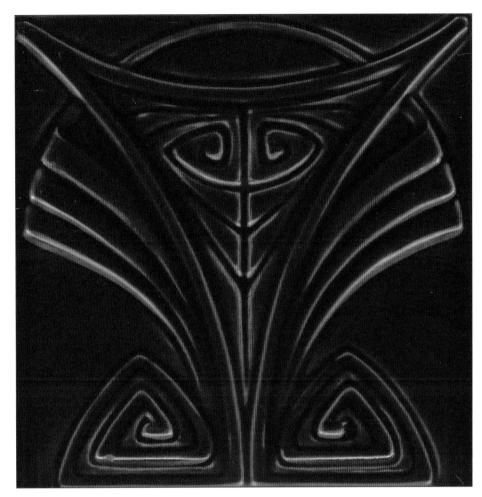

Wessel tile.

M.O.&P.F. tile.

Osterath/Ostara tile.

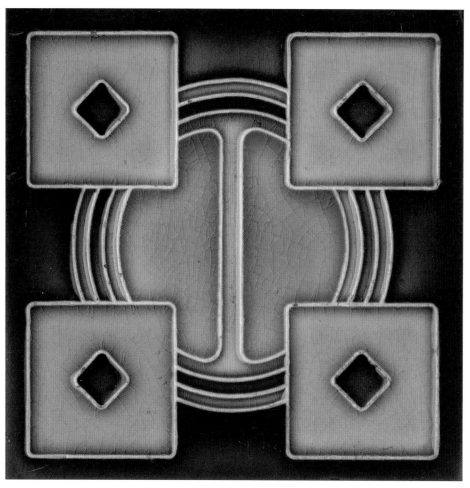

Osterath/Ostara tile.

Wessel tile.

Boizenburg tile.

Ernst Teichert tile

NSTG tile.

GWF tile.

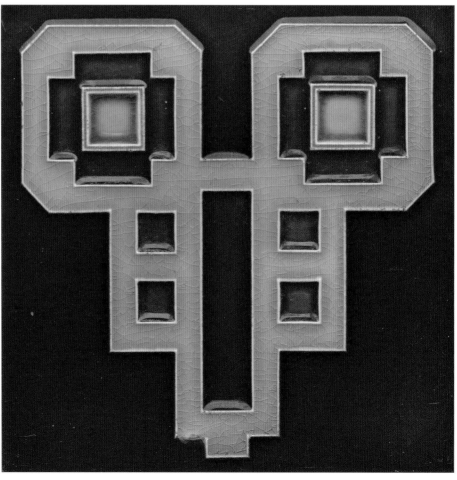

GWF tile.

Boizenburg tile.

Boizenburg tile.

Boizenburg tile.

Mügeln tile.

S. O. F. tile.

Osterath/Ostara tile.

Servais tile.

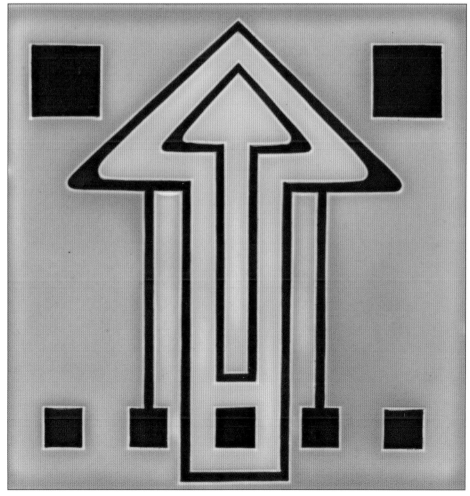

DTAG tile.

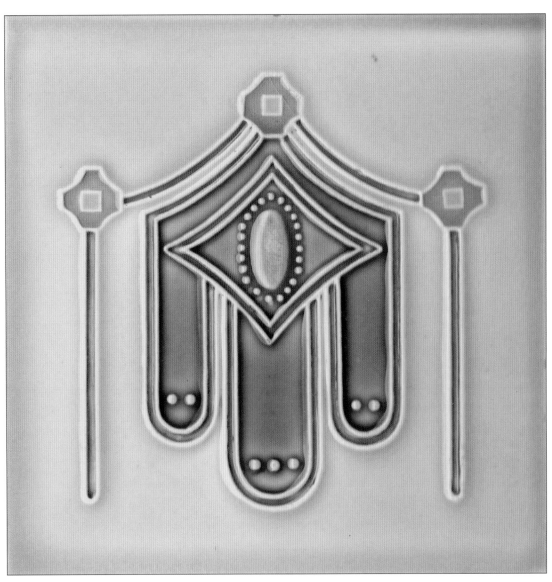

DTAG tile.

V&B M tile.

NSTG tile.

Servais tile.

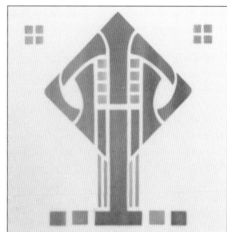

V & B D tile.

Boizenburg tile.

NSTG tile.

NSTG tile.

SOMAG tile.

Wessel tile.

Offstein tile.

A number of important German designers provided designs for production by manufacturers of wall, floor, and other tiles, some designs as originally conceived by the artist and others in free adaptation by the company in question. Some of these designs have been identified, including, for example: some for Villeroy & Boch Mettlach designed by Behrens, Van de Velde, and Eckmann; others for Wächtersbach by Christian Neureuther; and several for Villeroy & Boch Schramberg (and, possibly, Utzschneider) by Ludwig Hohlwein. Also, some Villeroy & Boch Schramberg tiles that have the initials "JB" incorporated into the designs could arguably represent the work of Jean Beck, who was associated with the Villeroy & Boch companies for much of his career.

V & B M floor tile, designed by Henry Van de Velde.

V & B M wall tiles, designed by Henry Van de Velde.

V & B M tiles, designed by Peter Behrens.

V & B M tile, designed by Otto Eckmann.

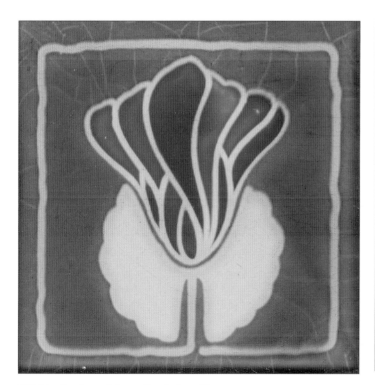

Wächtersbach special-use tile, designed by Christian Neureuther, 4" (10cm) square.

V & B S tile or, possibly, special-use tile, signed "JB," possibly designed by Jean Beck.

Still other designs were purchased or "borrowed" by various companies, including the Dusseldorf Claywares Factory – in respect of design(s) by Hans Christiansen – and the North-German Earthenware Factory and the Wessel company, with designs acquired from Paul Bürck or inspired by his designs. In addition, the Dusseldorf Claywares Factory manufactured an adaptation of their tulip tile with the addition of a stream or path in the background of the design, and the North-German Earthenware Factory adapted an image[89] by Eugen Gradl as a partial feature of one of that company's tiles.

Illustration in "Jugend," IV, page 284, of Hans Christiansen's 1898/1899 tulip design.

DTAG tile, from a design by Hans Christiansen.

DTAG tile, with a modified Hans Christiansen design.

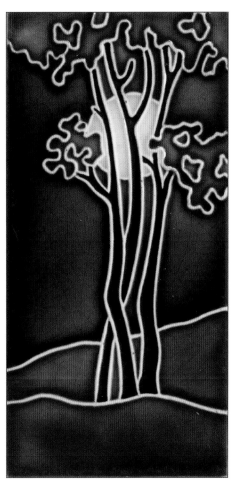

Half-tiles, by (left) NSTG and (right) Wessel, from designs by Paul Bürck.

NSTG tile, incorporating design motifs by Eugen Gradl.

Though it is often possible to identify the products of different manufacturers (through markings on the reverse, such as company name, initials, or insignia, or a characteristic surface structure that might allow attribution), without further documentary evidence in recognized sources, most of the popular designs can only be characterized as possibly "in the manner of" a documented designer or "inspired" by a known, published item, rather than "attributed" to a named artist. Included in this category are tile images reminiscent of the styles and motif choices/treatments favored by Behrens, Joseph Olbrich, and Van de Velde. Design elements, choice of imagery, and schemes of structural and spatial composition, so evident in Läuger's tile-work vocabulary, resonate strongly even in a number of Villeroy & Boch Mettlach's products. Furthermore, a Mettlach tile might indeed have been commissioned by the Mettlach firm from Behrens or could well be their "adaptation" of another design acknowledged as having been created by him, while another seems to bear an "adapted," simplified image of one of the company's floor tiles by Van de Velde. Indeed, the design of a Wessel tile seems to have been "inspired," in part, by a monogram/mark that often identifies the work of that designer.

V & B M tile, designed by Peter Behrens or adapted from his design..

V & B M tile, designed by Perter Behrens or adapted from his design.

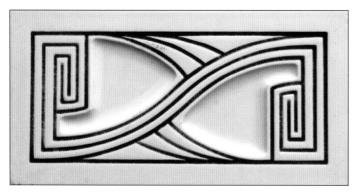

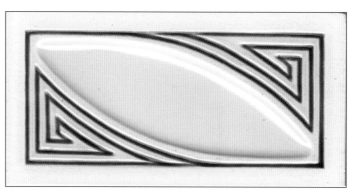

NSTG half-tiles, in the manner of Peter Behrens.

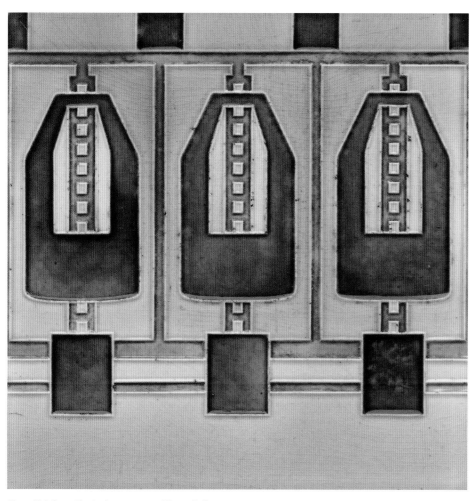

Ernst Teichert tile, in the manner of Peter Behrens.

(Above) V & B D tile in the manner of Joseph Olbrich.

(Left) V & B M tile in the manner of Peter Behrens or Joseph Olbrich.

Three tiles in the manner of Henry Van de Velde, by (left) V & B M, (top right) Wessel, (bottom right) V & B D.

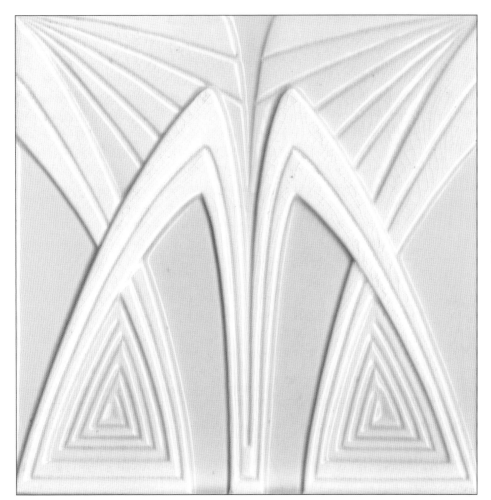

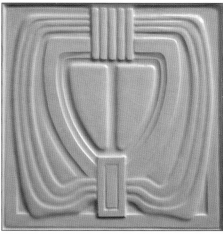

Three tiles in the manner of Henry Van de Velde: by (top left) Boizenburg, (bottom left) Wessel, (above) Osterath/Ostara.

Additionally – since Behrens taught at the Academy in Dusseldorf between 1911 and 1922 and because of the character of some examples from the company's production of that period – some collectors subscribe to the current hypothesis that, during his tenure at the Academy, designs by him – or, perhaps, his students – might have been acquired by the Dusseldorf Clayworks Factory.

In the absence of in-house designers – who produced designs or adapted others created by more important artists – manufacturers often requested members of their workforce with some artistic ability to copy artists' designs, though usually, of course, with some minor change. Indeed, the fact that so little information exists regarding the involvement of well-known artists in tile design indicates, glaringly, the significance of anonymous in-factory contribution.

At the same time, tile makers appropriated designs found in the literature of the time (with an abundance of different ornament), which, of course, encompassed those submitted for publication in periodicals, magazines, etc., by many important designers in the field of applied art, including, for instance, respected members of the Darmstadt Artists' Colony in Germany (and the Vienna Workshops in Austria). Many designs were used that were based on imitations of the work of other unknown – and, even, known – artists, who were, themselves, inspired by the example of the avant-garde designers already mentioned. Now and then, the work of students at neighboring arts and crafts / applied arts schools and technical schools could be of benefit to tile manufacturers. Also, versions of popular motifs (for instance, waterlilies), pirated by one company from a design magazine or book, were soon imitated by other firms. For instance, a round, special-use tile, mounted as a trivet, appears to be of the same design heritage as a square tile (or, possibly, special-use tile), since both display a Christiansen-type swan-scene.[90] It has been suggested occasionally, in the past, that the latter was produced at one of the Villeroy & Boch locations. On the other hand, the unidentified trivet in a silver-metal, galleried surround has been mistakenly attributed[91] to Schmider, while an otherwise identical tile – except with two swans – has been mistakenly attributed[92] to Von Schwarz. In fact, tile companies

DTAG tiles, in the manner of Peter Behrens.

copied from each other's design portfolios – avoiding copyright infringement, where deemed necessary, through adaptation and modification of designs – and also, on occasion, "adjusted" a number of published English and Belgian tile designs.

More legitimately, co-operative arrangements were sometimes concluded between companies for the exchange of designs, including, for instance, between the North German Earthenware Factory

in Grohn and the Belgian manufacturer Maison Helman, Céramiques d'Art.

In their sales catalogs, sample sheets, and other promotional literature, tile makers rarely, if ever, publicized designers or, indeed, included any information other than that concerning the company's own commercial production. Due to plant fires, war damages, and other reasons, few existing records remain, even in the archives of currently surviving or related businesses.

In the case of many designs, it is often difficult, too, to assign a date of origin, even from the evidence of accessible catalogs and sample sheets, since some examples, illustrated in some later company publication, were originated years – or even decades – earlier and continued to be offered for many years after, or might have been removed from production at some date and, later, made available again.

Certainly, design-attribution can NOT be based on stylistic consideration, alone, or on the artist's relationship/connection with/to a manufacturer. Exact identification of the design parentage of industrially produced decorative tiles is nebulously difficult or, frequently, even frustratingly impossible, except in the case of those few designs – in the artist's original conception or executed, sometimes, in adapted form – that are to be found illustrated and so captioned in such contemporaneous magazines as *Deutsche Kunst und Dekoration* or *Dekorative Kunst*.

In addition to such tile companies as Villeroy & Boch, Schmider, J. von Schwarz, and Wächtersbach, a number of earthenware factories, both small and large, that manufactured household china in Germany prior to the Second World War, also produced furniture tiles and wall plates of various kinds, as well as serving trays, trivets, coasters of different sizes (for glasses, carafes, and bottles), and items – mainly, "table plates" (Tischplatten) – for use in serving confectionery, etc. These latter – bearing stenciled, underglaze-printed and, only very rarely, handpainted decoration and sold unmounted or mounted in metal (or, sometimes, wood) – were of square, rectangular, oval, and, often, round shapes and were, frequently, totally flat or with a narrow, raised edges. One of these firms – whose items, only occasionally, bore identifying marks – was located in Grünstadt, in Rhineland-Palatinate, and another was in Sörnewitz (Coswig), near Meissen, in Saxony.

Von Schwarz tray, designed by Carl Sigmund Luber: 17.25" max. x 13.25" max. (43.82 x 33.66cm).

Wächtersbach tray: 11.5" x 7.75" (29.21 x 19.69cm).

Von Schwarz trays, designed by Carl Sigmund Luber: (left) 5.63" (14.3cm) square; (right) 17.5" max. x 13.75" max. (44.45 x 34.93cm).

Schmider special-use tiles: 0.25" (6.3mm) thick.

*Unidentified confectionery table plate: 9.75"
(24.77cm) diameter.*

Tiles for exterior use, plain or, occasionally, with sparse simple decoration, were sometimes used along with clinker bricks[93] in a variety of rich colors and surface textures (sometimes with glazed or enameled facings). The inclusion of tile and enameled brick together in an architectural scheme offered a distinctive form of ornamentation in the uniqueness of the patterns obtained. August Endell – shortly after he left Munich for Berlin in 1901 and began to renounce his prior predilection for ornate Art Nouveau decoration – integrated original exterior tilework with colorful, enameled-brickwork into his architectural work, there, for such projects as the still-existent Hackische Höfe residential/commercial courtyard complex in Berlin. In several of the architectural projects for which the Ceramic Manufactory of the Grand Duchy of Hesse, under Jakob Julius Scharvogel's direction, provided tile and architectural terra cotta, extensive use was made also of enameled brick on the outside of buildings and inside. Indeed, later, mostly in the 1920s, the combination of enameled brick and tile was often presented as the main visible building material in a fashionable, variant form of Expressionist architecture, known as "Brick Expressionism" (Backsteinexpressionismus) in Germany.

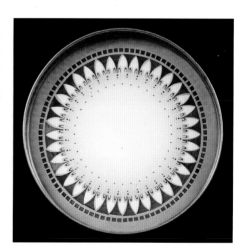

Unidentified, footed and galleried confectionery table plate: 6.25" (15.88cm) diameter.

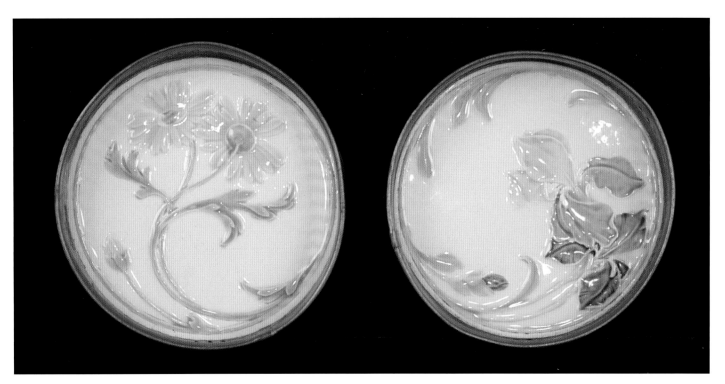

Two V & B M galleried coasters: each 3.25"
(8.26cm) diameter.

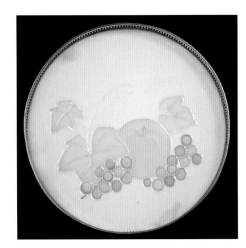

Unidentified, galleried confectionery table
plate: 8.75" (22.23cm) diameter.

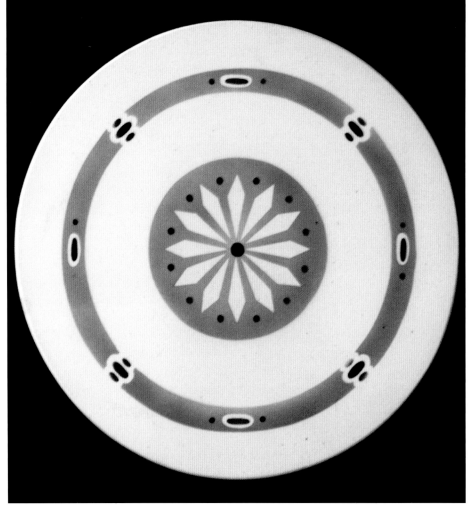

Unidentified trivet, in the manner of Hans
Christiansen, mounted in a silver-metal,
galleried surround: 4.25" (10.8cm) diameter.

Grünstadt Earthenware Factory confectionery
table plate: 9.13" (23.18cm) diameter.

SOMAG tile.

Though it may be said that Jugendstil, like most manifestations of International Art Nouveau, came to an end by the beginning of the First World War, at the latest, the production of Jugendstil tiles of one kind or another continued to be produced – or revived – during the war and afterward. Distancing itself, in the main, from other influences – though with occasional incursions into Art Deco / Modernist style in the later 1920s and later – wall-tile design in Germany and its sphere of influence continued, nevertheless, to represent Jugendstil decoration in all its variety into the 1930s, though eventually in more limited manufacture (especially during the cessation of the building trade in the Depression).

Tile or, possibly, special-use tile, marked (on reverse) "Iris Made in Germany."

Boizenburg tile.

For public and domestic architecture, particularly, and for other purposes, from the end of the nineteenth century almost up to the outbreak of the Second World War, German tile companies were responsible for an enormous output of colorfully glazed, decorative tiles for the home market, as well as for export to South America and other countries, especially those within the sphere of influence of the former German Empire. The high quality and diversity of design and decorative technique of those tiles and the extensive color range employed in production – surprising, at that time, in machine-produced wares of mass manufacture – account for their successful marketing at that time and also for their popularity for today's collectors.

AUSTRIAN SECESSIONIST TILES

For some Vienna Workshops commissions, ceramic tiles – designed by Josef Hoffmann and other members of the cooperative – were produced locally by the studio Vienna Ceramics, founded by Michael Powolny and Berthold Löffler in 1905/1906. For example, such major Gesamtkunstwerk architecture/interior design accomplishments of the Vienna Workshops as the Palais Stoclet (1905–1911) in Brussels incorporated extensive Vienna Ceramics tiling by Powolny and others. For the Fledermaus Cabaret (1907) in Vienna, Powolny and Löffler produced black-and-white, checkerboard flooring as well as an extraordinary, colorful, fantastical, and whimsical mosaic wall decoration consisting of around seven thousand individually different, though

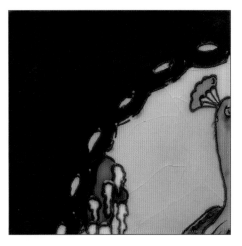

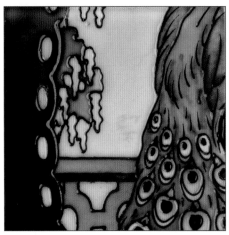

GWF wall-tile panel.

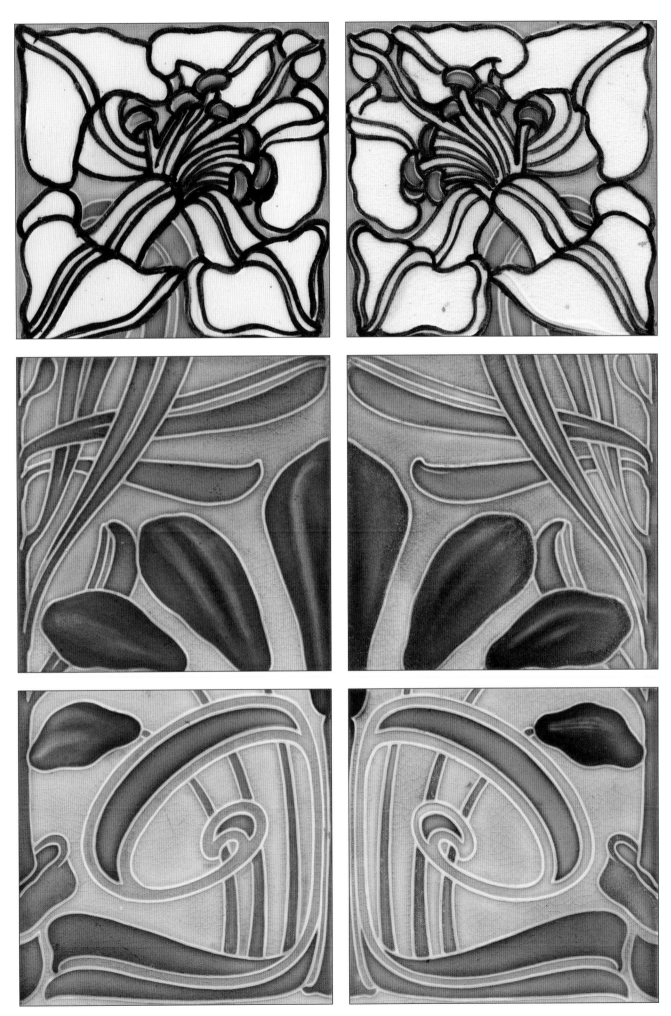

V & B M wall-tile panel.

Michael Powolny special-use tile or, possibly, stove tile (with two recessed cavities in reverse): 4" (10.16cm) square, 0.5" (1.25cm) thick.

Walter Bosse tile/plaque, 6.75" (17.15cm) square.

Gmundn tile/plaque: 10" (25.4cm) square, 1" (2.5cm) thick.

integrated, square tiles – of various sizes – randomly placed within the scheme and covering the cloakroom, walls, and bar of the Bar-Room.

Herta Bucher, a ceramist and longtime member of the Vienna Workshops, both designed and produced tiles for a number of projects; fellow collaborator Emanuel Josef Margold included tile design in his various architecture and craft programs.

Similarly, other small ceramics studios – such as the F. and E. Schleiss Ceramic Workshop, in Gmundn (Upper Austria), which executed commissions for Josef Hoffmann – also executed tiles by independent designers for various purposes on commission, along with architectural ceramics for architects. In 1913, as the studio Gmundn Ceramics, Franz and Emilie Schleiss joined forces with Powolny to form the United Vienna and Gmundn Ceramics and Claywares Factory. From

1916, the combined Schleiss/Powolny operation was also known as Gmundn Ceramics and, from around 1923 – with Powolny's continued collaboration – as Gmundn Ceramic Workshops.

The Powolny-trained ceramist Walter Bosse also designed and modeled items, including artistic tiles, plaques, and wall masks (as well as figurines) for the Vienna Workshops, Goldscheider, and Augarten.

In Austria, one of the few twentieth-century mass producers of ceramic floor and wall tiles and other architectural ceramics was the Wienerberg Brick Factory and Building Company. Earlier, with an extensive exhibit at the Vienna International Exhibition of 1873, the firm affirmed its position as the leading producer of architectural ceramics, tile, and terra cotta in the Austro-Hungarian Empire. At that time, it had a complement of eight thousand workmen and was thought to be the largest

brick works in the world, with extensive exports to Germany, Switzerland, Russia, Italy, England, the Far East, and the United States of America. In addition to pressed brick and glazed brick (in various colors) in construction, remarkable detail on the exterior of the company's exhibit hall at the exhibition included tiles, sculpture, and other ceramic-relief ornamentation in unglazed and glazed terra cotta, as well as a number of the medallions in glazed terra cotta, which, at that time, were counted among the company's specialties in architectural decoration.

By 1900, when its exhibits at the Paris Exposition Universelle received great acclaim, the Rudolf Sommerhuber Stove Factory in Steyr was already providing tiled stoves and fireplaces and other heat-storing, ceramic products to palaces, castles, and other aristocratic homes throughout Central Europe and Germany.

Wienerberg tiles.

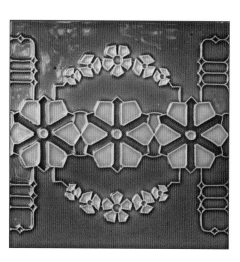

Unidentified Austrian plaque, c. 1900: 14.13" x 4.75" (35.9 x 12.1cm)

At first, many were in traditional styles but, later, others were ornamented with Secessionist designs by Michael Powolny, Herta Bucher, Robert Obsieger, et al, in addition to other decoration inspired by the work of students at the Imperial/Royal School of Arts and Crafts in Vienna and other technical (applied arts) schools in Austria and Bohemia.

From around the beginning of the twentieth century, wall-tile production in the Austro-Hungarian Empire was dominated by Zsolnay (in Hungary) along with Rako (in Bohemia), in addition to smaller manufacturers in other crown provinces, including Moravia. Discounting the Wienerberg company's production, Austria, itself, was not a prolific producer of industrial wall tiles in an Art Nouveau manner.

HUNGARIAN SECESSIONIST TILES

Along with other essential features, both the naturalistic and conventionalized variations of Szecesszio design were offensive to the taste of conservative critics in artistic, architectural, and political authority in Hungary, and a short-lived, official attempt was made to prohibit the use of state funds for architecture and decoration in the style in 1902. But, both before that year and afterward, the city of Budapest, in particular, gloried in the use of Zsolnay tilework and other architectural ceramic ornament in outstandingly attractive and fascinating new buildings, amongst which are the following:

i). the Museum of Applied Art, completed in 1896, with a mix of Gothic and Indo-Magyar ornamental detail, imagery from Hungarian folklore, and the use of Zsolnay's Pyrogranite, and

ii). the Hungarian Geological Society Building of 1899 (both designed by architect Odon Lechner); as well as

iii). the Franz Liszt Academy of Music of 1907; and

iv). the Gresham Palace of 1906.

Indeed, a consideration of the tile industry in Hungary, before, during, and after the turn of the century, is essentially the story of the Zsolnay company, as is also a study of the new architecture, of the time, in Budapest and a few other urban locations.

Interested in a synthesis of architectural styles, Odon Lechner – whose career changed course when, in the early to mid-1890s, he became aware of events in other parts of Europe – was responsible for many notable buildings in Budapest and other areas of the Austro-Hungarian Empire. Incorporating installations of Zsolnay wall tiles and other remarkable architectural detail, his Secessionist design for the Postal Savings Bank Building, of 1902, in Budapest, for instance, is striking, as are also those designs for buildings from the same period in Pressburg.

The Hungarian Royal National School of Arts and Crafts, founded in 1880 in Budapest, moved to the newly completed Museum of Applied Arts, which had been

designed by Lechner and Gyula Partos with a dome ornamented by Zsolnay tiles and other architectural ceramics. Around 1930, it is thought that the ceramics department at the School produced a decorative tile commemorating the ancient, royal, capital city Szekesfehervar, which,

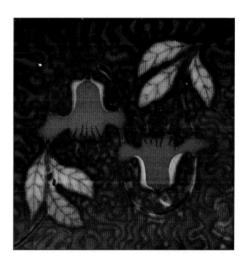

Zsolnay tiles: (top) 6.5" (16.51cm) square.

Detail of a (presumed) Rako tile panel on an architectural column in Prague Main Railway Station.

"Alba Regia" plaque: 8.25" x 6.25" (20.96 x 15.88cm).

at the time of St. Stephen, King of Hungary, was known by its Latin name Alba Regia.

As with the Secessionist development in Vienna and Prague, the Hungarian counterpart was, principally, a phenomenon of the city – Budapest and a few others – and, in neither country, did the popularity of the new style extend to the country as a whole.

BOHEMIAN/ MORAVIAN (CZECHOSLOVAKIAN) SECESSIONIST TILES

Inside and outside, the incomparable Municipal House – a cultural landmark designed by Antonin Balsanek and Osvald Polivka and built between between 1904 and 1912 in Prague – is one of the most important Secessionist buildings in the city. Its ornamentation in the form of reliefs, tiling, and woodwork, etc., is the epitome of the Czech (Bohemian/ Moravian) Secese style.

The magnificent, dazzling interior, furnished and decorated by leading Czech artists of the time and with floors covered with mosaic tiles, has an air of cultivated ease, its soft curves and free rippling effects giving way to sharp edges and prismatic forms. The walls of the staircase leading to the basement are decorated with Rako paneling that feature historical scenes of the city, while, in the basement, itself, there are more striking wall-tile installations, both pictorial and floral, as well as a decorative tiled floor. Other ornamental, mosaic-ceramic pictures by Rako were designed by the artist Jakub Obrovsky. The mosaic decorations on pillars in the American Bar and the Pilsen Restaurant – with tiles illustrating city emblems – complement the wood paneling in the Wine Bar, inset with relief ceramic tiles and mirrors. Furniture, sculpture, light fixtures, and frescoes/paintings – including those painted by the internationally renowned, Moravian-born artist Alfons Mucha after his glorious Parisian years and period of instructional activities in the United States – complete the impression

of an Art Nouveau confection with added Bohemian distinction.

The Main Railway Station in Prague – later, for some years, officially renamed the Wilson Station after President of the United States Woodrow Wilson – was originally designed in the Neo-Renaissance style and opened in 1871; it was rebuilt between 1901 and 1903. By 1909, enlarged and modernized, it included still-existent marquees, canopies, and stucco wall decorations, featuring an abundance of sculptural, two- and three-dimensional detail, such as female nudes, birds, foliage, grotesque masks, and historical figures, emblems, and crests. A restaurant/waiting-room area was installed with tall, floor-to-ceiling, square columns decorated, by 1905, with twenty-four remarkable, large, rectangular, pictorial panels (presumably, also, by Rako), featuring brightly colored, mosaic-tile representations of beautiful women – some in rural dress with traditional decorative patterning – from various parts of Bohemia and Moravia, and others representing such subjects as the Four Seasons and reminiscent of

French Art Nouveau advertising posters and other portraits by the legendary Mucha.

Other superb manifestations of Czech Secese decoration – especially tilework – in Prague include the Hotel Paris and the buildings lining Parizka Street, as well as the Imperial Hotel, opened in 1914, which was the most modern hotel at that time. Built by the previous owner of the Hotel Paris and designed by architect Jaroslav Benedikt – collaborating with Emil Sommerschuh – the Imperial Hotel is garnished with floral and figural ornamentation. Rako ceramic mosaic and relief decorations adorn walls and pillars throughout (including motifs taken from Oriental, as well as Egyptian, Babylonian, and other Middle Eastern art), many designed by Professor of Decorative Arts Jan Benes of the School of Arts and Crafts/ Applied Arts in Prague.

Elsewhere in Bohemia, outstanding Rako tilework in Secessionist style was placed in the sumptuous East Bohemia Theater in Pardubitz. For this building, also designed in Secese style by Prague architect Antonin Balsanek and opened in 1909, the painter and designer Frantisek Urban designed mosaic pictures made up of irregularly cut tiles to form complete images in a technique devised/patented by Emil Sommerschuh.

In the period 1885–1917, the Imperial/ Royal Technical School for Ceramics and Associated Applied Arts in Teplitz-Schönau, in Bohemia, offered specialized instruction not only in fine ceramics but also tile production and decoration (on Austrian Wienerberg blanks), as well as architectural stoneware and terra-cotta work. Included in the curriculum there, were "Modeling" and "Glazing" along with "Drawing and Decorative Painting." The last included lessons not only in the realistic and stylized depiction of plants, animals, drapery, and still-lifes, but also an emphasis on the reproduction of mixed floral/geometric ornament as preparation for possible future application in modern applied art and also for independent interpretation. Also, as part of the instruction in wall-tile design, decoration was practiced in the use of the lino-cut technique. By the first decade of the twentieth century, students' end-of-year examinations at this technical school in Teplitz required the production of a wall-tile panel, roughly 24" x 51" (60 x 130 cm), using floral and animal motifs. Designs by students and instructors of the school were occasionally accepted and executed by the local ceramic/tile industry.

Other technical schools in Bohemia and Moravia – also contributing designs for forms and decoration – cooperated, as well, with local industry, which, in turn, provided raw materials and products for instruction.

A close relationship was also maintained with the Schools of Arts and Crafts in both Vienna and Prague. Stanislav Sucharda – from 1899, a professor at the school in Prague – worked closely with architects Polivka and Kotera, designing Art Nouveau sculptural ornament for their buildings in Prague. At both schools, loans of historical material were received from museums and visits were arranged for students to touring exhibits. Lectures, on such subjects as the construction of plaster molds for relief tiles, were delivered by visiting teachers from other schools in Upper Austria, Bohemia, and Moravia, such as those from the Imperial/Royal Technical Schools for the Ceramics Industry in Znaim and Bechin.

The latter – now the Secondary School of Ceramics in Bechyne (in the Czech

Sucharda tile/plaque, 5.75" x 5.75" (14.6 x 14.6cm).

Republic) – was founded in 1884, with instruction beginning in March of that year for male students, only, at that time. The program of study was of three years duration, at first, for students wishing to enter the stove-fitter's trade. Later, pottery classes were introduced and, in 1890, ceramic decoration.

At the turn of the century, tile production in Bohemia/Moravia was dominated

Rako tile.

Rako tiles.

by the Rako company, which has continued its leading role in Central Europe (and, now, far beyond) to the present day.

Of other competing companies producing decorative wall tiles in a Secessionist manner in Bohemia/Moravia/Czechoslovakia, only Eichwald (or its successors) and, possibly, Oberbris seem to have survived up to the time of the Second World War. Tiles in a Jugendstil/Secessionist style were included in Oberbris advertising at least through the time of the First World War, together with stove tiles and, later, plain, white wall tiles, probably for overglaze decoration by client businesses and other decorators.

Not much is discoverable about the W. J. Sommerschuh company, after its 1899 listing as a manufacturer of ceramic wares and holder of an Imperial warrant awarded by the court in Vienna.

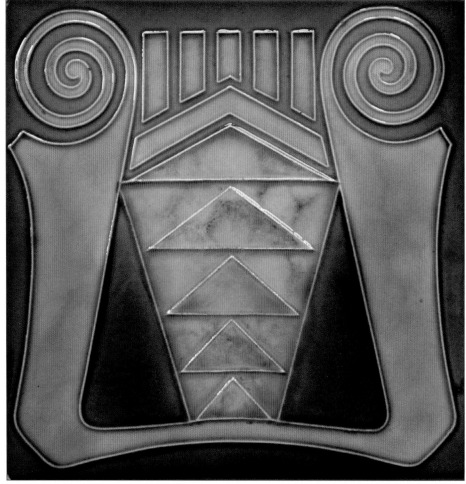

Oberbris tiles.

CHAPTER FOUR

THE MANUFACTURERS

Locations & Identifying Marks/Brand Names

GERMANY[94]

1. BANKEL

In 1889, Georg Bankel founded the Georg Bankel Stove Factory and Art Pottery, a factory in Lauf-on-the-Pegnitz, near Nuremberg (Bavaria), for the production of decorative earthenware, in addition to tiled stoves "in all styles" and stove tiles. The firm, which had its own clay pits, was later renamed the Georg Bankel Chamotte, Stove, and Wall Tile Factory.[95]

Between 1896 and 1906 – with a workforce, by then, of around four hundred employees – the company was awarded gold medals in Nuremberg and Berlin.

Around 1898, investigations were first made regarding the viability of producing wall tiles as an addition to the company's other products and, six/seven years later, the decision was taken to manufacture colorfully glazed wall tiles (later, occasionally, marked "G.BANKEL LAUF" and "GB LAUF") that were produced from 1905 through the time, c. 1921, when Georg Bankel's son Georg, Jr., took over the direction of the factory. At the same time, a new separate factory was built and equipped for the production, from 1907, of tiled stoves, with the later addition of architectural ceramics, fountains, and garden installations (from c. 1921, under the management of Georg Jr.'s brother Christof).

2. BENDORF

Founded in 1904 in Bendorf-on-the-Rhine (near Coblenz), in Rhineland-Palatinate, as the Erwin H. Niemann Wall Tile and Stove Factory with twenty-five employees for the production of wall tiles and tiled stoves, the company almost doubled its workforce within the first year.

Bankel tiles.

After the factory was damaged by fire in July 1906, it was rebuilt to re-open in September of that year as the Bendorf Wall Tile Factory – under new owner Hermann Büttner and with around sixty workers – to continue the production of wall tiles for interior and exterior decoration (later, under the brand name "BENDORF").

By 1909, there were about one hundred-ten employees but, by the beginning of 1911, less than sixty. Afterward, business did not improve and the company failed in October 1913. Seven years later, the facilities and equipment were sold to the Dutch merchant Dirk ten Cate Brouwer and re-named the D. Brouwer Rhine Area Wall Tile Factory, producing tile blanks for decoration at his factory in Holland using transfer-printing, stenciling, or handpainting techniques.

3. BOIZENBURG

In 1903, a factory was founded by Hans Duensing – later, with Max Bicheroux, co-proprietor of Duensing-Bicheroux-Works – in Boizenburg-on-the-Elbe (Mecklinburg-Western Pomerania) and, in 1904, wall-tile production was initiated there. By 1907, it was known as the Boizenburg Wall Tile Factory and, within the next two years, its workforce increased to over five hundred employees.

With proximity to the River Elbe and with a rail connection with the Berlin-Hamburg line, transportation presented no problem in the shipment of its manufacture. By late 1912, the factory was producing over two million tiles yearly (under the brand name "BOIZENBURG" or "Boizenburg," and often marked with the head of a mythological male person-age in profile – possibly Hermes or Mercury – with, sometimes, "BOIZENBURG / Made in Germany").

In 1913/1914, for one year, the premises of the Majolica Manufactory of the Grand Duchy of Hesse in Karlsruhe – under the administrative control, at that time, of Villeroy & Boch – was leased to Hans Duensing for operation by his Boizenburg works, but the operation was under-financed and closed due to the outbreak of the First World War.

In 1921, the Boizenburg Wall Tile Factory resumed production with increased funds from its main stockholder Dutch Tile Works, resulting in the opening of new markets for the company's products.

In 1928, with the addition of household crockery to its manufacture, the company was absorbed into the Duensing-Bicheroux

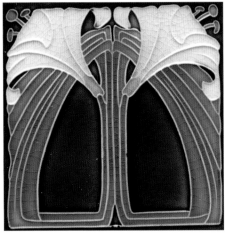

Bendorf tiles.

Works until interrupted by state ownership after the Second World War. In 1937, the company was reported to be the largest producer of wall tiles in Europe.

The Boizenburg Tile Factory is now, once again, privately owned.

4. BREMEN

This facility, the Bremen Wall Tile Factory, was opened in Aumund, near Bremen, in October 1911, as a subsidiary of the North German Earthenware Factory in nearby Grohn and, within the next ten/ eleven months, began the manufacture of color-glazed wall tiles.

Closed on the outbreak of the First World War, the factory was reopened by 1920/1921 and, then known as Plant III, continued in business until – along with other North German Earthenware subsidiaries – it was closed again in the late 1930s due to the Second World War.

Wall-tile work was resumed in 1950 and, from 1957/1958, together with the other North German Earthenware subsidiaries, it was owned totally by that company in Grohn and did business under that name.

5. BROITZEM

The Broitzem Wall Tile Factory or Marienberg Floor-Tile Factory, Broitzem Branch, was founded in 1921 in Broitzem, near Braunschweig (Lower Saxony), as a branch of the Marienberg Floor Tile Factory in Marienberg (Saxony), for the production of wall tiles (sometimes, when marked, bearing some version of the Marienberg mark consisting of an unframed, impressed, large, upper-case "M," or, alternatively, a small, upper-case "M" enclosed within a larger, upper-case "M," contained in a square).[96]

6. CARL TEICHERT, see: TEICHERT

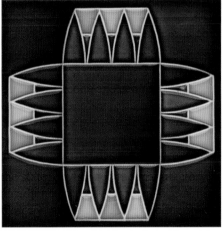 

Boizenburg tiles.

7. DARMSTADT

Summoned to Darmstadt in 1904, Jakob Julius Scharvogel consulted there with the Grand Duke Ernst Ludwig of Hesse and by Rhine on the organization – and eventual opening – of the Ceramic Manufactory of the Grand Duchy of Hesse in Darmstadt, which he directed from 1906 through 1913. The Grand Duke, who was eager to build up the local economy, improve the quality of local crafts, and promote cultural activities in the state, envisioned the manufactory as an adjunct to the Mathildenhöhe Artists' Colony, at first, for the production of garden terra cotta and ceramic vessels, as well as items to serve as models for the Hessian pottery industry. In addition, Scharvogel concentrated on work investigating the design and production of floor and wall tiles. This he was able to expand with ornamentation in glazed earthenware for use in interior architecture, as well as robust stoneware tiles for façades and weatherproof terra cotta for other exterior enrichment, such as figural capitals, pilasters, fountain figures, etc.

During the period he was at Darmstadt, Scharvogel supervised the production of tiles and terra cotta, including small 3" (7.5 cm), 4" (10 cm), and 6" (15 cm) square tiles, as well as large, decorative, rectangular, brick-like, terra cotta tiles/reliefs with a surface area of over 490 square inches (over 3200 square centimeters) and with a thickness of over 2" (over 5 cm). He continued to use the glaze formulations he had earlier researched and achieved in Munich[97] for both vessels and tiles and added new, more plastic features with slight surface relief, particularly in designs for rosette and abstract linear motifs.

Major installations were completed by a number of architects at important projects in various locations, including Darmstadt (Main Railway Station), Wiesbaden, Frankfurt-am-Main, Bad Nauheim, Freiburg, and Mannheim.

By 1912, though benefiting from the participation, in design, of sculptors Paul Haustein, Karl Huber, and Heinrich Jobst, and from Scharvogel's own wish for intensive collaboration with architects, the Ceramic Manufactory venture proved to be an economic failure due, at least partly, to architects' lack of interest in ceramic work, at that time, and the cost of architectural ceramic installation.

After Scharvogel's departure, the premises of the Ceramic Manufactory of the Grand Duchy of Hesse were leased, for some years, to the Majolica Manufactory of the Grand Duchy of Baden in Karlsruhe (Baden-Württemberg). Known as the Hesse-Darmstadt Ceramic Manufactory from around 1918, the facility was sold in 1921 to the Oldest Volkstedt Porcelain Factory in Volkstedt (Thueringia).

Scharvogel's work at Darmstadt in the period 1906–1913 is identified sometimes by an impressed, circular mark "GR K M DARMSTADT" (with "S") and an impressed, square mark "GROSSH. KERAM. MANUFAKTUR DARMSTADT" (with "S"), as well as his stylized-crane-in-a-circle mark (but without "SKM").

Some Ceramic Manufactory tiles and tile-related items bear the initials "EL" below a crown or the letters "Gr K M D" in a quartered-diamond mark.

8. DTAG

In 1900, the Dusseldorf Claywares Factory was founded in Reisholz, near Dusseldorf (now, Dusseldorf-Reisholz, in North Rhine-Westphalia), for the production of wall tiles (later, sometimes, bearing a raised mark consisting of a monogram formed of the letters, "D" and "T," above smaller "A" and "G"). Decorative pottery and architectural ceramics were also manufactured there. In 1913, prior to the First World War, the company employed about two hundred workers. After the war, in 1919, wall-tile manufacture was resumed until c. 1925/1926, when production ceased.

9. ELCHINGER

The Elchinger factory (now Céramiques Elchinger) was founded in Soufflenheim, in Alsace, France, in 1834.

After the end of the Franco-Prussion War in 1871, Alsace was annexed by the German Empire as part of the Imperial Territory Alsace-Lorraine.

Since the German victors preferred culinary articles in metal to those in ceramic materials at that time, the Elchinger family concern (Ph. Elchinger u. Söhne), in 1871, changed the focus of its manufacture for the German market

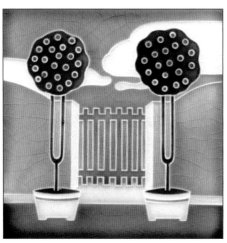

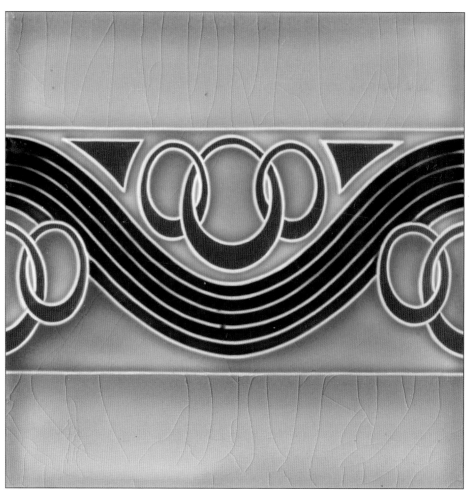

DTAG tiles.

and began producing garden faience and architectural ceramics. Included in the specialties, for which the company was renowned around the turn of the century, were tile panels, pressed medallions, and decorative tiles (especially those designed by Léon Elchinger), in faience, for building ornamentation.

10. ENGERS

By 1911/1912, the Engers Wall Tile Factory in Engers-on-the-Rhine (Rhineland-Palatinate) was manufacturing white, "fireclay"[98] tiles (later, occasionally, marked "E" with stars) for wall installation and industrial use.

11. ERNST TEICHERT, see: TEICHERT

12. FEUERRIEGEL

In 1910, the sculptor and ceramist Kurt Feuerriegel, who had studied under Karl Gross at the Dresden Arts and Crafts School, founded his Saxony Art Pottery Workshops in Frohburg, Saxony. While also teaching at the Dresden and Leipzig Arts and Crafts Schools, he directed a workforce of up to eighteen (in 1926) in the design and production of tiles for stoves and fireplaces, as well as earthenware and faience wares, terra cotta, and architectural ceramics.

13. GAIL

In 1903/1904, the architectural ceramics and wall-tile company Gail's Tile and Claywares Factory – founded in 1891 in Giessen (Hesse) – produced tiles to the designs of Josef Olbrich for the Darmstadt Exhibition at the Mathildenhöhe. Decorative brickwork material (Steinmaterial) was also supplied to Peter Behrens's specifications by the Gail company[99] for the park fountains he designed for the Dusseldorf Art and Garden Show in 1904. Later, other architectural work, especially fountain reliefs, was created with the cooperation of designer, graphic artist, and painter Daniel Greiner.

14. GRATHES

In 1888, Matthias Grathes moved his small cement tile factory from Dusseldorf to nearby Osterath (now, Meerbusch-Osterath) to expand his production of paving stones, roof tiles, and cement floor tiles there. With the introduction of ceramic wall- and floor-tile production, his company

experienced good growth and employed about one hundred-eighty to two hundred workers by 1900.

However, in 1903, Grathes was obliged to declare personal bankruptcy.

The factory continued as the Osterath Floor and Wall Tile Factory.[100]

15. GWF – GROHN

In 1906, the Grohn Wall Tile Factory was founded in Lesum (now Bremen-Lesum), near Bremen, and, in the fall of the following year, initiated wall- and floor-tile production – later, under the brand name "GROHN" and with infrequent markings, including "GROHN," "G," "GW," and "GWF" – in nearby Schönebeck (now, Bremen-Schönebeck). The premises were located close to the Bremen-Vegesack railway line.

In spite of strong competition from the North German Earthenware Factory, in Grohn (now, Bremen-Grohn), it was able to experience satisfactory growth

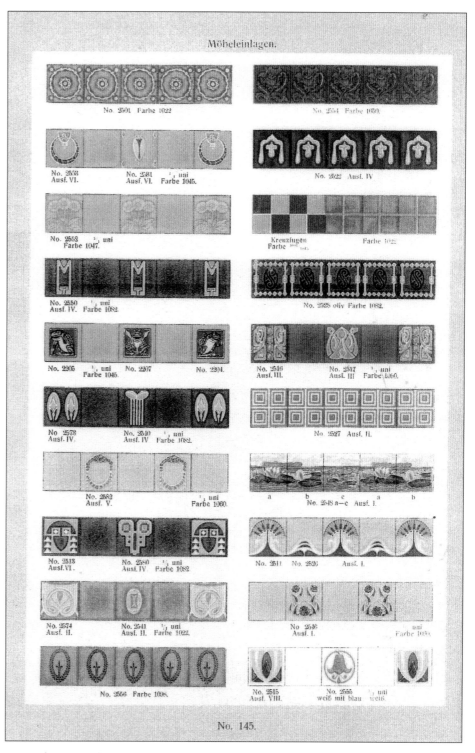

A page from an early GWF catalog: 8" x 10.5" (20.32 x 26.67cm).

GWF tiles.

and success, even winning a silver medal, in 1911, in Dresden.

In 1919, however, its much larger neighbor acquired an interest in the firm and, a year later, the Grohn Wall Tile Factory was wholly absorbed into the North German Earthenware Factory and, later, known as Plant II.

Consequently, from then on, numerous similar wall-tile models were produced by both factories in Grohn and Lesum/ Schönebeck.

In the late 1930s, along with the other two North German Earthenware subsidiaries, Plant II was closed down during – and for a few years after – the Second World War, with production resumed in 1948.

From 1957/1958, all of the subsidiaries of the North German Earthenware Factory in Grohn – Plants II, III, and IV – did business under that name.[101]

16. HESS & CO.

By 1891, Hess & Co. was producing floor tiles in Marienberg (Saxony).

17. KANDERN

Kandern Clayworks was founded c. 1835 in Kandern (Baden-Württemberg).

From 1887, as a joint stock company through 1910 – with a main production of industrial wares and floor tile – it won many awards at exhibitions at home and abroad. An art department was established by 1895 and was soon directed by Max Läuger, with his own studio there. Through 1913, this was known as Professor Läuger's Art Pottery. Uniquely decorated vases were first produced and, later, from the beginning years of the twentieth century,

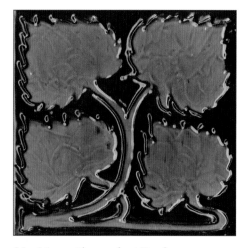  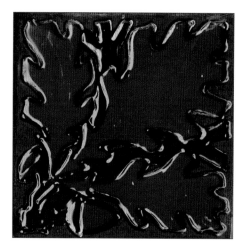

Max Läuger tiles, made at Kandern.

individual – though not unique – decorative tiles and panels (intended mainly for fireplace ornamentation), wall plaques, and picture tiles (produced under the brand name "KANDERN").

Recognized for his particular treatment of the underglaze-painting and difficult tube-lining techniques, Läuger's work won awards for the art department at several national and international expositions, most notably the Gold Medals received in 1900 and 1904 at Paris and St. Louis, respectively.

From 1913 through 1927, the art department at Kandern was under the direction of engineer Hermann Hakenjos, Sen., and, from c. 1914/1915 through 1929/1930, operated as Kandern Art Pottery, an independent enterprise.

Läuger marks at Kandern include the impressed/stamped "MLK" monogram, enclosing a small, simplified Baden emblem (shield with two diagonal stripes), sometimes contained in a square, occasionally above "GESETZL. GESCHZT." – also impressed/stamped; or his "LM" monogram, enclosing the same shield and contained in a square with rounded corners, impressed/stamped.[102]

18. KARLSRUHE

The Majolica Manufactory of the Grand Duchy of Baden was founded in 1901 in Karlsruhe, with a pottery building erected by Grand Duke Friedrich I of Baden.[103] The painter Hans Thoma was appointed adviser and director of design and the painter/ceramist Wilhelm Süs director of production (and, in 1904–1907, artistic director, as well). Their aim, as stipulated by the Grand Duke, was the promotion of art and crafts in Baden. The production of luxury ceramics – at first,

Max Läuger tiles, made at Kandern.

predominantly in majolica/faience and, later, with additional focus on stoneware – included single, pictorial tiles and tile pictures (made up of more than one tile) in addition to decorative plaques and wall plates, as well as trays and trivets, with the later addition of inlay tiles for tables, all featuring a diversity of motifs.

Artists, craftsmen, and ceramists were permitted to use the available equipment and materials for their own personal use and for co-operative production.

At first, in the years 1901–1904, unique, handpainted, single picture tiles – square or rectangular, with a maximum dimension a little over 5" (13 cm) – or tile pictures (usually consisting of 4, 6, or 12 such tiles) were designed by Thoma, Süs, and Hermann Haas, together with unique, handpainted wall-plates of various diameters.[104] Very soon, however, a program of serial production was introduced, with picture tiles and decorative plaques, etc. – as "individual" rather than "unique" items – produced to the designs of painters and sculptors by potters or modelers for reproduction by the casting technique and painting by decorators. These were molded, then colored, under the creating artist/designer's supervision. From the very beginning, duplication rights of these models remained exclusively with the company.

In 1905, production was expanded to include tiled stoves, as well as tiles for fireplaces, radiator covers, and fountains. From 1910, with slowly increasing demand for tile and terra cotta for interior design or architecture commissions (including state commissions), the company's marketing of its products covered both the domestic market and overseas export (including to South America).

Other architectural ceramics, manufactured under the supervision of architect Hans Grossmann as director of the architectural ceramics department from 1910, helped sustain the Karlsruhe operation, but, ultimately, collaboration with architects in the production of ceramic work (including decorative picture plaques) for private and public installation did not result in commercial success. Survival depended, largely, on the continued production of small decorative wares.

In 1909, the title of the enterprise was changed to include the designation Art Ceramics Workshops.

By 1910, the main focus in Karlsruhe was on the commercial production of individual (not unique) items with striking and unusual ornamentation, rather than the earlier art/craft emphasis. From that year, for three years (and, possibly, in other years, too), the sculptor and painter

Daniel Greiner collaborated with the manufactory on the design and production of relief tiles and plaques.[105] For many years from 1910 on, individual production – or, more and more, serial manufacture – replaced the more costly, original, unique pieces, resulting in a more economical variety of single tiles and tile pictures in larger formats, particularly in the 1930s (and also later), by freelance craftsmen/designers, including Gustav Heinkel, Hugo Ruf,[106] and Anton Kling.

Nevertheless, in spite of the industrial nature of manufacture at Karlsruhe, painters, sculptors, and craftsmen – with confidence in the co-operative arrangement – took advantage of the company's facilities to have their designs produced by factory methods and they continued to consult on the additional, hand-applied surface decoration by the Workshops' most capable employees.

By 1913/1914, when economic success remained elusive, the Grand Duke ended his involvement in the pottery (though retaining ownership of the premises) and, with the administrative management and artistic direction under the control of Villeroy & Boch, the Workshops were leased (for one year) by the Hans Duensing company of Boizenburg. As a result of the latter's under-financing from the time

Karlsruhe plaque, designed by Hugo Ruf: 10" x 9" (25.4 x 22.86cm).

Karlsruhe plaque, 1937, designed by Daniel Greiner: 7.25" x 8.5" (18.42 x 21.59cm).

of the outbreak of the First World War, the Karlsruhe facility – previously, with Richard Mutz as director of production through 1918 – passed into the possession of the State of Baden the following year. Two years later, when Villeroy & Boch's management ended, administrative control was assumed, once again, by the Art Ceramic Workshops of the Majolica Manufactory of the Grand Duchy of Baden, with master studios provided for Max Läuger from 1921 through 1929, Ludwig König from 1922, Paul Speck from 1924, and other designers and modelers.

Designs for tiled stoves (with brass framework) were provided by Fritz August Breuhaus; for architectural ceramics also by Breuhaus, and by Willi Schade and Paul Scheurich; for complete building exteriors by architect/designer Hans Poelzig; and for single interior elements and tiled stoves by Richard Riemerschmid. Other designers, on a freelance basis – including Emil Fahrenkamp, Josef Hillerbrand, Emanuel Josef Margold, Adelbert Niemeyer, Fritz Schumacher, and Joseph Wackerle – also collaborated with the manufactory in similar or different work or acted in consultation.

In 1922, after plant improvements and equipment replacement, the enterprise became a joint stock company. However, later in the 1920s, the production of stoves and decorative tile was reduced, along with the architectural ceramic work and ornamental ware for parks, gardens, and cemeteries, which, before the First World War, had become increasingly more important at Karlsruhe. Necessary reductions were made in the workforce and more economical production techniques were instituted to offset the effects of a diminished market. Nevertheless, under the threat of the company's financial collapse in 1924, the State of Baden took over financing, which inevitably led to State ownership of the company as the State Majolica Manufactory, Karlsruhe, in 1927.

Max Läuger, later artistic director of the Majolica Manufactory, first came to the city of Karlsruhe as an independent ceramic artist in 1916, with his own private studio at the premises formerly occupied by the manufactory, but, from the summer of 1921, he was employed by the company, retaining his master's studio facility there. From the mid-1920s, in addition to earlier work of the kind he had designed at

Kandern, he produced tile pictures and plaques for a few years with craquelé surfaces as an additional artistic feature. However, due to his dissatisfaction with its lack of the craftsman's personal touch in all facets of production, he became more and more opposed to the company's increasing series-production work and resigned in 1929.

After 1929, some of those artists who had enjoyed the privilege of their own studios at the Karlsruhe premises before the end of that year and who were interested in promoting the union of art and industry continued in co-operative work with the company through 1933.

From 1931, Erwin Spuler was an independent collaborator responsible for the introduction of new ceramic designs and techniques at Karlsruhe, including relief tiles (particularly with female-figural motif).

Though the bad economy continued in the ceramics and tile industry in Germany through the mid-1930s, including at Karlsruhe (in spite of increased state commissions), a decision was taken there in 1934 to hire Hermann Vollmer[107] to direct a newly organized faience department that continued the serial production of artistic tiles, wall plaques, and other items.

Most majolica/faience/stoneware items produced after 1901 by employees of the Majolica Manufactory at Karlsruhe bear an identifying mark, consisting of a crowned shield (emblem of Baden) above the cursive, conjoined initials "MM," all impressed, painted, or color-stamped, with the addition, sometimes, of "Baden" and "Germany." However, items originating from the early, independent masters'

studios might bear only the initials or monograms of the artists. Manufactured work, based on Läuger designs from 1921 through 1929, bears the impressed manufactory stamp, with impressed, upper-case "PROF. LÄUGER" below.

Among the marks identifying work produced by Läuger, earlier, at his Karlsruhe studio, are the following: around 1916, his "LM" monogram, incised; from 1919, his initials "M.L.," incised or painted; and from c. 1925, also, the initials "LK," incised.[108]

19. KAUFFMANN

Around 1871, Otto Kauffmann founded a company in Niedersedlitz (now, Dresden-Niedersedlitz), in Saxony, for the production, at first, of cement tiles. Intended for interior installation – and used extensively during the Gründerzeit and the first years of the Jugendstil era – these were made from a mixture of marble dust, cement, sand, and powdered stone, with color pigments added for surface decoration and applied by metal stencils for patterning. Hydraulically pressed, they were then dried, not fired.

In the 1880s – by that time, producing, also, ceramic floor tiles – the company was known as the Chemical Works for Chamotte and Floor Tiles of the Otto Kauffmann Company and began to develop a successful domestic and export business through the first decade of the twentieth century.

In 1905/1906, the firm was known as the Otto Kauffmann Chamotte Wares and Floor Tile Factory.

In 1938, the firm was taken over by Wessel Ceramic Works.

Max Läuger plaque, made at Karlsruhe, signed "M.L. / 1568 / Made in Germany," 5.63" (14.3cm) square.

Max Läuger plaque, made at Karlsruhe, signed "M.L. / 1570 / Made in Germany," 5.75" (14.6cm) square.

20. KLINGENBERG

In 1899, Ernst Albert and his partners founded the Klingenberg Clay Industry in Klingenberg-on-the-Main to produce ceramic floor tiles. In 1905/1906, its workforce numbered about one hundred-fifty employees.

Later, with production moved to nearby Trennfurt, the firm was known as the Klingenberg Clay Industry, Albert Works, and, by 1930, as the Klingenberg Floor Tile Factory, Albert Works. From c. 1937, the company was under the ownership of Heinz Albert and partners.

21. K.M.W.

In 1903/1904, in western Prussia, the modern Royal Majolica Workshops, later, Majolica Workshop Cadinen, was established by Kaiser Wilhelm II at the Hohenzollern estate at Cadinen (Elblag), near Elbing, for the production of plaques, tiles, and other wall decorations, as well as other majolica and terra cotta artwares, figures, figural groups, and fireplaces, and other architectural work. Artistic collaborators included sculptors Heinrich Splieth and Ludwig Manzel and sculptor/modeler Adolf Amberg. In the early years, work was often marked "K.M.W." or, particularly later, with an impressed cipher that incorporated the name "CADINEN." After 1918 (and through 1945), the factory, remaining the private property of the Hohenzollern family, was known as the Cadinen Majolica Workshops.

22. KPM

The Royal, later State, Porcelain Manufactory in Berlin is one of the three earliest and most important of German porcelain manufacturers.

Towards the end of the nineteenth century, portrait and scenic tiles and plaques and other artistic wall decorations – many in Classical and "old-German" styles, though some with more modern decoration – became a popular production specialty.

At the third German Exhibition of Arts and Crafts in 1906 in Dresden, the first prize was awarded to KPM, under the artistic directorship of Alexander Kips, in preference to the more senior Royal Saxony Porcelain Manufactory of Meissen,[109] which received the second prize.

When Theodor Schmutz-Baudiss succeeded Kips two years later, he continued his outstanding underglaze decoration, as well as the design of luxury items, household china, and porcelain decorations for inlay in furniture.

In the period 1925–1928, as part of a revitalization program, Nicola Moufang, the managing director of the Manufactory, was interested in opening up new, contemporary fields of application for china. Having promoted the use of ceramics in architecture at Karlsruhe, when he directed the State Majolica Manufactory there in 1910–1925, and, encouraged by influential architect, artist, and craftsman Bruno Paul, he wished to initiate the production of ceramic building materials at the Berlin factory. However, during his short tenure at KPM, the only architectural ceramics produced there were intended for use in interior decoration in a few individual projects involving the installation of relief porcelain plaques and other artistic wall decorations along with chimney-piece designs. Two of these were the outfitting – in historical style – of the Café Schottenhaml in the city in 1925/1926, followed by the refurbishing of the company's own showrooms in 1926/1927, with Paul's collaboration. In the latter case, the vestibule and foyer were decorated with single tiles and tile friezes with various motifs and in various techniques; also large plaques with ornamentation in painted relief were integrated into the scheme, together with an imposing, large, tiled fireplace.

23. MARIENBERG

From c. 1890/1891, the Marienberg Floor-Tile Factory in Saxony – by 1910, AG – was in full production of floor tiles at Marienberg (sometimes, when marked, bearing one of several versions of an impressed mark in the form of an unframed, impressed, large, upper-case "M," or, alternatively, a small, upper-case "M" enclosed within a larger, upper-case "M" contained in a square). In 1905/1906, it employed about two hundred workers.

Later, the production of wall tiles was initiated at a branch factory known also as the Broitzem Wall-Tile Factory in Broitzem, near Braunschweig (Lower Saxony).[110]

24. MEINHOLD:

The Meinhold Brothers Art Pottery was founded by Siegfried Meinhold in Schweinsburg (near Crimmitschau), in Saxony, around 1889. By 1903, decorative ceramic wares and wall tiles (mainly with cast images), designed by Mein-hold, himself, and other artists, were produced there. In 1903, the pottery executed tiles for a bathroom, which was exhibited in 1904 by the Dresden Workshops for Handicraft Art at the St. Louis World's Fair.

25. MEISSEN

The Royal Saxony Porcelain Manufactory, Meissen (the first European porcelain manufacturer) has an illustrious history from early in the eighteenth century through the twentieth century and beyond. Like KPM in Berlin the Meissen concern produced a long line of decorative plaques along with "artistic" tiles and plates of various sizes and shapes for wall decoration, in addition to ceramic sculpture and tablewares.

Between 1904 and 1907, the 1870 painting of an equestrian procession after a design by Wilhelm Walter – replacing an earlier painting of 1589 – was transferred to about twenty-four thousand tiles at the Meissen factory and mounted on a block-long wall in Dresden Old-Town. Along with heralds, musicians, and standard bearers of the court, as well as, later,

Detail of the Dresden wall installation "Procession of Princes" by Meissen, c. 1904-1907.

Detail of a Meissen stove, c. 1924-1934.

artists, craftsmen, miners, farmers, and students, this impressive, 102 meters-long, so-named "Procession of Princes" represents margraves of Meissen and electors/dukes/kings of Saxony – of the House of Wettin – in the period from 1123 to the beginning of the reign (1904–1918) of Frederick Augustus III.[111]

As managing director from 1918 and general director in the period 1926–1933, Max Adolf Pfeiffer led the Meissen Manufactory to new heights, while seeking to extend the scope of the production program there. Included was the design, manufacture, and decoration of tiled stoves in interesting, contemporary styles, some ornamented with Jugendstil motifs. Like other of the company's manufacture in 1924–1934, they bore the "Pfeiffer mark" (Meissen "crossed swords" with a point added between the blades).

26. M.O.&P.F.

In 1863, in Meissen (Saxony), Carl Teichert began to build new premises that opened two years later as the Meissen Stove and Porcelain Factory for the production, at first, of tiled stoves and, later, dinnerware and decorative items in porcelain. In 1879, after his death (in 1871), the company was renamed the Meissen Stove and Porcelain Factory, formerly C. Teichert, Meissen.

Through the 1860s and later, the production of tiled stoves and stove tiles grew well, concentrating, at first and for some time, on white, so-called "Berlin" stoves.

In 1873 – under a slightly different title – the company exhibited tiled stoves at the Vienna International Exhibition, reported as follows: "Meissner Ofen- und Chamottewarenfabrik (Meissen Stove and Chamotte Wares Factory) ... One of the largest manufacturers of stoves on the Continent, making annually about 3,000, which are sold in Germany and Austria. Many are of plain and unpretending design, but the best ones are characterised [*sic*] by very high artistic taste. This establishment employs 270 men and a 15 horse-power steam engine. It has only been in operation since 1865."[112]

The "Berlin" models were followed by stoves covered in green, brown, and polychrome tiles in the old German traditional design, which were sold not only in the surrounding area but also, through shipping and extended rail connections, in areas of northern and western Germany and beyond.

In 1885, the company had a workforce of about four hundred-sixty employees.

The following year, the Anton Tschinkel Majolica Factory in Eichwald, in Bohemia, was taken over to be run as a branch factory through 1899.

Between 1886 and 1891, the Teichert company's program focused on stoves and stove tiles with decorative ceramics produced more as a sideline for prestige purposes.

In 1891, the production of color-glazed wall tiles began at the Meissen Stove and Porcelain Factory, formerly C. Teichert, Meissen.

By 1896, its premises were expanded and equipment modernized for a full production in all categories of manufacture.

In 1907, the company had about seven hundred-fifty employees and, through the outbreak of the First World War – and after the war – continued to expand its domestic and export markets in tiled stoves and wall tiles, with representation in Berlin, Hamburg, Breslau, and overseas. This success was due, in small part, to designs contributed by experienced designers, such as Gertrud Kleinhempel, as well as the atelier of Josef Feller, and the benefit of consultation and advice from Karl Gross, Oswin Hempel, Fritz Schumacher, and other architects/artists/ interior designers, who commissioned wall and floor installations and stoves from the company. Also, stoves and wall tiles were featured in Teichert installations at various exhibitions, including an important stove design of 1914 for a livingroom by Peter Behrens for the Exhibition of the German Work Federation in Cologne.

Additionally, designs for Teichert's decorative pottery and porcelain sculpture were provided not only by the Teichert companies' own studios but also by recognized artists and sculptors throughout Germany, submitting designs and models for terra cotta, earthenware, and porcelain, including decorated vessels with colorful or lustered glazes. Also, "old Meissen" traditional dinnerware decors such as onion, straw-flower, and grapevine remained popular.

M.O.&P.F. tiles

In late 1919, the factory of the Meissen Stove and Porcelain Factory, formerly C. Teichert, Meissen, was destroyed by fire, but production continued elsewhere, including at the former location of the Heinrich Polko Claywares Factory[113] in Bitterfeld that had been taken over by the company in 1918.

Through the 1920s – beginning with its success in Vienna in 1873 – the company received many medals and prizes at various national and international exhibitions.

In 1923, the Meissen Stove and Porcelain Factory, formerly C. Teichert, Meissen, took over control of the Ernst Teichert Stove and Porcelain Factory, formerly Ernst Teichert, Meissen, together with all former components of the Ernst Teichert company, including the Saxony Stove and Chamotte Wares Factory, Meissen, formerly Ernst Teichert (S. O. F.) / Saxony Stove and Wall Tile Factory, Meissen, formerly Ernst Teichert (SOMAG). In 1928/1929, it also absorbed the "Saxonia" Cölln-Meissen Stove and Wall Tile Works GmbH.[114]

With the Meissen Stove and Porcelain Factory, formerly C. Teichert, Meissen, these companies – together with other stove and tile factories in the Meissen/ Dresden area taken over at various times by the Carl and Ernst Teichert concerns – formed the Teichert Meissen Works, an association of various Teichert family businesses focusing on artistic, traditional ceramics in porcelain and earthenware, including dinnerware and other household china, as well as industrial porcelain, "modern products in different fields," tiled stoves, white and colored stove tiles, and color-glazed wall tiles (with all wall-tile products manufactured under the brand name "M.O.&P.F. vorm. C.T.M.").

From c. 1930, the group advertised its production of tiled stoves and fireplaces – designed by important artists, executed in heatproof materials of the highest quality, and decorated with brilliant, matt, and artistic glazes, as well as wall tiles, architectural ceramics, radiator covers, and industrial/technical porcelain, though without mention of the former production of porcelain dinnerware and other household china, which had been discontinued due to economic difficulties in 1929.

After the Second World War – from 1948 – all Teichert companies operated under the name VEB[115] Max Dieter Tile Works.

27. MÜGELN

In 1895, the Mügeln Stove, Porcelain, and Claywares Factory was founded in Mügeln, near Leipzig, in Saxony – with its own clay and kaolin pits as well as kaolin extraction/cleaning equipment (Kaolinschlämmerei) – for the production of stoves, stove tiles, dinnerware, and other household crockery, with the addition, by 1906, of architectural ceramics and wall tiles (later, under the brand name "MÜGELN" and, sometimes, marked with a circle that enclosed a six-pointed star containing an upper-case "M").

In 1910, the company's workforce numbered about two hundred-fifty employees; in 1930, about four hundred; and, in 1935, about four hundred-fifty.

Known for its architectural ceramics (including exterior façades, etc.), color-glazed wall tiles (with designs in relief or handpainted or with artistic glazes), stove and fireplace tiles, tiles for wall-fountain installation and furniture inlay, and porcelain wares, the company received several awards at exhibitions in Germany, including a gold medal at Dresden in 1911.

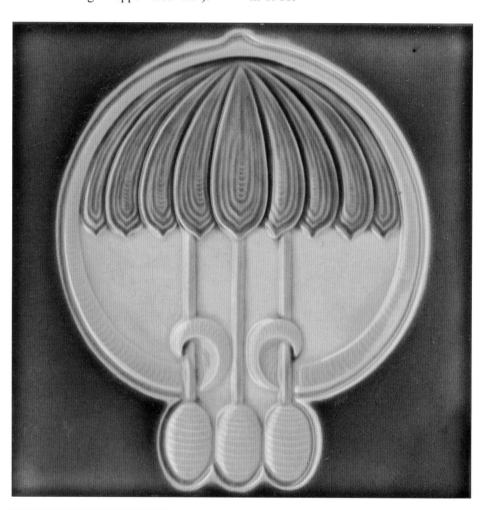

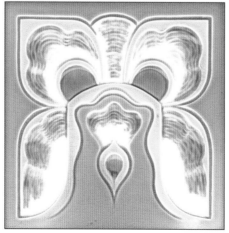

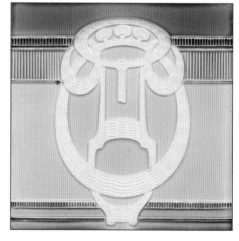

Mügeln tiles.

28. MÜHLACKER

Georg Steuler, with his brother-in-law Joseph Gillig, founded Steuler & Co. GmbH in 1908 in Grenzhausen (now, Höhr-Grenzhausen), near Coblenz (Rhineland-Palatinate), where they organized the manufacture of such industrial ceramics as acid- and heat-resistant ceramic products, including refractory brick and tiles, mainly for the chemical industry in the Coblenz area. Also, around this time, with other partners, they established an administrative parent company, the Industrial Factory for Heat-Resistant and Acid-Resistant Products.

The next year, a branch factory, the South German Claywood Works, was established in Mühlacker, near Pforzheim (Baden-Württemberg), for the addition of glazed wall tiles (later, under the brand name "MÜHLACKER" and sometimes marked with a raised "TM" monogram in a circle) to the production of industrial ceramics. From c. 1910, it operated under the name Mühlacker Pottery and Hard-Earthenware Factory.

In 1913/1914, the name of the parent company was changed to Coblenz Stone-ware Industry, which, by the time of the First World War, administered five factories, producing clay and chamotte products, not only in Grenzhausen and Mühlacker but also Wirges and Siershahn (in the Westerwald region of Rhineland Palatinate).

The company's production of industrial ceramics as war material expanded during the First World War. Afterward, the Mühlacker works was re-equipped in 1919 for wall-tile manufacture, with the addition of household crockery.

Through 1926, the company's products were advertised and marketed under the Mühlacker Clayworks name and, then, under both that name and that of Steuler Industries.

In 1935, under the name Steuler Industrial Works, all subsidiary companies were combined under the control of Georg and Hans Steuler and there was no further listing for the Mühlacker Clayworks in trade registers under that name.

29. MUTZ

The ceramist Richard Mutz[116] produced wall tiles and other ceramic wares between 1906/1907 and 1915 at the Richard Mutz & Rother Workshops for Ceramic Art in Liegnitz, Silesia; in 1920–1922, at his own Richard Mutz Ceramic Works, Stove and Claywares Factory in Velten; and, between 1923 and 1929, at the R. Mutz Ceramic Workshop in Gildenhall (Brandenburg).

Between 1915 and 1919, he was director of production at the Majolica Manufactory of the Grand Duchy of Baden in Karlsruhe.

30. NSTG

With a location close to the River Weser – allowing direct access to the seaway – the organization of the North German Earthenware Factory began in 1869 in Grohn, near Bremen (now, Bremen-Grohn), by businessmen from Bremen and Vegesack (now, Bremen-Vegesack).

Two years later, with about one hundred employees, full production was reached in household china, beginning with domestic utilitarian ware. It was not until the mid-to-late 1880s that wall tiles (later, known under the brand names and with markings "NSTG" and "N.St.G.") were first manufactured there – by the wet-clay process – to take advantage of the current condition of the domestic and export marketplace, in which there was little competition at the time.

As demand grew, it was decided by 1891 that the company would concentrate its production on wall tiles. However, a slump in sales occurred in the next few years, so that, in 1894, a restructuring of the works was undertaken. After a fire loss in 1897, wall-tile manufacture was resumed at the end of that year, along with earthenwares and sanitary fittings, for almost two years, before those categories were again discontinued.

Around the turn of the century, the North German Earthenware Factory tiles were reduced in thickness from over 0.33" to about 0.25" (from about 8 to about 6 mm), contributing to a lighter item weight. Consequently, the cost of transportation became cheaper, affording more competitive delivery prices to the German market. More importantly, the reduced size and weight were able to offset part of the high import tariffs in the foreign market, allowing the company's exports to increase by up to 65%.

In 1904 – by which time its raw materials (previously shipped from England) could then be ordered and shipped by rail from the Rhineland and when its wall tiles were awarded gold medals at the World's Fair in St. Louis – the company decided that future demand from South

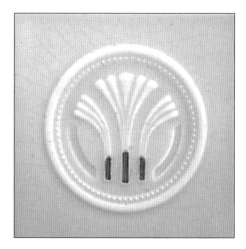

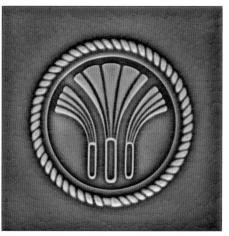

Mühlacker tiles.

America, Africa, and Southeast Asia would necessitate greater production and, therefore, a move to new, larger premises in Grohn.

Between 1905 and 1910, North German Earthenware entered into collaborative agreements with the Belgian tile company Maison Helman, Céramiques d'Art, especially regarding the sharing of designs, overseas representation and negotiation, and filling customers' orders, etc.

Floor-tile manufacture was added in 1909, after production at the Grohn factory, employing some eight hundred workers, had reached about a hundred thousand wall tiles per day in 1907 – with about two-thirds exported. This permitted further expansion, though at the expense of household china, which was discontinued around that time.

The continued success of the Grohn wall tiles at this time – both at home and abroad – was accounted for, in part, by their use of traditional, popular motifs with local color, such as rural scenes and maritime themes that included persons, animals, and familiar and attractive flora. In particular, many of the factory's models featured motifs in high relief contained within medallions.

As demand grew from around the world, it was necessary to open a subsidiary, established in 1911/1912 as the Bremen Wall Tile Factory in Aumund, near Bremen (to be known, later, as Plant III). However, due to the First World War, the manufacture of wall tiles at Aumund was suspended, totally, in 1914–1918, and production at the North German Earthenware Factory in Grohn was converted to ceramic materials important for the war effort.

With the end of hostilities, the Witteburg Earthenware Factory in Farge (now, Bremen-Farge) was acquired and run as a subsidiary, to be re-equipped seven years later for floor-tile production (and, later, known as Plant IV).

Also, in 1919, North German Earthenware purchased a majority interest in the Grohn Wall Tile Factory in nearby Lesum/Vegesack (also, now, parts of the city of Bremen), and from 1920, took over full ownership of this neighbor and competitor (later known as Plant II).

In 1925, 41% of Grohn-area inhabitants were employed in the local tile works.

Two years later, about twenty-two hundred employees worked at the North German Earthenware and Grohn Wall Tile factories, but after a disruption of business of almost a year in 1932 (due to the international economic climate at that time) only about fifteen hundred workers were employed there in 1935.

In the late 1930s, all manufacturing activities ceased at the subsidiary Plants II, III, and IV, and, c. 1942/1943, the Grohn premises of the North German Earthenware Factory, itself – Plant I – closed down, to resume production of household china and other ceramic wares in 1945, after post-war rebuilding, and, soon thereafter, wall tiles. Plant II at Lesum/Vegesack resumed wall-tile work in 1948; Plant III at Aumund in 1950; and – for just four years – Plant IV at Farge with floor tiles only in 1949.

From 1957/1958, the North German Earthenware Factory was the sole owner of the former subsidiaries that conducted all "Grohn" business under its name.

31. NYMPHENBURG

In Munich, the Royal Bavarian (later, State) Porcelain Manufactory, Nymphenburg, entered a period of considerable artistic renewal in the first years of the twentieth century. Its eclectic products (with Neo-Classical, Neo-Baroque, Biedermeier, and contemporary style elements) – including

NSTG tiles.

figural and other luxury ceramics and table-wares – received awards at a number of national and international expositions. With commissions for architectural work (some exterior, but mainly interior) – and from c. 1905/1906 with the collaboration of artist/craftsman Josef Wackerle (through 1958) – the output included large-size terra cotta and majolica works, including wall, column, and niche decorations (with polychrome tiles, reliefs, and medallions, often in contrasting colors and with luxurious floral, fruit, and figural motifs). Along with garden statuary, fountains, openwork covers for cast-iron radiators, and other custom-designed, architectural ceramics in modern designs, these were originated by such architects and artists/designers as Ludwig Gies, Emanuel von Seidl, and Gabriel von Seidl. Josef Hillerbrand and Adelbert Niemeyer also collaborated with the manufactory.

32. OFFSTEIN

In 1899, the Offstein Clayworks, formerly Dr. G. Lossen, was organized in Offstein, near Worms-on-the-Rhine (Rhineland Palatinate) by Ernst Albert, Albrecht Hildebrandt, and Ferdinand Lossen. A few years after the turn of the century, the production of wall tiles in earthenware (later, under the brand name "OFFSTEIN" and, sometimes, marked with a raised "TO" monogram in a circle) was added to the manufacture of floor tiles there.

By 1911, when its workforce had increased to over two hundred-forty employees, the Clayworks was under the control of the Worms and Offstein Clay Industry, Albert-Works, which had been founded in Worms and was, later, known – after the First World War and through 1930 – as the Offstein and Worms Ceramic Works.

After the premises were destroyed by fire in the spring of 1913, an expanded facility was erected for increased wall-tile production, with a closer connection to the Worms railway line. After the First World War, weather-resistant facing bricks and other architectural ceramics were added to the production line.

In 1931, the factory was closed due to bankruptcy.

33. OSCHATZ

The Oschatz Hard-Earthenware Factory was founded c. 1911/1912 in Oschatz, Saxony, and included the manufacture of wall tiles (later, under the brand name

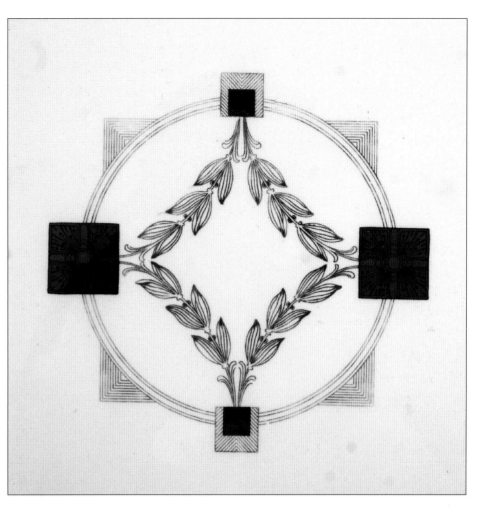

Offstein tiles.

"OSCHATZ" and with markings including a monogram of the initials "H" and "O" with either "m.b.H" or numbers).

By 1927, it was taken over by the Colditz Earthenware Factory in Colditz (Saxony) and managed as a branch.

34. OSTERATH/OSTARA

When, in 1903, Matthias Grathes declared personal bankruptcy, his factory in Osterath (now, Meerbusch-Osterath), near

Dusseldorf, continued in production there as the Osterath Floor and Wall Tile Factory. In 1905/1906, it employed about one hundred-fifty workers.

In 1910, with a successful business in floor tiles, particularly, and wall tiles (later, marked with two enclosed, raised letter "R"'s, divided by a vertical line and with the first "R" reversed), it was renamed the Ostara Floor and Wall Tile Factory and, from the beginning of the First World

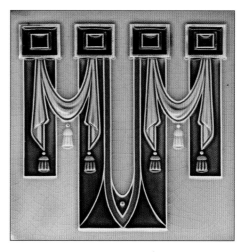

Oschatz tiles and half-tiles.

Osterath/Ostara tiles.

War, it was known as the Osterath Ceramic and Chemical Industries Factory, with a continuing manufacture of ceramic products and the introduction of "clay soap" production. This latter soon resulted in damage to the kilns and, by 1918, rendered them useless for two years.

Around 1920, after the financial difficulties arising from this, the company passed into different ownership and the premises were enlarged and equipment replaced. Again known as the Ostara Floor and Wall Tile Factory, it conducted a successful business by 1923 for the next several years. However, with subsequent financial difficulties – by the time of the onset of the international Depression and with the breakdown of technical equipment in the early 1930s – the company entered bankruptcy in 1932. By the mid-1930s, all of the movable plant assets were transferred outside Germany (for political reasons) and the premises were purchased by new owners, who possessed clay pits in the Westerwald region and continued production for several years.

On the outbreak of the Second World War – by which time the workforce had increased to about one hundred-forty employees – the factory ceased all tile manufacture. However, despite the severe wartime damage suffered by the plant, production was resumed in 1945.

The business was, later, absorbed into – and exists, today, as part of – Cremer & Breuer German Stoneware.

35. POLKO

The Heinrich Polko Claywares Factory was established in 1861 in Bitterfeld (Saxony-Anhalt) for the production of pottery items – often identified by the mark "H. POLKO BITTERFELD" together with the Bitterfeld coat of arms – with, particularly, stoneware floor tiles as a specialty and, possibly later – after the turn of the century – also wall tiles.[117]

In 1918, it was acquired by the Meissen Stove and Porcelain Factory, formerly C. Teichert, Meissen, as a subsidiary, exclusively for the production of glazed wall tiles. When the Meissen factory was destroyed by fire the following year, the company was in a position to expand production at the Bitterfeld facility.

The location had the advantages of a nearby rail connection for coal supply as well as favorable transportation of finished goods.

Saxonia tile and two half-tiles.

36. RANSBACH

A factory was established by 1894 in Ransbach (now, Ransbach-Baumbach, Rhineland-Palatinate), which operated under the names Ransbach Floor Tile Factory and Ransbach Floor Tile and Wall Tile Factory.

Around 1905/1906, the factory supplied floor tiles for installation in an Augsburg (Bavaria) bank building designed by Henry Van de Velde.

37. SAXONIA

Fourteen years after its founding in 1874 by Richard Müller – for the production of stoves and floor, wall, and fireplace tiles – ownership of the Cölln-Meissen Chamotte and Clay Products Factory in Cölln (now, Meissen-Cölln), in Saxony, was transferred from the Christian Seidel & Son Stove Tile Factory to the "Saxonia" Cölln-Meissen Stove Factory, owned by

Arthur Baarmann and directed by Hermann Karl Max Simon.

By 1915/1916, this factory employed about three hundred workers manufacturing single-colored or polychrome wall tiles (under the brand name "SAXONIA MEISSEN"), along with floor tiles, fireplace tiles, stove tiles, tiled stoves in either old-German or modern design, and other ceramic products.

In 1928/1929, it was taken over by the Meissen Stove and Porcelain Factory, formerly C. Teichert, Meissen. By c. 1930 and through 1941, it was a branch of Teichert Meissen Works.

38. SCHARVOGEL

From 1897 through 1905/1906, Jakob Julius Scharvogel organized his own Art Pottery for Decorative Vessels and Earthenware Articles in Obersendlin, near Munich (Bavaria), collaborating with a number of artists/designers – including Ludwig Habich, Paul Haustein, Walter Magnussen, Theodor Schmutz-Baudiss, Karl Soffel, and Emmy von Egidy – in the production of decorative and functional objects in earthenware (vessels, lamps, desk sets, figural ceramics, etc.), as well as, from 1900, tiles for wall decoration and mantel and furniture inlay. His experimental work with tiles – especially those 4" (10 cm) and 6" (15 cm) square – included the use of high-fired stoneware, the execution of ornament without contours, and the formulation of enamel, flambé, and other unique glazes with various color nuances, achieved through the addition of different metallic oxides in the glaze batch. As a member of the United Workshops for Art in Handicraft, he produced vessels and tiles in the early years of the twentieth century that he exhibited in Darmstadt, Leipzig, Paris, and Turin. Since his methods and techniques were craft-intensive, his work was restricted to the creation of individual designs produced in small series, as well as unique items. In 1904, not only were Scharvogel tiles installed in furniture and featured in interior design schemes shown at the second Darmstadt exhibition, they were also used in an interior designed by Bruno Paul and exhibited at the St. Louis World's Fair.

After seven years in Darmstadt,[118] Scharvogel returned in 1913 to a studio in Munich, which he maintained for the next eleven/twelve years, producing tiles for numerous architectural installations, while lecturing on architectural ceramics at the city's Technical High School. The emphasis in his work in Munich continued in designs in a painterly manner, with the surface decoration of each motif – in a color applied by stencil technique – melting into the background of the base color without separating outlines. This achievement, first developed c. 1902/1903, together with his experimentation in firing temperatures and reduction techniques and the unique coloration of his tiles – due

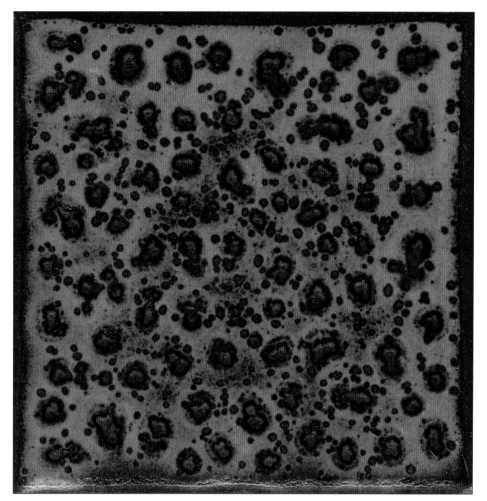

to often accidental effects in firing – resulted in the serial production of tiles with individuality. He discovered color-shaded, flambé, flowing, wavy, rippled, speckled, and, sometimes, even interestingly streaky surfaces and, often, combined various glaze elements to produce brilliant enamel colors in intensive blue/green/red/violet tones that were additionally enlivened by irregular, crystalline, gold-dust, and aventurine effects.

Scharvogel's personal signature in this Munich period is also revealed frequently in a high-fired glaze, sometimes matt or semi-matt, in such color combinations as green/brown, gray/brown, and blue/brown, with the brown coloration often enhanced by a copper-red effect. Some of his tiles for larger wall installations bore simple, graphic decoration, while Haustein and other artists – in the early years, before Scharvogel's stay in Darmstadt – produced, with his collaboration there, single tiles, tile friezes, column coverings, and fireplace surrounds with slightly textured surface ornamentation, inspired by flora and fauna of land and water, in the manner of early Jugendstil design.

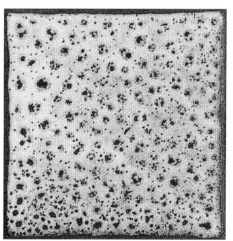

Scharvogel tiles.

An impressed circular mark consisting of a stylized depiction of a crane, with the addition of "SKM," identifies the work Scharvogel produced in 1898–1905 and c. 1916–25 in Munich, along with the, c. 1906, impressed mark "J.J.SCHARVOGEL MÜNCHEN;" a printed, lower-case "Scharvogel" mark is also known.

39. SCHMIDER

In December 1890, as part owner, Georg Schmider joined Haager, Hörth & Co. – a firm producing earthenware and porcelain in Zell-on-the-Harmersbach (in Baden-Württemberg) – later, in 1898, taking over sole ownership. In 1907, he bought the Porcelain, Earthenware, and Majolica Factory of Karl Schaaff, formerly Jakob Ferdinand Lenz, also in Zell, and united the two companies under the name Georg Schmider Zell United Ceramic Factories to continue production of all kinds of ceramics, including dinnerware (that both companies had previously produced), as well as tiles.

Schmider's company – with an increasing workforce, totaling about five hundred employees in all branches of manufacture by 1926 – produced special-use tiles with either naturalistic, floral decoration or fantasy designs of stylized flowers and plants (sometimes with insects). Seldom, if ever, marked with the Schmider name or Schmider company insignia, they were decorated in mainly pastel tones, for subdued coloration, and without distinct separation between areas of different colors, suggesting a painterly effect. Schmider's use of negative-relief pressing to produce this "intaglio" kind of design was a technique rarely employed by other tile makers.

For about twenty-nine years through c. 1936, tiles – roughly 6" square, with a thickness of between 0.19" (5 mm) and 0.3" (8 mm) – were designed by in-house draftsmen as well as freelance artists/ ceramists Alfred Kusche, Elisabeth Schmidt-Pecht, and others, and delivered frequently to furniture businesses (for ornamentation of cabinetry) and metal workshops (for mounting as trays, trivets, wall plaques, etc.)

40. SERVAIS

i). In 1877/1878, the **SERVAIS-EHRANG CLAYWARES FACTORY OF LAMBERTY, SERVAIS & CIE.** was organized in Ehrang, near Trier (Rhineland-Palatinate), by Paul Servais and others. With about seventy employees, its production included floor tiles that were, at first, formed in wet-clay presses from black-, red-, yellow- or white-colored clay bodies and unglazed. The factory also specialized, from the early years, in floor tiles shaped and/or cut for placing in mosaic patterns, as well as paving stones, ceramic piping, and fireproof bricks, etc. Later, tiles were dust-pressed and glazed.

Though foreign import tariffs presented economic difficulties for the company in Austria and the overseas market, growing domestic demand allowed it to increase its workforce by 1885 to about one hundred-thirty-five employees.

In 1898, glazed wall tiles (later, under the brand names "LAMBERTY SERVAIS & CIE. EHRANG," "SERVAIS," and "SERVAIS WERKE A.G. EHRANG") were introduced – which, along with floor tiles (sometimes marked "Ehrang"), were designed by in-house designers, including Eduard Becking (for many years) and Karl Scriba – and, soon afterward, architectural ceramics, including chimney pieces, columns, gargoyles, water fountains, etc., were put into production

Four years later, the Servais-Ehrang Factory and its Servais-Witterschlick Factory branch (opened in 1889/1990) merged to form the United Servais-Works, Ehrang-Witterschlick, and, by 1905/1906, the two facilities employed about one thousand workers.

By the time of the outbreak of the First World War, the Ehrang factory's workforce had decreased drastically in the past four/five years from around seven hundred-fifty to about one hundred-fifteen employees and, by 1919, all production ceased until resumed in the early 1920s.

In the 1920s, the connection with the Witterschlick concern was severed, which allowed the Ehrang business to merge, later, with tile factories in Friedland (Mecklinburg-Western Pomerania) and Sinzig (Rhineland-Palatinate) as the United Floor and Wall Tile Works, Friedland-Sinzig-Ehrang for the production of unglazed, red-clay, stoneware tiles and mosaic-pattern tiles, as well as single-color and polychrome, glazed wall and floor tiles. In 1921 the Servais-Ehrang headquarters moved from Ehrang to Trier.

In 1931, the Servais-Ehrang firm closed, due to the imposition of increased import-tariffs abroad and the continuing slump in the domestic building industry, but it resumed floor-tile production two years later.

In the early twentieth century, Servais-Ehrang tiles were installed in the Old Elbe Tunnel in Hamburg (opened in 1911); the Roman Catholic Cathedral in Batavia, Java; the Church of the Holy Spirit in Buenos Aires; and the China Export-Import Banking Company building in Shanghai.

From c. 1912/1913, tile designs were solicited from various sources, including the Trier Arts and Crafts School that was

Schmider special-use tiles, 0.25" (6.3mm) thick.

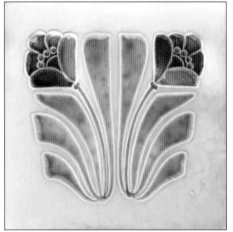

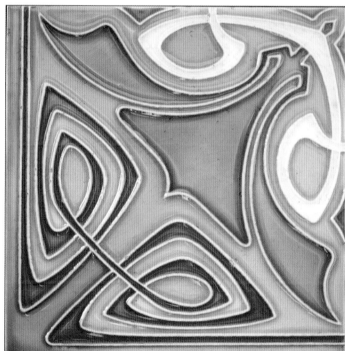

Servais wall-tile panel.

established at that time. Also, the company received many medals and awards and honorable mention at exhibitions in Germany and abroad.

ii). Around 1889/1990, a Servais-Ehrang branch factory for floor tiles, the **SERVAIS & CIE. WITTERSCHLICK CLAY-WORKS** was opened in Witterschlick, near Bonn (North Rhine-Westphalia), by Paul Servais and other shareholders, for

the manufacture of brick products, paving stones, piping, glazed facing stones, and tiles, as well as other fireproof, ceramic materials for steel companies and manufacturers of stoves and furnaces.[119] Clay was dug from the company's own neighboring clay pits for its own use and supply to other businesses.

In 1902, the Witterschlick factory merged with Paul Servais's other concern in Ehrang as the United Servais-Works,

Ehrang-Witterschlick, but, two years later, was destroyed by fire.

By 1905, the factory was rebuilt with added facilities and equipment for the production of glazed wall tiles (also under the brand name "SERVAIS") and, with considerable success due to increased demand for its products, further significant enlargement and modernization of the plant was undertaken between 1912 and 1914, which, later, proved especially

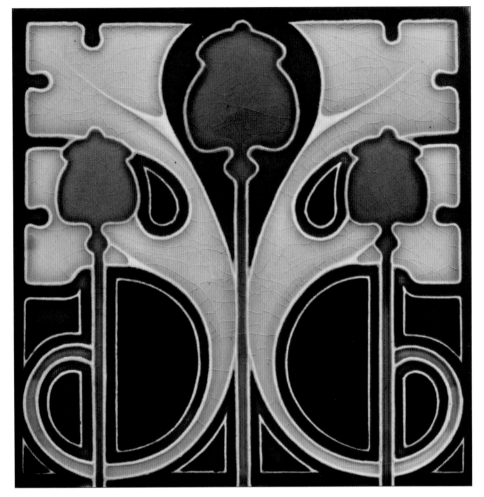

Servais tiles.

favorable for the production of fireproof materials needed in the war effort. Another factory – with close-by clay pits – was acquired in 1915 in Hangelar, near Siegburg (North Rhine-Westphalia), and converted to the manufacture of additional fireproof products.

In the late 1920s, the Witterschlick connection with the Servais-Ehrang concern was severed – though with Witterschlick representation on the new United Floor and Wall Tile Works AG, Friedland-Sinzig-Ehrang, company's board – and, from 1921, the Servais-Witterschlick factory was known as Witterschlick Clayworks.

In 1927 – two years after the separation of the Sinzig undertaking from the United Floor and Wall Tile Works – the Hangelar plant was expanded to allow for the manufacture of floor tiles there, in addition to its fireproof products.

In 1940, a majority holding in what had been the Servais Witterschlick Works / Witterschlick Clayworks was acquired by the Wessel Works of Bonn and it is,

now, part of Cremer & Breuer German Stoneware AG Alfter-Witterschlick.

41. SINZIG

In 1865, after the death of the Mehlem brothers, the Franz Anton Mehlem Porcelain and Fayence Factory in Bonn was taken over by the Krefeld-based businessman Ferdinand Frings, prior to his re-locating to Sinzig (Rhineland-Palatinate).

In 1870, his Sinzig Floor and Paver Tile and Claywares Factory began the production of floor tiles and other ceramic ware[120] (sometimes, later, identified by the name "SINZIG MOSAIK FABRIK AG SINZIG AM RHEIN" or a circular mark "SINZIG AM RHEIN" encircling a large "S" over conjoined "MF").[121]

Forty years later, the Sinzig factory merged for some years with the Friedland Floor Tile Factory in Friedland – founded in 1906 – under the name United Sinzig and Friedland Floor Tile Works. Later, the Sinzig and Friedland factories merged with the United Servais Works AG, Ehrang, to form the United Ehrang, Sinzig,

Friedland Floor and Wall Tile Works AG. However, in 1925, a joint sales agreement was agreed upon with the Sinzig branch of the United Friedland-Sinzig-Ehrang Works that resulted in the organization of the "Mowa" Floor and Wall Tile Company, with its main office in Bonn and, therefore, independent of the headquarters of the Servais group of companies by then located in Trier.

More recently – from about 1943 – the Sinzig operation was part of Agrob Tiles, which, in 1992, was taken over by the Cremer Group and, in 1994, became Cremer & Breuer German Stoneware AG.

42. S. O. F.

In 1872, the Saxony Stove and Chamotte Wares Factory, Meissen, in Cölln (now, Meissen-Cölln), took over the factory of Ernst Teichert Meissen, which had been founded three years earlier for the production of stoves and ceramic wares. From then on – with about one hundred-thirty employees – it continued the production of utilitarian and decorative pottery items, stoves, and stove and floor tiles as the Saxony Stove and Chamotte Wares Factory, Meissen, formerly Ernst Teichert, Meissen.

Through the mid-1870s, production concentrated on white-tiled stoves and white stove tiles, mainly for the German market (since tariffs on such goods imported by other countries, at that time, rendered German tiles too expensive for overseas markets.)

Silver medals were awarded at exhibitions in Munich in 1876; Halle (Saale) in 1881; and Görlitz (Silesia) in 1885; a first prize was received in Cologne in 1889.

In 1883, the factory employed around four hundred- five workers.

Stove and stove-tile manufacture increased, particularly in the 1880s, necessitating a workforce almost tripled by the 1890s, when wall-tile production was introduced at the factory (under the brand names / and with markings "S. O. F. vm. E. T. M.," "S. O. F. vorm. E. T. M.," and "S. O. F. vorm. E T C M."[122])

The takeover of the Theodor Alexander Markowsky Stove Factory, c. 1905, allowed substantial expansion of the wall- and stove-tile departments of the Saxony Stove and Chamotte Wares Factory (S. O. F.) and also made possible the addition of heat-resistant fireplace tiles, radiator covers, and architectural ceramics.

By 1905/1906, the company's workforce numbered about five hundred workers.

By 1918 – after the addition, eight years earlier, of a branch works to concentrate the undertaking's wall-tile production – the company was most often referred to as the Saxony Stove and Wall Tile Factory (SOMAG).[123]

Gertrud Kilz, Anna Gasteiger, and Margarethe von Brauchitsch are known to have supplied designs for the Saxony Stove and Chamotte Wares Factory.

S. O. F. tiles.

43. SOMAG

Between the time of its founding in 1868/1869 and 1893, the Saxony Stove and Chamotte Wares Factory (S. O. F.) introduced the production of wall tiles in earthenware and, in 1910, maintained a branch works for the undertaking's wall-tile manufacture.

From around that time or later, the company was known as the Saxony Stove and Wall Tile Factory,[124] producing wall and stove tiles (under the brand names / and with markings "SO Meissen," "SO Meissen SOMAG," "Somag Meissen Verbandsfabrik," and "SOMAG Meissen"[125]), along with tiled stoves, façades, and other architectural ceramics.

In 1918, it became a public limited company.

Around 1923, the Saxony Stove and Chamotte Wares / Wall Tile company (S. O. F. / SOMAG) was taken over by the Meissen Stove and Porcelain Factory, formerly C. Teichert Meissen.

By c. 1930, when it joined with other Teichert companies to form the Teichert Meissen Works, it had a workforce of about eight hundred workers.

44. TEICHERT

i). CARL TEICHERT, MEISSEN: The name Carl Teichert has long been an important one in the Meissen ceramics

SOMAG tiles.

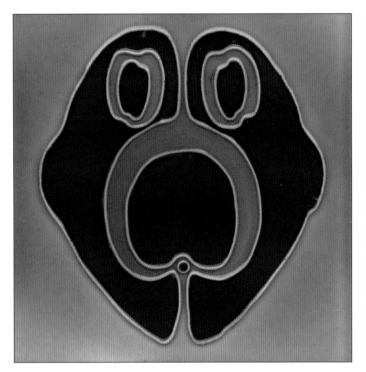

Ernst Teichert tiles.

area of Saxony, beginning with the founding in 1857 – by the master potter and, later, entrepreneur Carl Teichert – of the Carl Teichert Factory / Carl Teichert Porcelain Factory, later, known as Carl Teichert, Meissen, and, finally, by 1930, absorbed into Teichert Meissen Works. The initial manufacture of stove tiles – produced under the "Meissen Tile" patent (Meissner Patentkachel), filed in 1855 by Gottfried Heinrich Melzer, covering the manufacture of tiled stoves and stove tiles that would tolerate great heat and show no glaze-cracks for many years – was closely followed there by the production of household china and decorative ceramic products in earthenware or porcelain. Soon, the company became one of the biggest and most successful companies in the Dresden area.

A new factory was planned in 1863 and opened two years later in Meissen as the Meissen Stove and Porcelain Factory.[126]

ii). ERNST TEICHERT, MEISSEN: Through 1868, Johann Friedrich Ernst Teichert was employed by his brother Carl as supervisor of Carl Teichert's stove-tile factory until he, independently, opened his own factory the following year for the production of tiled stoves in Cölln (now, Meissen-Cölln), in Saxony. Three years later, the business was taken over by the Saxony Stove and Chamotte Wares Factory.[127]

In 1884, in Cölln, Ernst Teichert opened another operation, Ernst Teichert, Meissen, for porcelain production. After his death in 1886, it was converted to

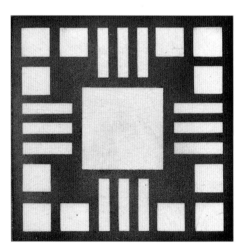

stove-tile production and directed by his son Christof. Still under the father's name as the Ernst Teichert Porcelain Factory, formerly Ernst Teichert, Meissen, this factory then enjoyed a steady expansion through the later 1880s, when, c. 1889, color-glazed wall tiles in earthenware (later, from c. 1901, under the brand name "ERNST TEICHERT G. m. b. H. MEISSEN") were added to stove tiles, requiring a total workforce, by c. 1890, of over four hundred employees.

By 1913, the company was successfully producing, marketing, and exporting its products, employing about seven hundred workers in the manufacture of earthenware wall tiles, stove tiles, tiled stoves, architectural ceramics, and household china.

Around 1923, Ernst Teichert Porcelain Factory GmbH, formerly Ernst Teichert, Meissen, was taken over by the Meissen Stove and Porcelain Factory, formerly C. Teichert, Meissen, along with the Saxony Stove and Chamotte Wares Factory, Meissen (S. O. F) / Saxony Stove and Wall Tile Factory (SOMAG), and, around 1930, these companies joined the Saxonia Stove and Wall Tile Works, Meissen – taken over in 1928/1929 – to form the associated Teichert Meissen Works.[128]

Tiles made by the Ernst Teichert, Meissen, firm generally measure around 5.63" (14.29 cm) square, rather than 6" square.

45. UTZSCHNEIDER

By 1800, François-Paul Utzschneider was the sole owner of a French faience/majolica factory in Sarreguemines, Lorraine, that had been founded in 1785. In 1836, management of the factory was taken over by Utzschneider's son-in-law Baron Alexandre de Geiger.

After a market-sharing arrangement was agreed upon with the Villeroy family of Wallerfangen and the Boch family of Mettlach, the Sarreguemines factory, known by 1838 as Utzschneider et Com-

pagnie, opened three other factories there, between 1858 and 1869, to increase production of household ceramics of various kinds. The company was directed in 1871 by Alexandre's son and Utzschneider's grandson Paul de Geiger and under his management employed over three thousand workers around 1890.

After the 1870–1871 Franco-Prussian War, part of Lorraine – with most of Alsace – was annexed by Germany, with Saarguemines becoming known for the next forty-eight years as Saargemünd in Imperial Territory Alsace-Lorraine.

In France, Utzschneider & Cie. established a new factory in 1876/1877 in Digoin (for decorative and household ceramics), and its subsidiary in 1881 in Vitry-le-François (for architectural and industrial ceramics), in order to evade taxes and to continue serving the French market.

In Saargemünd, Utzschneider & Cie. produced all kinds of ceramics, faience stoves, and tiles, including, from c. 1880, wall tiles (seldom, if ever, bearing registered Utzschneider company marks) and other architectural ceramics. From the mid-1890s, these wall tiles began to appear on the market with Jugendstil decoration.

In 1905/1906, thirty-two hundred workers were employed by the Utzschneider company.

In 1913, the firm's interests were divided into Utzschneider & Co. AG and Établissements Céramiques Digoin, Vitry-le-François et Paris SA. Through 1918, the company head office and general direction remained in Saargemünd, but, after the First World War, the Alsace-Lorraine territory was returned to France, with all three Utzschneider works there re-united as Faienceries de Saareguemines,

Digoin et Vitry-le-François, formerly known as Utzschneider & Cie., with the head office in Paris.

Luxury items were produced in faience, majolica, and earthenware, and utilitarian ware and dinnerware were made in porcelain and earthenware, along with sanitary ware, tavern fixtures, wall tiles, stove tiles and tiled stoves, fireplace tiles, and picture tiles; some of the latter bore designs by Jules Chéret, Theodore Steinlen, and other celebrated artists.

Utzschneider & Cie. produced most of the original tiles for use in the Paris Métro system.

During the Second World War, Alsace-Lorraine was again under the control of Germany[129] and tile production ceased at the faience works in Saareguemines/ Saargemünd (Administrative Division West March / Reichsgau Westmark). Between 1942 and 1945, the three Utzschneider locations were under the administration of Villeroy & Boch and, after suffering severe war-damage, underwent extensive rebuilding after the end of the war.

46. UTZSCHNEIDER & ÉD. JAUNEZ

In 1864/1865 – employed by Utzschneider & Cie. – Édouard Jaunez (from 1904: Édouard von Jaunez), the grand-nephew of Paul Utzschneider and son-in-law of Alexandre de Geiger, joined his uncles Charles Joseph and Maximilien Joseph Utzschneider in opening a separate tiling and flagging company, Utzschneider & Éd. Jaunez, also in Sarreguemines. After the initial introduction of floor-tile production there, greater success was achieved with the development of a clay

Utzschneider tile.

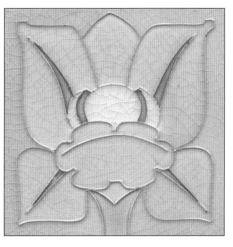

Two Utzschneider tiles with tube-lined decoration.

body for the manufacture of what became known as "carreaux de Sarreguemines," which contained a concentration of blast-furnace slag (French: "laitier de haut fourneau") that made it suitable for extensive use in exterior pavements.

In 1908 – by which time, production was extended, from 1873, to locations in Belgium and France (Burgundy and Picardy), as well as Luxemburg (Wasserbillig); Alsace (Oberbetschdorf); eastern Germany (Zahna in Saxony-Anhalt); and western Germany (Birkenfeld-Neubrücke in Rhineland-Palatinate) paving/tiling commissions were obtained for railway installations in eastern Germany and all Imperial Army barracks throughout Germany.

Of these branches, the Utzschneider & Éd. Jaunez Floor Tile and Claywares Factory at Zahna, established in 1890/1891, was planned there because of its proximity to nearby clay pits, and, more, because of the anticipated market for pavements and floor coverings in the fast-growing capital city of Berlin. In 1905/1906, it employed around four hundred workers (whereas the workforce at the Wasserbillig factory numbered about one hundred-eighty at that time, and the other plants functioned with even fewer employees).

After the First World War, the Utzschneider & Édouard Jaunez partner-ship, previously with its headquarters in Saargemünd, divided its administration between the three separate companies, Sarreguemines-Wasserbillig, Zhana, and Birkenfeld-Neubrücke. In the fall of 1921, the Sarreguemines-Wasserbillig central office formed the Compagnie Générale de la Céramique du Bâtiment (CERA-BATI), based in Paris, to direct the then-French factories in Sarreguemines, Betschdorf, and Pont-Ste.-Maxence, as well as the Wasserbillig location in Lux-emburg and the two Belgian facilities.

In the 1930s, the workforce at the Zahna works increased to over six hundred employees, which made it the third-largest tile factory in Germany at that time. After the Second World War, it became a manu-facturing branch of the Boizenburg Tile and Sanitary Ceramics industrial combine.

The majority of ceramic tiles produced by Utzschneider & Éd. Jaunez before the Second World War measured 5.5" (13.97 cm) or 6" square, with the indoor floor tiles 0.5" (1.3 cm) or 0.7" (1.8 cm) thick and the outdoor surface coverings in four thicknesses ranging from 0.9" to 1.6" (22/28/33/41 mm). Other floor tiles were made in roughly 5" (12.5 cm) or 4" (10.16 cm) square formats.

47. VELTEN / BLUMENFELD

In 1884, Richard Blumenfeld took over the direction of the Velten Stove Factory, his father's stove factory in Velten (Brandenburg), and, later, renamed it the Richard Blumenfeld Stove and Claywares Factory with the head office in nearby Berlin-Charlottenburg.

In 1913–1917, it was under the artistic direction of architect/sculptor John Martens.

In 1926, by which time it was the biggest firm in Velten, its workforce numbered three hundred-fifty and, in 1929, it was five hundred-twenty, manufacturing not only stoves but also architectural ceramics and tiles of different kinds, as well as functional and decorative pottery wares.

In the early 1930s, there were still fifteen stove factories in the town, with five of them belonging to Richard Blumenfeld AG (including some of his factories producing wall tiles in addition to stove tiles and architectural ceramics).

In 1932/1933, under the National Socialists, the company – without Blumen-feld – was merged with Velten Ceramics as Veltag Stove and Ceramics AG, Velten.

Some of the Richard Blumenfeld company's tiled stoves were designed by Malve Unger, who, by the late 1920s, operated her own sculpture studio in Berlin. Others were designed by Ludwig Vierthaler.

The firm also produced color-glazed wall tiles, designed by architect Alfred Grenander, for at least one of the U-Bahn stations opened in 1929 in Berlin. Interior and exterior architectural decorations were manufactured for buildings by Bruno Taut and Max Taut. Other designs were executed for other important architects and sculptors of the time, including Peter Behrens, Bruno Paul, Walter Gropius, Erich Mendelsohn, and Mies van der Rohe.

48. VELTEN-VORDAMM

The company known as Velten-Vordamm Earthenware Factories was founded in 1914 after the establishment of an earthenware factory in 1902 in Vordamm (Brandenburg) and a sister factory, built in 1913/1914, in Velten. Both closed in 1931/1932.

Employing a total of eight hundred workers in 1926, luxury items and household china were produced at both locations, with the collaboration of independent artists/designers (including Ludwig Gies). In addition, wall tiles, architectural ceramics, and garden decorations were manufactured at the Velten plant.

49. V & B DÄNISCHBURG

In 1906, a branch works of the Mettlach firm Villeroy & Boch was opened under René von Boch in Dänischburg, near Lübeck (Schleswig-Holstein), a location favorable for the transportation of raw materials from the Meissen/Dresden area, by barge on the Elbe River (and, from 1900, the Elbe-Trave Canal), also for export shipments overseas due to the factory's proximity to the Lübeck and Hamburg harbors.

Production began in 1907 and, within the next five years, kilns were increased from three to twenty for the manufacture of functional ceramics, sanitary ware, and twenty-five thousand square meters, per month, of white and single-color floor and wall tile (in various sizes).

In 1913, the factory employed about three hundred-sixty workers. That number increased after the First World War through the mid-to-late 1920s – with expansion and improvements to equipment and continued business growth – until the time of the international Depression. Then, due to decreased demand and, therefore, production and employment requirements, the workforce continued to fluctuate downwards from a high point of almost one thousand workers to eighty-seven after the Second World War.

By the end of the 1930s, the thickness of the white tiles manufactured at Dänischburg was reduced to about 0.17" (4 mm) – in order to qualify for reduced shipping costs and lessened export tolls (based on weight) – thus allowing a greater number of the thinner, lighter-weight tiles to be shipped at an equivalent cost. By 1938, the factory was producing one hundred-twenty-five thousand square meters of tile per month, with significant exports of tiles (for bathrooms and kitchens, fireplaces and hearths, etc.) in white and, possibly, other single colors, especially to Britain.

At the end of the Second World War, production was converted to household crockery, with the resumption of wall/fireplace tiles in 1946.

To counteract the revenue lost as a result of the take-over of the Villeroy & Boch concerns around that time, in the German Democratic Republic (DDR), the manufacture of sanitary ware was also initiated at Dänischburg, along with the re-introduction of floor-tile production.

Tiles with polychrome decoration for wall installation in public and domestic buildings are not known to have been produced there, but tiles and border tiles with relief enhancement were already appearing in company brochures and other advertising material by around 1910.

The Dänischburg factory tiles were occasionally acquired for decoration (and, possibly, sale afterward) by professional, private retail artists and teachers,[130] and by amateur enthusiasts.

Tiles bearing a mark "V & B DÄNIS-CHBURG Made in Germany" are known.[131]

50. V& B D

Between 1853 and 1856, the Villeroy & Boch Earthenware and Floor Tile Factory was organized in Dresden-Neustadt (Saxony), in northeastern Germany. This location had access to raw materials and coal and was also favorable for sales in other areas of the country, particularly northern, central, and eastern Germany.

With the most modern machinery for the manufacture of functional ceramics, it was also equipped to begin filling, immediately, the increased demand for floor tiles produced by mass-manufacturing techniques and to introduce the production, later, of wall tiles (under the brand name "VILLEROY & BOCH" and with marks including "VILLEROY & BOCH DRESDEN" or "VBD").

From c. 1886/1887, the factory added the manufacture of decorative ceramics in earthenware as well as color-glazed wall and stove tiles and tiled stoves, which it marketed locally and exported through the time of the Second World War.

By 1889, the Dresden branch employed about twelve hundred workers.

Around 1896, the production program was again increased with the addition of sanitary ware.

Before that time – in 1892 – Villeroy & Boch designed and completed, in Dresden-New Town, the tile installation at the famous and still-existent Pfund Brothers Dairy Store, called the "Most

V & B Dresden tile page from the Villeroy & Boch Mettlach and Dresden 1910 catalog: 8" x 11" (20.32 x 27.9cm).

Beautiful Milk-Store in the World." Its walls, ceilings, floors, pillars, counter, fountain, and other historical store fittings, were – and are[132] – entirely covered in decorative tile representing flora and fauna, children, animals, insects, and mythical creatures, as well as milk industry motifs and other images, in an opulent and richly colored, Historicist, Neo-Renaissance manner. The treatment of the vividly colored and linear-bordered decoration anticipates Art Nouveau/Jugendstil ornamentation.

The Dresden factory of Villeroy & Boch was the first factory in Germany to produce earthenware with flowing, colored

glazes and luster decoration. From the mid-1890s, it produced wall tiles and tile-trays with Jugendstil decoration and, around 1905, it introduced, most notably, its famous wall decorations and trays/trivets incorporating variations of a scene with swans from an Art Nouveau design, first produced by Hans Christiansen, c. 1898, in Paris. It also produced tile decoration for washstand mirrors and wall-mounted towel rails, as well as fountains for apartment houses, and columns and wall reliefs for large entry halls and corridors in public buildings and business properties.

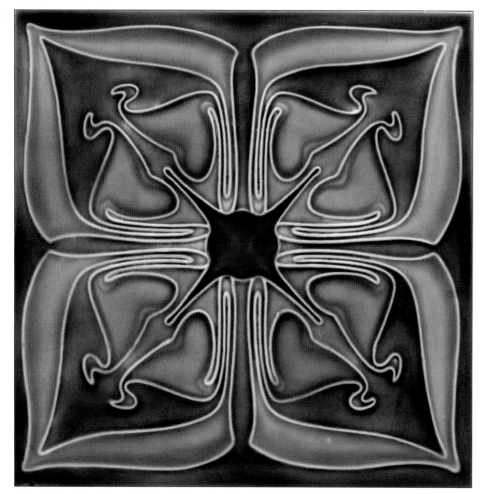

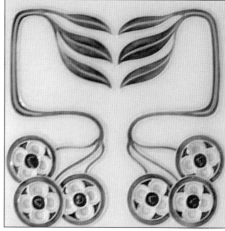

V & B D tiles.

By the turn of the century and at the beginning of the twentieth century, Villeroy & Boch Dresden maintained a good relationship with the Arts and Crafts School in the city. It contributed clay and glazes for student use and fired student work, prior to 1907, when the Meissen Porcelain Manufactory adopted those roles.

By 1912, the factory employed about fifteen hundred workers.

During the period 1923–1935 – when Mettlach, in the Saarland, was already located in territory annexed by France and, thus, participating in the economy of that country – the head office of the German Villeroy & Boch firms was in Dresden.

In 1945, the Dresden factory was expropriated by the German Democratic Republic and the company's name changed, there, to VEB (State-Owned Enterprise) Dresden Earthenware Factory.

51. V & B M

Since the nineteenth century, the Villeroy & Boch company has been one of the most important enterprises in Germany for the production of porcelain and ceramic wares, with its first high point – in the very long history of the firm – around the end of that century.

That history began, in 1809, with Jean François Boch's acquisition and conversion of an old Benedictine abbey in Mettlach-on-the-Saar (Saarland) – later, the Villeroy & Boch Earthenware Factory – to begin the manufacture of items in earthenware. In 1829, the management of this factory was taken over by Jean François's son Eugen. Seven years later, father and son joined with the manufacturer Nicolas Villeroy – owner of a factory, from 1815, in Wallerfangen – to achieve a more effective, cooperative production partnership. With shares in a pottery works in Septfontaines, in Luxemburg – inherited by Jean François, in 1818, from his father Pierre Joseph – Eugen Boch shared in the control of three works, with the administration coordinated in Luxemburg.

At Septfontaines, Jean François Boch first began making single-color floor tiles in the 1840s, from wet, plastic clay and, then, in 1846, from dry, powdered clay. Soon, his work was continued by Eugen Boch at the factory in Mettlach. There, around 1850, single-color floor tiles were produced, on an industrial basis, by means of hand-operated (and lever-assisted) screw presses, until the introduction, c. 1851/1852, at Mettlach, of hydraulic presses,[133] allowing greater mass production.

In 1852, with the company's invention of a dry-press method for the inlaying of colored designs with clay dust, "Mettlacher Platten" – dust-pressed, multicolored, encaustic floor tiles – were first made by Villeroy & Boch at the Mettlach location by means of metal stencils placed in the molds and the tiles then pressed hydraulically.

Between 1853 and 1856, new premises were organized in Dresden, with raw materials nearby. However, despite the increasing demand for floor tiles, especially in northern and eastern Germany, their manufacture, still in the mid-to-late 1850s, remained only a sideline – alongside architectural ceramic decoration and figures (made from the late 1840s) and terra cotta ornamentation (introduced in 1856) – subsidiary to the company's production of household china and other ceramic wares.

When his father died in 1858, Eugen Boch – from 1892, Eugen von Boch – took over the direction of the four branches (in Septfontaines, Mettlach, Wallerfangen, and Dresden), with the assistance of his sons René – from 1907, René von Boch-Galhau – and Edmond.

Around 1860, the manufacture of, at first, plain and, then, decorated wall tiles by the wet process (later, under the brand name "VILLEROY & BOCH" and with marks including "VILLEROY & BOCH METTLACH," "VILLEROY & BOCH MOSAIKFABRIK METTLACH," "VILLEROY & BOCH IN METTLACH," and "V & B M") was added to that of floor tiles by Villeroy and Boch Mettlach.

In 1862, the exhibit of floor tiles by Villeroy & Boch was awarded a medal at the London International Exhibition.

In 1869, a new building, housing the Villeroy & Boch Earthenware and Floor Tile Factory under the direction of René, was completed in Mettlach for an expanded production of color-glazed wall tiles (from wet, plastic clay) in addition to encaustic floor tiles (manufactured by the dust-compression method). The original earthenware factory in Mettlach was, from that time, managed by Edmond.

By 1873 – in which year it was awarded a medal for merit for its display of encaustic floor tiles at the Vienna International (Universal) Exhibition – the company's workforce in Mettlach numbered over eighteen hundred employees.

In 1875, color-glazed wall tiles were first produced by the company using compressed clay dust.

Soon after the take-over, in 1879, of the Merzig Earthenware and Terra Cotta Factory in nearby Merzig (Saarland) for additional production of tiles and architectural ceramics,[134] Villeroy & Boch was recognized as being, at that time, the largest manufacturer of floor tiles and terra cotta in the world. Moreover, from around this time and through the beginning of the twentieth century, major clients in Germany and overseas markets appreciated,

and benefited from, the Mettlach company's staff of traveling tile-installation specialists.

By 1882, a decision was taken to focus on sanitary ware at the original, older factory at Mettlach – with large-scale production from c. 1899 – while manufacture at the other locations continued in other specialized fields.

In 1883 (and through 1912), earthenware and majolica items were produced at yet another location, Villeroy & Boch Schramberg in the Black Forest (Schwarzwald). Thus, by the time of René's death in 1908, there was a total of nine Villeroy & Boch factories in Germany and Luxemburg, employing more than eight thousand workers. With a diversified production, the company continued its success for almost forty years, despite the loss of business in times of financial crisis and periodic slumps in the building industry. However, at the end of the First World War, with the loss of control of the factories when the Saar region was ceded to France, and, also, a destructive fire at the Mettlach location, there were only two Villeroy & Boch facilities remaining in Germany, namely, the factories at Dresden and Dänischburg. This situation led to the acquisitions, from that time, of

Two V & B M tiles and a V & B M half-tile.

Franz Anton Mehlem's Earthenware Factory & Art Pottery in Bonn (North Rhine-Westphalia), operated through 1931; the Deutsch-Lissa Floor Tile Factory[135] near Breslau, in Silesia, through 1945; and the Torgau Earthenware Factory in northwestern Saxony, from 1925 through 1945.

Between 1923 and 1935, the main office of all Villeroy & Boch concerns in Germany was located at Dresden and, afterward, again at Mettlach.

By 1930 – in spite of the closure that year of the Dresden location for several months and its re-opening with only forty percent of its former employees – the workforce had again been built up to around ten thousand workers at eleven Villeroy & Boch factories, producing not only decorative wares (including dinnerware), tiles, and other architectural ceramics, but also technical porcelain. Tiles for wall and floor installation had again approached record production, along with wall tiles advertised – from c. 1910 – for use as furniture inlay in washstands, cupboards, etc.

In 1948, the Villeroy & Boch factories in the German Democratic Republic – in Dresden, Torgau, and the Breslau area – were nationalized and the company's name changed, there, to VEB Dresden Earthenware Factory, producing household china, there, until 1965.

From before the end of the nineteenth century through the beginning of the twentieth, designers of Villeroy & Boch's products – mainly tablewares and decorative ceramics – included Jean Beck, Peter Behrens, Hans Christiansen, Otto Eckmann, Hermann Gradl, Ludwig Hohlwein, Albin Müller, Adelbert Niemeyer, Joseph Maria Olbrich, Richard Riemerschmid, Henry Van de Velde, Franz von Stück, et al. Those who are known to have contributed designs for wall/floor tiles, or to whom designs have been attributed, include Beck, Behrens, Christiansen, Eckmann, Hohlwein, Riemerschmid, and Van de Velde.

52. V & B S

In 1883, the Schramberg Majolica Factory, founded in 1820 in Schramberg (Baden-Württemberg), was bought at auction – jointly, with Utzschneider & Co. – and renamed the Villeroy & Boch Earthenware Factory Schramberg. This new undertaking was modernized and directed by Eugene Villeroy and, later (by 1906 and up to 1912) managed by Dr. Lindhorst.[136] By 1906, about three hundred workers were employed there, producing earthenware and majolica items, but, six years later, due to railway work in the area, the factory was torn down.

Around 1910, the Schramberg factory produced a series of tiles designed by Munich poster artist Ludwig Hohlwein.

Tiles of square or, even, circular form were always glazed, possibly on the front, back, and edges and, often, identified by a mark incorporating the letters "V," "B," "S." They were produced, with or without foot rings, to be used as trivets – that are, sometimes, to be found mounted in metal or wire frames – or as wall pictures in appropriate, patent-protected frames. Usually featuring flowers, plants, birds, or scenes, they were painted under clear, shiny glazes and probably designed by Jean Beck (since the initials "JB" are often to be found on the front of the tile) or other in-house or freelance artists. Prior to 1913, they, also possibly, ornamented furniture in the same manner as Schmider and J. von Schwarz tiles.

Occasionally, Schramberg tiles are to be found marked "Schramberg, Majolika, SMF," sometimes with numbers.

53. VON SCHWARZ

In 1859, Johann Christof David von Schwarz founded the Johann von Schwarz Factory for Soapstone Gas Burners in Nuremberg (Bavaria), where he, first, produced gaslight parts (of soapstone) and insulators, as well as, from 1867, architectural elements (including garden ware) that resulted in a rapidly increasing demand. In 1870, he introduced the manufacture of tiled stoves – with tiles, composed of a body containing soapstone/steatite with a high talc content, which allowed good heat absorbency, retention, and distribution – together with small ceramic items with Historicist (mainly Rococco-styled) ornamentation. These latter – which included circular plaques decorated with historical views of Nuremberg – were made from a body combining soapstone/steatite and fire-clay, which had a similar potential application as terra cotta.

By 1870, the company was known as the J. von Schwarz Majolica and Terra Cotta Factory.

Seven years after the award of a medal for merit for statuary and other ornamental objects at the Vienna Interna-

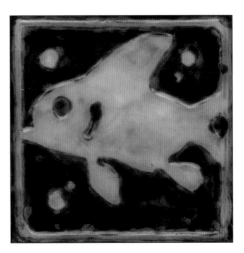

V & B S tiles, designed by Ludwig Hohlwein: each approximately 5" (12.7cm) square.

tional (Universal) Exhibition of 1873, one fifth of the company's workforce (of about one hundred-fifty employees) was engaged in the production of decorative ceramics.

Like its pottery vessels at the time, J. von Schwarz's architectural ceramics – for the ornamentation of home and business façades – incorporated various art styles. Soon, a department was established for the manufacture, by casting, of ceramic balustrades, friezes, masks, rosettes, and capitals and, afterward, expanded to include such other artistic, architectural ceramics as garden figures, columns, and urns of glazed terra cotta.

In 1885, after wall tiles were, arguably – though improbably – added to the factory's program, by 1883,[137] stove and stove-tile manufacture was discontinued. In 1890, the firm moved to larger quarters for the production of faience and, in 1896, the artist Carl Sigmund Luber was hired as designer of vessels, plaques, and artistic tiles, etc., supported, eventually, by over thirty assistants, skilled in decorative painting, to execute his designs.

With a clay body (with a high steatite content) and extensive glaze range devised by the company's chemist Dr. Lindhorst,[138] tiles from Luber's designs – including tile pictures, furniture tiles, tiles for mounting as serving trays, etc., and tile shapes adapted for other uses – were pressed using the cuenca technique of raised outlines for the separation of colors and glazed on both sides and all edges. Of a thickness, usually, between 0.25" (6 mm) and 0.44" (1.12 cm) – most often about 0.4" (1 cm) – they were produced in a variety of shapes and sizes, with the basic forms, most frequently, rectangular, oval, square, and round. Often about 6" x 12" (15 x 30 cm) or, sometimes, as small as 2.75" x 3.75" (7 x 9.5 cm),[139] others might have a maximum dimension measuring up to about 20.25" (51.5 cm).[140]

Artistic tiles, in various formats and in a large selection of designs, including floral and figural decoration, were specially created for sale to furniture makers for installation in sideboards, wall cupboards, tables, side chairs, hall stands, wall shelving, umbrella stands, and jardinieres. Others were sold to art suppliers/ wholesalers and other manufacturers to be retailed as tile pictures in wooden frames for wall-hanging.

In other categories of tile usage, a number of tiles were enhanced by the addition of metal mounts[141] in complementary style and, often, of highly ornamental and intricate design, for sale as serving trays and trivets; others were incorporated into clock cases or sconces and other lighting devices.

Also, small objects in a vast range of shapes, sizes, and pictorial designs were pressed to be used as unmounted trivets. Incorporating integral, self-framing, low walls, some with a dimension as small as 3" (7.62 cm)[142] or as large as 12.25" (31.12 cm),[143] they were alternatively intended to serve as pen, jewelry, or dresser trays, etc., or even to be used for advertising purposes and as souvenir items by client companies.

At the Paris Exposition of 1900, the company was awarded a bronze medal.

Between 1900 and 1906, the Von Schwarz factory advertised their "artistic faience items" ("Artistische Fayencen") and, particularly, their inventory of decorative tiles – with inlaid colored glazes, in the "modern style" ("in moderner Art") – for home decor as wall pictures, for furniture inlay, and for everyday household use.

Most, if not all, designs by Luber for the Von Schwarz firm feature the emphasis on the use of the dynamic line – so characteristic of early Franco/Belgian Art Nouveau – in floral depiction, with poppies, irises, and waterlilies predominating, or, more often, figural representation, including human and animal motifs, with full-length, standing figures, busts, or faces, mostly in profile. Seldom do such single, female figures appear without accompanying imagery, often, with flowers and luxuriant foliage and/or integrated into nostalgically scenic landscapes, including castles and other motifs related to ancient myths and sagas. Many are rendered as images of a pure, unspoiled ideal, removed from seductive womanhood, despite an aura of tender eroticism, displaying bejeweled, luxurious and, frequently, swirling hair treatments, very much in the Alfons Mucha manner, and flowing garments reminiscent of Parisian, fin-de-siècle fashion. Wistful, dreaming faces, enhanced by handpainted details – in addition to technically superb cuenca decoration – reflect attractive, otherworldly innocence, with an air of Oriental mysticism and unattainability. Dancing, making music, picking flowers, or "alone

Von Schwarz plaques, designed by Carl Sigmund Luber: (left) 18.75" x 13.75" max. (47.63 x 34.93cm); (right) 15.25" x 9.75" (38.74 x 24.77cm).

and palely loitering" (in Keats-ian
language) and gazing towards some far-
off horizon, beautiful, slender women
demand the beholder's attention, yet
remain sensuously aloof.

The stylized representation apparent
in Luber's designs resulted specifically
from the application of the cuenca
technique – with narrow lines of separation,
between large areas of usually vibrant
color – strengthening the ornamental
nature of the image. In many instances,
the floral background relates to the
foreground figure in a way that enhances
the rhythmic dynamism of the Art Nouveau/
Jugendstil linear design.

Luber's sense of fantasy and his
delight in illusion and idyll – what has
been called "escape from the world"[144]
and "aestheticisation of life"[145] – combined
with his concern, as a painter and designer,
for elegant refinement and his love, as a
craftsman, for skilful execution in a two-
dimensional medium, marked his personal

Von Schwarz plaques, designed by Carl Sigmund Luber: (top left) 4.75" x 14.38" (12.07 x 36.53cm); (bottom left) 6.25" x 4.38" (15.88 x 11.13cm); (right) 4.75" x 14.38" (12.07 x 36.53cm).

signature in this singular achievement – of little more than ten years – in Von Schwarz's production of artistic faience.

With the departure of Sigmund Luber (also, Dr. Lindberg) in 1906, the manufacture of art ceramics – artistic tiles and "Norica" vessels and other objects – ceased in Nuremberg but an expanding business continued in industrial ceramics, including electrical insulators, manufactured by an increasing workforce that reached about eleven hundred employees by the end of the first decade of the twentieth century.

Moreover, from 1902, in Holenbrunn, in Upper Franconia (Bavaria), a separate factory – J. v. Schwarz Holenbrunn Floor Tile Factory – was maintained for the production of floor tiles. These tiles were smooth or exhibited, alternatively, a ribbed, grooved, blistered, or "hammered" surface texture, in a variety of shapes and with a variety of thicknesses ranging from almost 0.75" (1.9 cm) to almost 1.25" (3.2 cm). Single-color, 4- and 6-sided tiles, with dimensions of almost 6" square or 6.5" x 5.75" (16.51 x 14.61 cm) were available in tones of white, yellow, red, brown, black, gray, blue, and green, and in plain or impressed, geometric, and imitation-parquet designs. For 6" border tiles, abstract patterns were designed, sometimes, in more than one color or more than one tone (e.g., dark and medium olive green). The larger, 8-sided tiles, with maximum dimensions 6.75" x 6.75" (17.15 x 17.15 cm) – for entryways, corridors, etc. – could be ordered in white, with brown, red, gray, black, or blue, encaustic, inlaid patterns. Occasionally tiles – 6.75" square, with a thickness of less than 0.75", and bearing abstract decoration in negative relief – were manufactured for use, possibly, in floor installation or even as wall tiles in exterior architecture. The reverse sides of all floor tiles were, usually, marked "J. von Schwarz Holen-brunn" (in raised, impressed, or black-printed letters).

In 1921, the J. v. Schwarz Factory merged with other companies as Steatite-Magnesium AG, Berlin.

It is, indeed, only very rarely that artistic tiles, trays, trivets, etc., with decoration to Luber's designs can be identified by such impressed markings as the "NORICA" or "J.v.S" brand names. However, once witnessed and studied, it is highly unlikely that an admirer should mistake their outstanding quality and appeal for other equivalent Jugendstil/ Secessionist/Art Nouveau manufacture of German, Central European, or French/ Belgian origin.

54. WÄCHTERSBACH

By the late 1870s, the Wächtersbach Earthenware Factory, founded in Schlierbach, near Wächtersbach (Hesse), in 1832, established a department for the production of decorative wares that was added to the company's manufacture of kitchen items and household crockery in earthenware. From 1879, this department collaborated with independent artists/designers to produce ornamental ceramic articles, as well as, later, polychrome tiles mounted as serving trays, trivets, etc.

With the founding, in 1885, of a kitchen-furniture factory in Neuenschmidten (Hesse), tile designs were solicited and executed for inlay in tables, washstands, cupboards, etc.

In 1900, a program of work began in the execution of decorative ceramic articles commissioned by members of the Mathildenhöhe Artists' Colony at Darmstadt, including designs by Hans Christiansen and Joseph Maria Olbrich, followed by collaboration, in later years, with Paul Haustein, Albin Müller, and Ernst Riegel.

The following year, with the support of the factory's ownership, Christian Neureuther organized his own ceramic art studio in Schlierbach, which, in 1903, became affiliated with the Wächtersbach factory as its art department "with special status," under the name Chr. Neureuther's Wächtersbach Ceramic Studio. Neureuther designed plates, vessels, and tiles (the latter, sometimes for mounting), with interesting abstract-linear designs, at first influenced by Olbrich and, later, in his own mature manner. After his death in 1921, the studio continued under the direction of Eduard Schweitzer prior to the closing of the art department in 1928.

Marks identifying items with Neureuther designs and originating in Schlierbach include the printed Wächtersbach shield mark with "K.A.W." above and "C.N." below; also, sometimes, the initials "CN.," painted in an oval; "CHR.N.," incised; or his surname "Neureuther," painted.

Wächtersbach trivet or confectionery tray, designed by Christian Neureuther: 5.75" (14.5cm) diameter, in a footed, silver-colored metal surround.

55. WESSEL

The Ludwig Wessel Porcelain and Earthenware Factory in Poppelsdorf, near Bonn (North Rhine-Westphalia), was named for the founder of the forerunner Wessel company. Ludwig Wessel was the father of Franz Joseph (who, from 1838, headed the company) and grandfather of Nicholas and Louis (born Joseph Karl Ludwig). From 1868, the firm was jointly directed by Nicholas and Louis and, from 1888, by Louis, alone, producing functional and decorative wares, including toilet articles, kitchen items, and dinnerware and other household china.

In the late 1870s, trials were conducted in the production of color-glazed wall tiles, which were, shortly afterward, added to the manufacturing program.

In 1888, the company's name was changed to the Ludwig Wessel Porcelain and Earthenware Manufacturing Company, from which time, glazed wall tiles were made in a specially equipped production department. These were, later, to be marketed under the brand names and/or with company markings "WESSEL," "LUDWIG WESSEL Akt. Ges, POPPELSDORF-BONN," "WESSEL BONN," "WESSEL'S WANDPLATTEN-FABRIK BONN," and, in a double circle, "WWF BONN" with a crown.

In 1890/1891, a wall-tile plant was added at the premises in Bonn-Poppelsdorf and, in 1896, a separate Wessel Wall Tile Factory was opened in Bonn-Dransdorf for the production of glazed wall and furniture tiles. This was under the direction of Louis (later, Consul Louis) Wessel. With the installation of improved equipment over the next fifteen years, the company, in 1925, became a limited liability stock corporation under Louis' son Wilhelm Wessel and, from c. 1930, was known as Wessel Works AG.

With an average of about two hundred-sixteen workers in the period 1899–1904, the company increased its workforce to an average of three hundred-two employees in 1905–1907, before a reduction to two hundred-forty-two in 1908–1909, and prior to reaching a high of three hundred-eleven in 1910–1912.

Between 1902 and 1910, the company gained considerable prestige at home and abroad, with the receipt of awards at international expositions in Buenos Aires, Dusseldorf, and St. Louis.

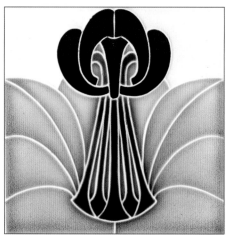
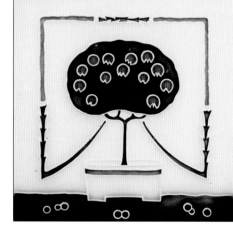

Wessel tiles.

From 1925, the conversion from coal to gas for kiln-firing facilitated easier maintenance, as well as an economy of energy costs, during the difficult time in international business, beginning in the late 1920s.

In 1938, the Wessel Works absorbed the Chemical Works for Chamotte and Floor Tile Manufacture of the Otto Kauffmann Company,[146] which had been founded originally, in 1871, by Kauffmann in Dresden-Niedersedlitz for the production of cement floor tiles. And in 1940, it also acquired a majority holding in the Servais Witterschlick Works[147] in Witterschlick, near Bonn, which is now known as Cremer & Breuer German Stoneware in Alfter-Witterschlick.

During the Second World War, in 1944, Wessel Works was destroyed by fire but, after the war, a new factory was built and operated until 1970.

56. WITTEBURG

In 1852/1853, a factory was organized – later known as the Witteburg Earthenware Factory – in Farge (now Bremen-Farge), by three owners, of whom two were Englishmen with experience in the pottery business. With deliveries of coal and ceramic raw materials (including chamotte), directly by sea, from England to Farge on the River Weser, production started and continued with the manufacture of household crockery and utilitarian earthenware, prior to the introduction, in 1885, of color-glazed tiles (later, under the brand name "Steingutfabrik Witteburg Farge a/d Weser," and sometimes so marked or marked "Witteburg Farge").

Due to the lack of a rail connection from Farge, progress in sales was, at first, slow, until an extension of the Bremen-Vegesack line was completed. But, by the late 1890s, a vigorous business was developed in the domestic market and exports were made to Austria, Italy, Norway, Sweden, Netherlands, Belgium, Russia, India, Argentina, Brazil, and Mexico.

However, between 1898 and 1912, the company experienced constant fluctuations in its income – with profits highest in 1898 and lowest in 1908/1909 – due to strong competition from the North German Earthenware Factory.[148] From c. 1904/1905, particularly, there was a rapid decline in demand for all Witteburg products, including tiles, despite an inventory, by that time, of over two hundred-fifty tile designs (including some adaptations of models produced by Villeroy & Boch in Mettlach).

After closing during the First World War, Witteburg Earthenware was taken over by North German Earthenware, which modernized the facility in 1919 and operated the company as a subsidiary (later, known as NSTG Plant IV), at first continuing its production of functional ware and wall tiles and, in 1926, re-equipping it to concentrate on floor-tile manufacture.

Around 1931/1932, the factory was temporarily closed and, by 1943 – along with the North German Earthenware Factory (Plant I) and NSTG's other subsidiaries (Plants II and III) – ceased production as a result of the Second World War.

In 1949, floor-tile production resumed at Farge and continued until 1953, when the factory closed down permanently.

55. OTHER GERMAN FIRMS

Other German firms operating by the end of the nineteenth century or after the beginning of the twentieth century (and prior to the Second World War) and producing/decorating tilework (for walls, floors, or stoves, etc.) included:

i). in Brandenburg: "Adler" Stove and Claywares Factory and Schmidt Lehmann Stove Factory in Velten;

ii). in Rhineland-Palatinate: Grünstadt Earthenware Factory in Grünstadt;

iii). in Saxony: Ernst Hermann Hörisch Stove Factory and Christian Seidel and Son Faience, Majolica, and Stove

Witteburg tiles.

Factory in Dresden; Hermann Berger Leipzig Chamotte Stove Factory in Fuchshain, now Naunhof-Fuchshain; J. Bidtel Ceramic-Chemical Factory, Theodor Alexander Markowsky Chamotte & Stove Factory, and Meissen Chamotte and Stove Factory, formerly Theodor Alexander Markowsky in Meissen; Sörnewitz-Meissen Earthenware Factory in Neusörnewitz, now, Sörnewitz (Coswig); and Torgau Earthenware Factory in north-western Saxony;

iv). in Silesia: Deutsch-Lissa Floor Tile Factory in the Breslau area; and

v). in Strassburg: Cesar Winter-kalter's Ceramic and Cement Floor-Tile Factory:

In addition there were a number of other small earthenware/stoneware factories across the country that were involved in tilework of one kind or another.

AUSTRIA

1. BOSSE[149]

2. JOSEF DE CENTE
One of the largest tile makers by the 1870s in Austria – with an Imperial warrant – the Josef de Cente Stove and Tile Factory in Vienna-New Town exhibited ceramic floor and stove tiles at the Vienna International (Universal) Exhibition, in 1873, and was awarded a medal for progress, there.

In 1878, the company also exhibited at the Paris International Exhibition.

By 1905/1906, it was continuing to manufacture stoves of all kinds, along with fire-resistant products, stoneware crockery, and other claywares.

3. FESSLER
Holder of an Imperial warrant from 1874, the long-established E. Fessler Stoves and Claywares Factory, in Vienna, enjoyed sales of tiled stoves and other ceramics to the palaces, castles, and mansions owned by members of the Austrian court. Particularly impressive business was achieved at the time of the Ringstrasse construction in the city. Eduard Fessler died in 1910 but the company continued, for many years afterward, under the ownership of family members.

From 1921 until some time between 1955 and 1960, Herta Bucher maintained a studio at the premises and provided stove and fireplace designs for execution by the company.

4. GOLDSCHEIDER WIEN
In 1885, the famous company of Friedrich Goldscheider opened a factory in Vienna, along with others in Pilsen and Karlsbad, for the production of earthenware and porcelain, as well as, later, design and decoration studios in Leipzig and Florence (Italy) and trade outlets in Berlin and Paris. Apart from the artist-designed figures and busts, for which the company is celebrated, the Friedrich Goldscheider Vienna Manufactory also manufactured other decorative ceramics, including tableware, vases, jardinieres, lamp bases, and clock cases.

Artistic tiles and plaques, reliefs, and wall masks were also made, marked with the usual oval "Goldscheider Wien" mark (impressed or printed) and painted mono-grams or initials of designers/decorators.

5. PERLMOOS
In 1873, the Perlmoos Hydraulic Lime and Cement Company[150] exhibited a floor covering of cement floor tiles in a colorful, decorative, mosaic design at the Vienna

Goldscheider tile/plaque, 3.88" (9.86cm) square.   *Goldscheider tile/plaque: 3.88" (9.86cm) square.*

Goldscheider tile/plaque, 12" x 10.25" (30.48 x 26.04cm).

International (Universal) Exhibition. As the leading Portland cement company in Austria, it conducted a long and successful manufacture of this sideline well into the twentieth century.

6. PRÄGARTEN

Tiles for furniture inlay were included in the production program of the First Upper-Austria Earthenware Factory, in Prägarten, which, in 1918, was taken over by the Di Giorgio Earthenware Factory.

7. SCHLEISS/GMUNDN

In addition to independent, creative, ceramic wares, as well as commissioned tile work for Josef Hoffmann, the F. and E. Schleiss Ceramic Workshop, in Gmundn (Upper Austria), also produced tiles and architectural ceramics for other designers and architects.

In 1913, Franz and Emilie Schleiss – at that time, operating under the name Gmundn Ceramics – merged their studio with Michael Powolny's Vienna Ceramics to form the United Vienna and Gmundn Ceramics and Claywares Factory. From 1916, the business was also known as Gmundn Ceramics and, from around 1923, as Gmundn Ceramic Workshops. At the German Applied Arts Show in Munich – reported on in *Deutsche Kunst und Dekoration*[151] – Gmundn Ceramics received acclaim for their stove exhibit.

The Schleiss company enjoyed a long collaboration with Herta Bucher.

8. SOMMERHUBER

By the end of the third quarter of the nineteenth century, the Rudolf Sommerhuber Ceramic Stoves Factory began manufacturing decorative tiled stoves, fireplace surrounds, and radiator covers, as well as other tile products, in Steyr, in Upper Austria. Later, in the twentieth century, art pottery production was added, with designs by Herta Bucher, Robert Obsieger, Michael Powolny, Franz Schleiss, et al. Having exhibited at the Paris International Exposition in 1900, the company grew to employ eighty workers by 1910, maintaining production at twelve kilns and two muffle-kilns. It was a member of the German Work Federation by 1912 and joined the Austrian Work Federation in 1913. Students at the School of Arts and Crafts in Vienna – including Powolny and Obsieger – gained practical experience during apprenticeships at the Steyr factory.

Today, Sommerhuber Ceramic Manufactory, Steyr, is still celebrated for its manufacture of modern-styled tiled stoves, fireplaces, design radiators, spa ceramics, and other contemporary, heat-storing, ceramic products.

9. UNITED VIENNA AND GMUNDN CERAMICS AND CLAYWARES FACTORY

In 1913, Franz and Emilie Schleiss merged their studio in Gmundn with Michael Powolny's Vienna Ceramics, forming the United Vienna and Gmundn Ceramics and Claywares Factory.

10. VIENNA CERAMICS

The Vienna Ceramics studio was founded in 1905 by Michael Powolny in partnership (through 1913) with Berthold Löffler and produced tiles, particularly in the first decade of the twentieth century, for some of the Vienna Workshops' major commissions. In 1913, Powolny merged Vienna Ceramics with Franz and Emilie Schleiss's Gmundn Ceramics to form the United Vienna and Gmundn Ceramics and Claywares Factory (from 1916, also known as Gmundn Ceramics and, from 1923, Gmundn Ceramic Workshops).

11. WIENERBERG

After its founding in Vienna earlier in the nineteenth century, by 1869, the Wienerberg Brick Factory and Building Company[152] manufactured industrial wares and tiles for hearths, mantels, fireplaces, etc. By 1872, there were nine different plants, located in the southern half of Vienna. One of these was the clayworks in the Inzersdorf area of the city, manufacturing terra cotta, majolica, ornamental and building brick, and roofing tile. That year, a tenth factory was established, also in Vienna, for the production of "stove tiles, glazed and decorated wall tiles, hard-burnt encaustic and mosaic floor tiles, terra cotta, majolica and (Della) Robbia ware."[153] Later, other branches were opened in other areas of Austria – to specialize in the manufacture of ceramic floor tiles and other architectural ceramics – and in Hungary and Croatia.

In 1873, the company received an award for its exhibit at the Vienna International (Universal) Exhibition of 1873. In 1878, in Paris, it was similarly honored.

From 1908, the company also produced decorative ceramic wares.

Single tiles, friezes, also tile pictures of two, four, or more tiles (seldom, if ever, bearing registered marks of the Wienerberg company) displayed decoration featuring organic motifs, floral bouquets, fruits, animals, and fish, as well as still-life depictions and landscapes, in a variety of different techniques, including, particularly, printing. With a thickness of about 0.4" (1 cm), multi-tile pictures of fairly large size were also designed, thickly painted in vibrant colors, and, often, surrounded by a striped Vienna Workshops-type framework consisting of squares and/or ovals as decoration. Some single tiles enclosed self-framed, vertical, oval-shaped designs with flower or fruit motifs and others featured self-framed, circular designs containing landscape scenes; in both instances, the colorful decoration was accomplished with inlaid glazes in cuenca technique, with the designs, themselves, surrounded by vacant, white space within the tile's square format.

The Wienerberg company supplied tile blanks to the Imperial Teplitz-Schönau Technical School for Ceramics and Associated Applied Arts, in Bohemia, for decoration by its students. And, later, the company's own training institution, the Wienerberg Ceramics Workshops School – constructed, between 1919 and 1921 in Vienna and directed by sculptor and ceramist Robert Obsieger – offered instruction in the technical and artistic aspects of ceramics and glaze chemistry, along with classes in stove-fitting.

Wienerberg's catalog of 1926 included ceramic designs by decorative artist and ceramist Michael Powolny, architect and designer Otto Prutscher, sculptor Gustav Gurschner, ceramist and designer Herta Bucher, and other artists, as well as students at the School of Arts and Crafts in Vienna.

In 1927, there were twenty-seven hundred employees in all Wienerberg factories.

HUNGARY

1. SCHOOL/COLLEGE OF THE HUNGARIAN MUSEUM OF APPLIED ARTS (Iparmuveszeti Muzeum)[154]

2. ZSOLNAY

In 1868, the company – named for the Zsolnay family – was registered in

Wienerberg tiles.

Wienerberg tiles.

Fünfkirchen/Pecs to embark on the production of all kinds of ceramics, including household china, luxury items, stoves, sanitary ware, and insulators.

By the early 1870s, glaze testing was undertaken and, by the mid-to-late 1870s, analysis of clay bodies and study of high-fire glaze technology. Along with this experimentation came the introduction of new materials and machinery for the manufacture of architectural ceramics (from fireproof clay), including tiles for exteriors and interiors. In 1873, the factory's exhibit of fine, white earthenware with enamel glazes received great acclaim in Vienna, at the Universal Exposition, as did also its ornamental terra cotta that was, by the early to mid-1880s, successfully marketed throughout the Austro-Hungarian Empire.

As early as 1878, when the company received gold medals at the Paris International Exposition for its vessels in "porcelain-faience" and "high-fire enamel technique," wall plates and plaques became popular, some designed and painted with figural decoration by Vilmos Zsolnay's daughters Terez and Julia. In different formats and dimensions, hand-shaped or jiggered, these were painted in colored enamels and also high-fired.

By the 1880s, wall-tile production was introduced at Pecs and, in 1885, a separate stove department was established.

Tiles with floral patterns, printed, painted, or in molded relief, in Historicist or aesthetically naturalistic styles (through the turn of the century) were also created by Armin Klein and Sandor Apati Abt.

In 1885, work began to develop a fireproof, acid-resistant, and frost-resistant stoneware body for building purposes, and soon Zsolnay's trials in this high-fire technology were completed. The material, named "Pyrogranite," resulted from the addition of fine-grained quartz and pulverized chamotte to refractory clay. Unglazed or covered with various glazes (including majolica and, later, eosin glazes), it could be fired at a high temperature with a first firing at between 1200° and 1300° C (2200° and 2350° F) for installation – along with the already well-received earthenware-tile products – as decorative, indoor wall tiles (both pressed and cast) and in fireplace and stove manufacture, in addition to its major architectural use in exterior façades, including ornamental sculpture and tiling.

By the end of the 1880s, pyrogranite had found favor with local architects and builders and was used in numerous new buildings in Budapest, as well as, in 1888, the reconstruction of the Matthias Church in the city, incorporating colored roof tiles and ceramic floor covering by the Zsolnay company. For the eclectic, Historicist architecture of late nineteenth century Budapest, the factory supplied façades with ceramic cladding of colorfully patterned tile accompanied by richly sculpted, ceramic elements for embellishment. Architects and builders accepted the cooperation of Zsolnay professionals in their construction projects in Neo-Gothic, Neo-Renaissance, Medieval, Oriental, and Middle-Eastern styles in Budapest and also in Vienna (where Zsolnay competed with the Wienerberg Brick Factory and Building Company). New synagogue buildings in Moorish or Romanesque styles also benefited from a choice of the new, enduring material, which allowed endless possibilities of form and color and lent a weather-proof and strikingly impressive, artistic appearance.

From 1888 – one year after Miklos Zsolnay, Vilmos's son, visited Turkey, Persia, and Egypt to study sixteenth and seventeenth-century tiles made there – Near-Eastern motifs were introduced in ceramic decoration at Pecs. Also, around this time, an increased interest in reduction firing was beginning to lead to further extensive experimentation at the factory to produce a glaze material that was to be known as "Eosin." The first such glaze, with metallic luster, was a red eosin that was developed by the early 1890s, with industrial production beginning within a few years of that date. Other glaze colors were soon to be added to the eosin palette.

By around 1895, when there was a widespread boom in the building industry in Central Europe, the Zsolnay company (known at that time in the Austro-Hungarian Empire as the Zsolnay Budapest Porcelain and Faience Factory AG) began mass-producing tiles of various kinds, together with sanitary fixtures, for new apartment residences, particularly in Budapest. Also, by the turn of the century, pyrogranite was dominating the domestic market in the Austro-Hungarian Empire, as a result of its vast, diverse potential for architectural use.

In a transition from Historicist, architectural styles and traditional building decoration in the mid-to-late 1890s, Se-

cessionist influences were already apparent when the Zsolnay company supplied pyrogranite tile panels for a Viennese apartment building – designed by Otto Wagner – that was opened in 1898. Soon, the growing appeal of the new Hungarian style was acknowledged as an important aspect of Zsolnay ceramic design after being introduced and adapted for the company's production of luxury art pottery and architectural ceramics.

By 1896, the appeal already had been reflected in the Zsolnay output for the Millennium celebration, for which the architectural planning, though still stylistically bound to Eclecticism, introduced forms, techniques, and a new decorative approach that foreshadowed the arrival of Szecesszio. Built between 1893 and 1896, some of the entryways at stations of the underground electric railway, opened that year to mark the occasion, were entirely of Zsolnay's color-glazed, ceramic elements applied to the ornate, Neo-Renaissance, architectural style of the new system, as well as pyrogranite roof tiles and decorative, pyrogranite wall decorations mounted in iron framing.

At the Paris Universal exposition of 1900, Zsolnay's exhibit was applauded and rewarded. Also, Zsolnay's vessels, figures, and other small decorative and functional items – some produced, by then, in collaborative work with the artist Joszef Rippl-Ronai – met with great success in the domestic and foreign markets. This was due, principally, to the combination of artistic, sculptural (including figural) forms and the rich, reduction glazes that proved to be an inexhaustible source of strikingly bright eosin colors (greens, reds, and purple/blues) and created an iridescent, metallic effect that heightened the impression of exoticism and fantasy.

Decorative tiles – cast or hand-pressed in earthenware or pyrogranite – were already produced with floral and abstract designs in lustrous eosin colors or in majolica and other glazes in an infinite variety. In addition to in-house, Art Nouveau designs, some commissioned from or by individual, local architects and applied artists – such as Pal Horti, for example – were selected to embellish wall installations, staircases, fountains, stoves, and fireplaces in designs, patterns, and colors eminently suited to each client's personal taste.

Zsolnay plaque: 27.75" x 19.75" (70.49 x 50.17cm).

Also, around the turn of the century, ornamental, eosin-glazed wall panels composed of tiles in a variety of sizes and mosaic pictures of irregularly shaped, polychrome, ceramic tiles, occasionally mounted with glass pieces in plaster, were featured in the interior decoration of commercial and public buildings and private town houses and villas.

After 1900, Zsolnay's tile decoration – with floral and other motifs and even with Symbolical or Expressionistic overtones by such artists as Henrik Darilek, Sandor Pillo Hadasy, Lajos Mack, Geza Nikelszky, and other artists under the leadership of Tade Sikorski (as artistic director, from 1883, and director of architectural ceramics) – tended to be more conventionalized and abstracted than before. Later, however, architects and designers began to favor decoration that owed something to the restraint and more geometric abstraction of the Arts & Crafts style. Otherwise, up to the time of

the First World War, some Zsolnay tiles relied, solely, on the pleasing effect of brilliant eosin glazes, combined in various colors (without further decoration), or other "artistic" glazes.

Also included, very occasionally, in Zsolnay's production program, were tiles for use as small frames of one kind or another or in square and rectangular formats for assembling as larger frames for wall mirrors or pictures. And, from about 1900, wall tiles of pyrogranite or another ceramic body were designed and produced – mostly in square formats of 3" (7.5 cm), 4" (10 cm), 6" (15 cm), 6.5" (16.3 cm), or, perhaps, even larger – that could be used, as well, for installation in furniture. These were usually hand-pressed, high-fired, glazed in a number of colors – sometimes with a crystalline effect – and, often, covered with a transparent eosin glaze. Others bore marbled, engraved, or acid-etched patterns or other textured surfaces that, after an initial firing, were

refired to invest one or more eosin glazes over the original base glaze.

In 1905/1906, about nine hundred workers were employed by the Zsolnay company that was then recognized internationally for its high quality of craftsmanship.

Through the mid-1910s – with a workforce of over one thousand – production continued at Pecs and the Budapest branch works, opened in 1895, including tiles for stoves and fireplaces and for wall and floor installation, along with architectural ceramics and industrial porcelain. But, with the advent of the First World War, it was limited to industrial porcelain, alone, for the war effort. After the war, most of the normal program of manufacture was resumed but, in the early 1920s, when building activities ceased in Austria and Hungary and insulator production slumped, Zsolnay was able to take advantage of the situation only with reconstruction, reorganization, and the replacement of antiquated equipment. By the late 1920s, the reintroduction of art pottery and architectural ceramics, on a smaller scale, was added to the remaining porcelain and household crockery production.

Later, the company suffered the effect of the worldwide economic crisis, then the Second World War, and, afterward, expropriation and Soviet nationalization.

Today, the evidence of Zsolnay tiles and other decorative building ceramics in architectural use is to be seen everywhere in Austria and Hungary – but rarely elsewhere, with the exception of public buildings, spas, and public baths in Prague and Trieste.

Throughout the Zsolnay company's history, an eclectic trend in tile production benefited from many factors of industry and influence, including the advances in technology and a progressive interest in special glaze effects, along with an admiration for pluralist, revivalist styles in printed or relief decoration and local/national affection for the repetition of popular old ornament (particularly, traditional, Hungarian, naturalistic and abstract patterns and folk-art floral motifs). But much of Zsolnay's claim to fame has been due – both during the period of Szecesszio and, again, from the mid-1960s (during the revival of interest in Art Nouveau) through the present time – to its adoption, treatment, and continued marketing of elegant Secessionist ornament and sculptural form in striking color.

BOHEMIA, MORAVIA (CZECHOSLOVAKIA)

1. DITMAR
Before 1910, the firm Rudolf Ditmar Heirs – founded, originally in 1878, by Karl Rudolf Ditmar as his Art Pottery and Claywares Factory in Znaim, Moravia – passed into the ownership of Richard and Oskar Lichtenstern. With about six hundred workers, around that time, and offices in Vienna, Prague, Lemberg, Milan, Lyons, and Bombay, it continued under the name of the founder's successors through its affiliation with the Triptis AG porcelain factory in Thueringia. In 1919, it merged with Urbach Brothers in Turn as Ditmar-Urbach AG.

At the Znaim works, wall tiles, sanitary wares, and household china were produced.

2. EICHWALD
In 1886, the Meissen Stove and Porcelain Factory, formerly C. Teichert, based in Meissen, Germany, took over the Anton Tschinkel Majolica Factory in Eichwald, near Teplitz, to run as a branch factory producing porcelain wares and tiles for a number of years.

After the later purchase of this factory in the mid-to-late 1890s by Bernard Bloch, it was amalgamated with Bloch's other pottery/terra cotta/ironstone companies in Eichwald and Hohenstein, to form the Bernard Bloch Porcelain, Stove, and Terra Cotta Factories, engaged in the manufacture of tiles, tiled stoves, and terra cotta, as well as household china. Later, these businesses were separated as B. Bloch (Proprietor: Stella Bloch) in Eichwald and Hohenstein, and the Bloch & Co. Eichwald Porcelain and Stove Factories in Eichwald.

Enjoying worldwide exports of dinnerware and decorative ceramics, as well as sales of stoves, in Germany, Switzerland, Italy, Turkey, and Rumania, the factory in Hohenstein and the two factories in Eichwald sent a joint B. Bloch Company exhibit to the German/Bohemian Exposition

in 1906 in Reichenberg. There, it received the Chamber Prize for a varied selection of ceramics, including majolica figures, other luxury wares, household crockery, architectural terra cotta, colorfully glazed stoves, and wall tiles, as well as tile pictures and plaques with figural decoration.

The following year, there were about four hundred employees in all three factories.

After Bernard Bloch's death, the Bloch company was owned by Oskar, Arthur, and Otto Bloch and, by 1922, Arthur Bloch, alone.

By 1914, for three years, orders were received from the Vienna Workshops to execute ceramic designs by Josef Hoffmann and Dagobert Peche, which were later, from 1917, commissioned from Gmundn Ceramics / Gmundn Ceramic Workshops in Upper Austria.

In 1938 and through the end of the Second World War, the Bloch factories were known as the Dr. Widera & Co. Eichwald Porcelain, Stove and Wall Tile Factories.

3. HARDTMUTH[155]
In 1873, the L. &. C. Hardtmuth company in southern Bohemia – makers of "bricks

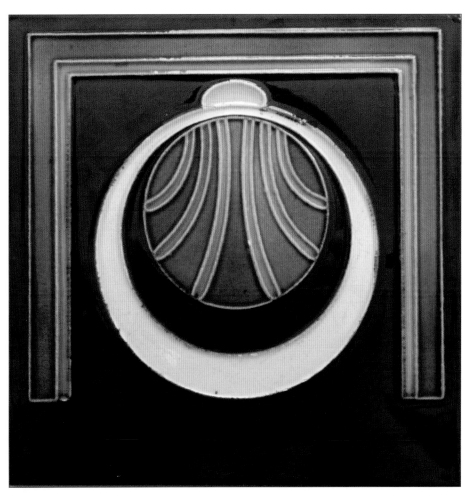

Hardtmuth tile.

and stoneware" – was awarded a Medal for Merit at the Exposition in Vienna, where their "stove ware-rooms...presented a beautiful exhibit of porcelain stoves which were manufactured in Budweis, Bohemia."[156] By the 1890s and afterward, plain white and decorated wall tiles – infrequently marked "L. & C Hardtmuth" – along with tiled stoves were produced at the L. &. C. Hardtmuth Stove Factory, with the occasional collaboration, around 1900, of Rudolf Hammel. At the Exhibition of Austrian Arts and Crafts in 1899 at the Imperial/Royal Museum for Art and Industry in Vienna, "the pièce de resistance [was] the excellent chimney front by the well-known Vienna firm L. & C. Hardtmuth and the artist Herr Georg Klimt," and with tiles designed by Hammel.[157]

4. KNOLL
Already, in the 1890s, Carl Knoll's Porcelain Factory – founded in 1846 in Fischern, near Karlsbad, and holding an Imperial warrant – was producing porcelain tiles there.

5. OBERBRIS
In 1882, in Oberbris (or Ober Bris), the Western Bohemia Kaolin and Chamotte Works, formerly J. Fitz, was established for the manufacture of clay, kaolin, and chamotte products. Other related factories were in Kaznau, Zliv, and Koenigsaal.[158]

A small tile production was active through the first decade of the twentieth century, and possibly later, when the company's workforce in Austria-Hungary increased to about fourteen hundred employees manufacturing porcelain, stoneware, faience and majolica, etc., as well as gas stoves. It possibly continued through – or, perhaps, it was resumed by – the time of the German occupation of Czechoslovakia, when Oberbris tiles were, sometimes, if not always, marked "Made in Bohemia – Moravia."

6. RAKO
In 1882, in the Rakonitz region of Bohemia, about thirty miles west of Prague, the Rakonitz Floor Tile and Stove Factory was founded in a previously flooded coal mine that was adapted for the manufacture of ceramics using local clay. The following year, it was equipped with clay processing machines, hydraulic presses, and kilns to include the production of floor tiles.

In 1898, Emil Sommerschuh – son of Wenzel Johann Sommerschuh, a well-known Prague ceramist, who, earlier in the century, had founded his own company there for the manufacture of pottery wares, stoves, and stove tiles – purchased the business, with a partner, and began a diversified production of floor tiles, wall tiles, stove tiles, picture mosaics, tiled stoves, and other ceramic products. By 1900, architectural ceramics were manufactured for the domestic and export markets until, by 1910, tiles made by the Rakonitz Tile and Stove Factory (under the brand name and also, sometimes, marked "RAKO") were being transported to many European countries and, also, shipped elsewhere in the world.

In the last three years of the nineteenth century, the first elements of the Secessionist style were to be found in Rako-tile decoration with curvilinear accents. With the cooperation of painters, sculptors, and architects, new designs were introduced for tiles, tiled stoves, ceramic mosaic pictures, building façades, and other architectural ceramics, along with garden and cemetery ware. For walls in hotels,

Oberbris tiles.

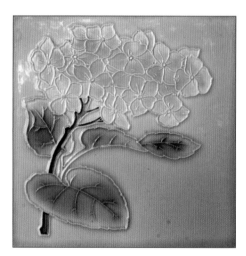

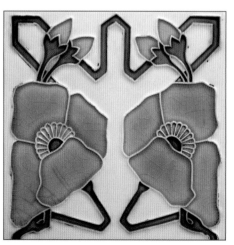

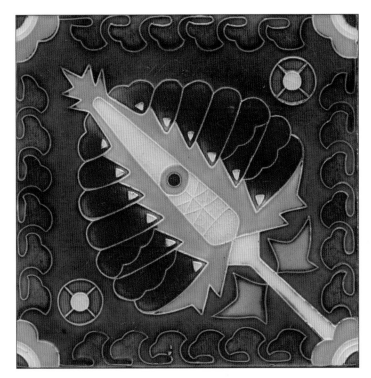

Rako tiles.

theaters, the Main Railway Station (in Prague), etc., Sommerschuh developed and patented a method of manufacturing and installing mosaic pictures (made up of irregularly cut tiles and tesserae) representing intricate, large pictorial/narrative presentations from history and myth, etc.

In 1907, for a number of years, the company was bought by Prince Johann II of Liechtenstein – who already owned stove, stove-tile, ceramics, and brick plants, employing over 700 workers, by 1905/1906, in the Unter-Themenau area of Lower Austria[159] – with Sommerschuh continuing as director general, overseeing installations at the Municipal House in Prague and various museums and hotels.

In 1920, a controlling interest was sold to Zivnobanko, a joint stock company, and the business became known as the Rakonitz and Unter-Themenau Ceramics Works of Rakovnik and Postorna in Czechoslovakia. Modernization followed, with innovations in mechanization and technique. This allowed for a greater production of glazed floor and wall tiles (including handpainted wall tiles) and tiles for furniture inlay, together with architectural ceramics (including wall fountains, etc.). Also, porcelain wares were introduced, with designs by modern artists, and manufactured through the beginning of the Second World War.

By then, with Czech, Austrian, and German workers, the work force totalled about fourteen hundred employees.

During the war, Rako tile production – with tiles manufactured during the German occupation of Czechoslovakia sometimes marked "Made in Bohemia" – was restricted. After the war, the company was expropriated and consolidated with other Czech national plants, at first concentrating on the manufacture of floor tiles as replacements in restoration work at buildings in a number of European cities. Later, a flourishing export market was reestablished.

In 1991, the firm was privatized and, afterward, passed through various ownerships.

It is still, today, producing ceramic facing material.

7. SCHATTAU

The First Schattau Claywares Factory in Schattau was one of the largest Moravian potteries, employing around seven hundred workers by 1905/1906.

Shortly after 1900, it donated an instructive collection of floor and wall tiles, clinker bricks, and stoneware items to the Imperial Technical School for Ceramics and Associated Applied Arts at Teplitz-Schönau.

8. W. S. & S. / SCHILLER

Around 1900, the Wilhelm Schiller & Son Faience, Majolica, and Terra Cotta Factory in Obergrund, near Bodenbach, introduced work with Art Nouveau decoration. Included in the company's manufacturing program of luxury items were wall plaques and candle sconces – produced (or partially produced) by the pressing process (and, sometimes, adapted, for use, with the addition of molded, ceramic elements) – as well as tiles, decorated for installation or, possibly, plain (for decoration outside of the factory). Sometime between 1910 and 1914, the factory closed.

Usually, Schiller production was marked "W. S. & S."

9. SCHÜTZ

After the award of a gold medal at Munich in 1876, the Schütz Brothers Majolica and Earthenware Factory – opened in 1854 – continued to prosper, throughout the 1880s and into the 1890s, in the production of luxury goods for the domestic and export[160] markets, together with artistic wall decorations and tiled stoves. With design assistance and commercial representation in Vienna, the two brothers Arnold and Ludwig Schütz decided, in 1889, to divide the business activity, with Arnold retaining control of the main factory in Olomuczan, near Blanz, in the Brünn area of southern Moravia, and Ludwig taking over responsibility for the subsidiary Majolica, Earthenware, and Chamotte Factory that had been opened in 1870 in Liboje, near Cilli, in the area of Lower Styria.

Around the turn of the century, Arnold was succeeded as proprietor, in Olomuc-zan, by his son-in-law Wilhelm Julinek, assisted by his brother Frank Julinek, but soon the factory passed into the owner-ship of Oskar Basch.

By the middle of the twentieth century, if not earlier, the Olomuczan factory closed, but the facility near Cilli continues today to manufacture ceramics of various kinds.

Schütz Brothers was renowned, particularly, for the quality of the company's plaques and wall plates and reliefs, which, through the 1890s, bore either the impressed mark "GEB. SCHÜTZ" in an oval (sometimes with other details or "MADE IN AUSTRIA") or the stamped figure of a kneeling archer surrounded by an upper-case "G." Later stamped marks were "SCHÜTZ BLANSKO" and "SCHÜTZ CILLI."

10. SOMMERSCHUH

By the 1870s, the W. Sommerschuh Stove and Pottery Factory of Prague produced tiled stoves, tiles, and other ceramic products. The firm exhibited earthenware tiles at the Vienna International (Univer-sal) Exhibition in 1873 and a wider range of tiles and pottery items at the Centen-nial Exposition, in Philadelphia, three years later.

By 1900, Wenzel Johann Sommer-schuh's son Emil, who had been trained by his father in Prague, was listed as the owner of his father's factory, manufactur-ing ceramic wares and supplying the Austrian court as a holder of the Impe-rial warrant. Emil was shortly to be one of the guiding forces behind the early success of Rako, even prior to his purchase of the factory at Rakonitz.

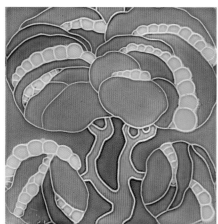
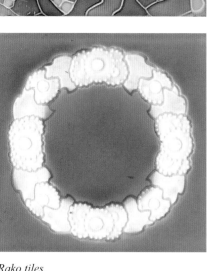
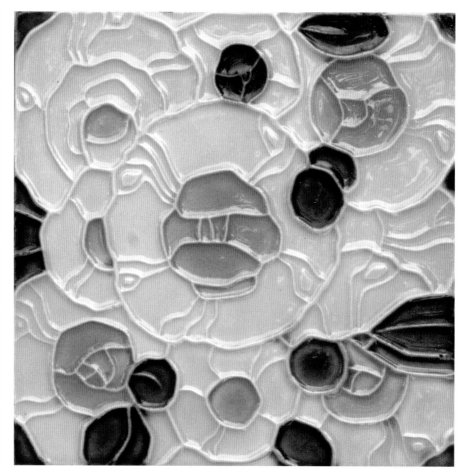

Rako tiles.

DESIGNERS

SANDOR APATI-ABT (1870–1916) studied at the Royal Hungarian School of Applied Art in Budapest in the period 1885–1888 and, later, also in Munich. A Symbolist painter, sculptor, and ceramist, he worked for the Zsolnay company, from 1898 for ten years, under the leadership of Tade Sikorski. His production there included the design of luxury ceramics, tiles, and mosaics. From 1903, he also taught at the Zsolnay factory school (established in 1886), where professional instruction for workers and apprentices included ceramic decoration. In 1909, he was appointed instructor at the Museum School of Applied Arts in Budapest.

JOHANN LUDWIG (JEAN) BECK (1862–1938), a designer of ceramics and glass, received training in ceramics, as a youth, at Villeroy & Boch in Mettlach. Afterward, he studied for several years from around 1880/1881 at the Arts and Crafts and Technical High Schools in Munich and, later, in France and England. In the later 1880s and into the 1890s, he headed the design studio at Villeroy & Boch in Mettlach, after which, from 1898 for many years, he operated his own studio in Munich, where he specialized, principally, in designs – for ceramic and glass objects in serial production – for a number of companies. His freelance work for Villeroy & Boch continued through the end of the 1920s.

It is argued that some Villeroy & Boch Schramberg tiles are derived from designs by Beck since they bear the initials "JB" near the bottom of the image.[161]

EDUARD BECKING (1861–1934), an artist, architect/draftsman, and designer, received on-the-job training at Villeroy & Boch in Mettlach, before joining the Servais-Ehrang Ceramic Wares Factory Lamberty, Servais & Cie. (later, United Servais Works Ehrang-Witterschlick), for many years from 1888, directing the drawing office there and completing designs for the production of floor and wall tiles, etc. Around 1897, he supervised the building and equipping of a Servais branch factory near Radom, in the Ruthenian area of eastern Poland. From c. 1912/1913, he commissioned designs from the Arts and Crafts School in Trier for execution at Servais-Ehrang.

PETER BEHRENS (1868–1940) was a painter, graphic artist, craftsman, and architect. After studying painting in the late 1880s in Hamburg, Karlsruhe, Dusseldorf, and also, later, in Italy, he designed industrial buildings, public offices, and private villas, as well as furniture, household goods, script/ typography, and advertising material. Continuing to evolve his own formal geometric vocabulary in the twentieth century, he was responsible – directly and indirectly – for many acclaimed designs in different media, including ceramic designs executed by German porcelain, stoneware, and tile companies.[162]

From 1890, he was active in Munich, co-founding there the Munich Secession in 1892 and the United Workshops for Art in Handicraft in 1898. In the late 1890s (through the first years of the twentieth century), most of his innovative, applied-art designs were for works in two dimensions, particularly carpets, wallpapers, textiles, and book illustration, though the earliest of his celebrated silver and porcelain achievements also date from this time.

Summoned to Darmstadt in the summer of 1899 – as a member (through the spring of 1903) of the Grand Duke's Artists' Colony – he built his own house on the Mathildenhöhe there, with complete interior decorations.

In the early 1900s, as well as participating at international exhibitions in Paris and Turin and holding master classes at the Bavarian Arts and Crafts Museum in Nuremberg, he acted as design consultant for stoneware factories in Westerwald, as well as the earthenware factory of the Franz Anton Mehlem Company in Bonn.

Appointed director of the Arts and Crafts School in Dusseldorf in 1903 (through 1907), Behrens began to design for the Dresden Workshops for Handicraft Art.

For his Jungbrunnen Restaurant installation in 1904 at the Dusseldorf Art and Garden Show, he designed floor tiles, 6.75" (17 cm) square, bearing a spiral design[163] that were manufactured by Villeroy & Boch Mettlach[164] and decorative brickwork material for his park fountains there was supplied to his specifications by Gail's Claywares Factory, at Giessen.[165]

From 1904/1905, he was associated with the Delmenhorst Anchor-Mark Linoleum Factory in Delmenhorst, near Bremen. Within the next five years, for this company – along with Albin Müller, Josef Hoffmann, and other designers of note, who were members of the German Work Federation (which Behrens co-founded in 1907) – he designed floor- and wall-covering patterns in linoleum and lincrusta.[166]

For six years from 1907, he was hired as artistic consultant for AEG (General Electricity Company), Berlin.

Around 1911/1912, he taught at the Academy in Dusseldorf[167] through 1922, during which time he designed a tiled stove, constructed at the Meissen Stove and Porcelain Factory, for a "Saxony House" living-room exhibit at the 1914 German Work Federation's exhibition in Cologne.

In 1921–1922, he was instructor in architecture at the Dusseldorf Academy, after which, from 1922 (for fourteen years), he was professor of architecture at the Academy of Fine Arts in Vienna.

Appointed a member of the Academy of Art in 1927 in Berlin, he also, from 1936,

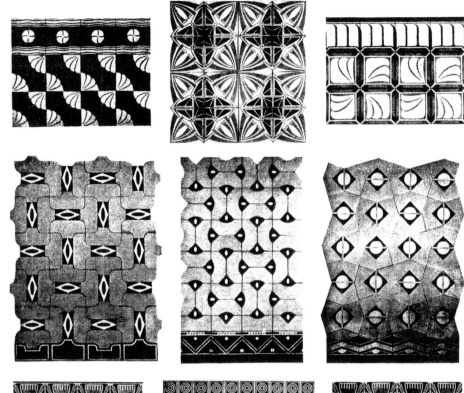

Illustration from "Die Kunst / Dekorative Kunst" (1904/1905, p. 427) of Peter Behrens' designs for floor tiles manufactured by Villeroy & Boch Mettlach.

maintained a master's studio there at the Prussian Academy of Arts and Sciences.

JOHANN BELZ (1873–1957), after studying in Frankfurt-am-Main, Munich, and Berlin, was active as a sculptor in Frankfurt, also designing, particularly, fountains and architectural ceramics. Around 1907, in collaboration with Scharvogel, he produced tile designs for the Ceramic Manufactory of the Grand Duchy of Hesse in Darmstadt.

WALTER BOSSE (1904–1979) was a designer, ceramics modeler, and metals craftsman, who trained under Michael Powolny at the Arts and Crafts School in Vienna and studied under Richard Riemerschmid and Adelbert Niemeyer in Munich. He opened his own ceramics studio in the early 1920s in Kufstein (relocated in 1937 in Vienna). He also designed and modeled items, including artistic tiles, plaques, and wall masks, for the Vienna Workshops, Goldscheider, and Augarten and collaborated with Arno Fischer (at his porcelain factory in Ilmenau-Thuringia), Metzler & Ortloff and F. & W. Goebel in Oeslau-Bavaria, and the Majolica Manufactory in Karlsruhe.

RUDOLPH BOSSELT (1871–1938), in addition to being a medalist, sculptor, and writer, was a designer of jewelry, metalwork, and lighting equipment. After studying in 1891–1897 at the Arts and Crafts School in Frankfurt-am-Main and

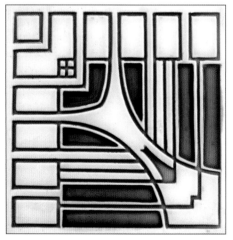

V & B M wall tile, designed by Peter Behrens.   *V & B M wall tile, probably designed by Peter Behrens or, possibly, adapted from a Behrens design.*   *V & B M wall tile, designed by Peter Behrens.*

in 1897–1899 at the Académie Julien in Paris, he was a member of the Artists' Colony at Darmstadt through 1902/1903. A founding member in 1907 of the German Work Federation, he is reputed to have created designs for the Dusseldorf Claywares Factory.

FRITZ AUGUST BREUHAUS (1883–1960), an architect and designer, later active in Dusseldorf, Bremen, Munich, Lucerne (Switzerland), Berlin, and Cologne, studied in Wuppertal (North Rhine-Westphalia), Munich, Darmstadt, and, under Peter Behrens, in Dusseldorf. By 1921, for the Majolica Manufactory in Karlsruhe, he produced designs for architectural ceramics and tiled stoves.

HERTA BUCHER (1898–1960), a German-born ceramic artist, who studied, c. 1911–1919, under Michael Powolny and Franz Cizek at the School of Arts and Crafts in Vienna, produced work – including floor tiles, relief tiles, and architectural decorations – for the Vienna Workshops from 1916. With her own studio between 1921 and c. 1955 at the Eduard Fessler Stove and Claywares Factory, in Vienna, she also executed designs for fireplaces and radiator covers there – including some for installation in interiors designed by Josef Hoffmann – as well as wall and floor tiles for municipal buildings. From 1924, for many years, she collaborated with a number of potteries, porcelain factories, and tile manufacturers in Vienna, including the Wienerberg Tile Factory and Building Company, as well as the Rudolf Sommerhuber Factory in Steyr, and the Gmundn Workshops in Gmundn, where she created designs for tiled stoves, stove tiles, and other tile work. Around 1931, she collaborated in the design and production of garden figures and fountain statues at the State Majolica Manufactory in Karlsruhe.

PAUL WILHELM BÜRCK (1878–1947) was a member of the Artists' Colony at Darmstadt in the years 1899–1902. The design he entered in the wall-tile competition arranged by *Deutsche Kunst und Dekoration* in 1898 received an honorable mention. Also, two designs of his were, later, freely adapted by Wessel's Wall Tile Factory and the North German Earthenware Factory, respectively.

HANS CHRISTIANSEN (1866–1945), an artist and designer, an important representative of Jugendstil, and a member of the German Work Federation, studied painting and graphic design in Munich, Paris, Antwerp, and, also, Italy. After publishing *New Surface Ornament* in 1892, exhibiting at the Arts and Crafts Exhibition in Darmstadt in 1898, and further study in Paris in 1898/1899, he joined the Darmstadt Artists' Colony for three years through 1902. At the World's Fairs in Paris and St. Louis, he won, at the first, a Gold Medal – as a contributor to the Darmstadt Artists' Colony's exhibit – in 1900 and, at the second, a Grand Prize in 1904. In the early 1900s, he was again active, for a time, in Paris and, after returning to Germany, continued to produce designs for many media, particularly, ceramics (for Villeroy & Boch, Wächtersbach, and others) and silverware. The Dusseldorf Claywork Factory not only produced a tile from a tulip design by Christiansen, but also adapted that design to include a stream or path in the background; both variations were available to buyers. It is believed that a design of his was adapted by Villeroy & Boch and Offstein Clayworks and it is further reported that he might have provided design work – or at least design inspiration – for the J. von Schwarz company.

HENRIK DARILEK was an Austrian-born painter, graphic artist, also interior designer, who, after graduating from the Royal Hungarian School of Applied Arts in Budapest, was hired at Zsolnay in 1898 to design vessels, tiles, and fireplace installations through c. 1905.

OTTO ECKMANN (1865–1902), after studying in Hamburg, Nuremberg, and Munich, was soon acknowledged to be a master of form and line, famous for the two-dimensional quality and spareness of his designs for pottery and porcelain. In 1894/1895, he gave up painting to devote himself to applied art and, as a contributor to the magazines *Pan* and *Jugend,* began to specialize in graphic art (particularly, color woodcuts), as well as design for craft (ceramics and weaving) and book illustration. Between 1897 and 1901, he was an instructor for courses in ornamental decoration at the School of Arts and Crafts in Berlin.[168] His celebrated fox-head design, featured in 1900 in

Deutsche Kunst und Dekoration, was reproduced in 1902 as printed decoration on tiles executed by Villeroy & Boch.

LÉON ELCHINGER (1871–1942), grandson of the founder of the Elchinger pottery company in Süfflenheim (Imperial Territory Alsace-Lorraine) – previously and, also, today, Soufflenheim (Bas-Rhin, Alsace, France) – enjoyed a short apprenticeship at the age of seventeen at Villeroy & Boch in Mettlach. Around 1889/1890, he first studied ceramic science and technique at the Royal Technical School for Ceramics in Höhr-Grenzenhausen (Rhineland-Palatinate), then painting, modeling, and sculpture at the School of Fine Arts in Nancy, France. As a student and, later, assistant to professor Anton Seder at the Arts & Crafts School in Strassburg, he executed – at his family's pottery – Seder's monumental ceramic panels and other tiles for installation on the façade and interior walls and doorways at the school's new premises. By the beginning of 1893, he returned to Süfflenheim/Soufflenheim to work alongside his brothers Charles and Victor, for many years, as an innovative, artistic ceramist designing and creating luxury items and decorative tiles there. In 1896/1897, in England, Hungary, and Italy, he visited potteries, ceramic studios, and museums.

EMIL FAHRENKAMP (1885–1966), an architect and designer, collaborated, occasionally – from around 1922 and, particularly, in the 1930s – in architectural ceramics work with the State Majolica Manufactory in Karlsruhe and, later, supplied designs for tiled stoves.

ANNA SOPHIE GASTEIGER (1877–1954), a painter and designer at Schloss Deutenhof, near Dachau, won both first prize and one of three third prizes in the wall-tile design competition, organized in 1898/1899 by *Deutsche Kunst und Dekoration*.

Her first-prize entry, "Two Greens," was soon offered in the catalog of the Saxony Stove and Chamotte Wares Factory, formerly Ernst Teichert Meissen (S. O. F.), after the company purchased the design.

LUDWIG GIES (1887–1966), after studying in 1904–1912 at the Arts and Crafts School and Academy of Fine Arts

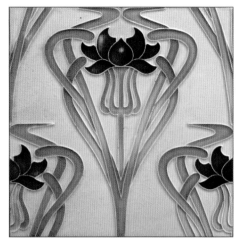

S.O.F. tiles, designed by Anna Sophie Gasteiger.

in Munich, was a sculptor, medalist, and designer. From 1917, he was professor at the High School of Fine and Applied Art in Berlin and, in the period 1927–1937, professor at the United State Schools for Fine and Applied Art. He produced designs for tiled stoves and architectural terra cotta / majolica work and, occasionally, collaborated with the State Porcelain Manufactory (KPM), in Berlin. For the Nymphenburg Porcelain Manufactory in Munich, he designed terra cotta sculpture in addition to a tiled stove that was manufactured there. Among his other designs were some for the Schwarzburg Workshops for Porcelain Art in Unter-weissbach (Thuringia) and the Velten and Velten-Vordamm Earthenware Factories in Velten and Vordamm.

EUGEN GRADL, a painter, graphic artist, and designer, was born, c. 1880, possibly in Eberbach (Baden-Württemberg). Border and panel designs by him – in an abstract Jugendstil manner – were illustrated in *Dekorative Vorbilder*, vol. 17, of 1906. One of these was adapted for inclusion in a tile image by the North-German Earthenware Factory.[169]

DANIEL GREINER (1872–1943) was a painter, designer, and sculptor, who studied in Berlin and Paris in 1901–1904 and was a member, from 1904 to 1907, of the Artists' Colony in Darmstadt. He was, later, active in art and literature and renowned for his religious paintings, graphic art, and cemetery sculpture, as well as art criticism. In 1910–1913 and, possibly, at other times, he collaborated with the Grand Ducal Majolica Manufactory in Karlsruhe on the design, mainly, of relief tiles and plaques. It is thought that he might have resumed this collaboration in 1937 or that the State Majolica Manufactory might have reintroduced some (or at least one) of his earlier designs that year.[170] He also designed fountain reliefs and other architectural ceramics for Gail's Tile and Claywares Factory in Giessen.

KARL GROSS (1869–1934), a sculptor, designer, and teacher, was hired, in 1898, to teach modeling and metalwork at the Arts and Crafts School in Dresden and, in 1914, was appointed director there. He was a sometime consultant to the Meissen Stove and Porcelain Factory (M.O.&P.F.) and other businesses in the Dresden area. Most notably, he designed an impressive, green-glazed stove for the German Art Exhibition in Dresden in 1899, executed by the Christian Seidel Factory of Dresden, as well as another for the International Art Exhibition, there, in 1901, that was executed jointly by the Markowsky and Bidtel firms in Meissen. He also designed a mask relief for Villeroy & Boch Dresden.

HANS GROSSMANN (1879–1949) studied in Zurich (Switzerland) and Karlsruhe, before opening his own architecture office in 1906 in Karlsruhe. He was also, from 1906 for eight years, director of the drawing office and, from 1910, head of the architectural ceramics department and artistic controller of finished wares at the Majolica Manufactory of the Grand Duchy of Baden in Karlsruhe, with particular responsibility for the design of tiled stoves and lighting fixtures; from 1914, he continued to collaborate with the manufactory, but only on an occasional basis.

HERMANN HAAS (1878–1935) studied in Berlin and Karlsruhe and was, later, active as a painter, architect, craftsman, and teacher. Between 1901 and 1903, he assisted Hans Thoma at his studio in Karlsruhe, occasionally working with him there on the creation of scenic picture tiles, as well as designs for functional ceramics, for the Majolica Manufactory of the Grand Duchy of Baden. He, later, provided designs for Villeroy & Boch in Mettlach. In 1904–1907, he was director of the Technical School for Ceramics[171] in Landshut (Bavaria) and, from 1925, director of the Technical High School in Munich.

RUDOLF HAMMEL (1862–1937) was a Viennese architect, designer, painter, craftsman (ceramics, glass, metal, textiles, wood), and teacher. He briefly studied painting at the Academy of Fine Arts in Vienna in 1879, prior to training in architecture and design and traveling in Germany, France, and Italy. By 1886, he began his career as an independent architect. Artistic advisor to the Imperial/Royal Austrian Museum for Art and Industry in Vienna from 1899, he also continued to collaborate with several arts and crafts schools in Austria and Bohemia. After teaching in Salzburg in 1901–1902, he was appointed professor and director of the crafts department of instruction at the Museum for Art and Industry the following year and, in 1909, named national head of the department of arts and crafts / technical schools in the Austrian Empire.

For the exhibition of Austrian arts and crafts at the Museum in 1899, he designed a bachelor's bedroom featuring a tiled chimneypiece by L. & C. Hardtmuth and also displayed "many designs for little objects" there.[172] He was honored at many other international exhibitions, including those in Paris and St. Louis in 1900 and 1904 respectively.

In 1900 and afterward, he continued his association with the Hardtmuth tile and tiled stove company in Budweis, Bohemia, and also supplied designs to the Josef Bock Porcelain Manufactory and other companies in Vienna and elsewhere.

KARL OTTO HARTMANN (1861–1934), an architect and designer, designed tiles for the Meissen Stove and Porcelain Factory.

PAUL HAUSTEIN (1880–1944), a craftsman, designer (of metalwares, jewelry, pottery, and enamel), and teacher, studied in Dresden and Munich. He collaborated with Jakob Julius Scharvogel, sporadically, in Munich – around 1898–1902/1903 – assisting in designs for tiles, as well as metal heating-covers with tile inserts. Later – after (or, possibly, even during) his activity, from late 1903 for almost two years, as a member of the Artists' Colony at Darmstadt – he also created ceramic designs for the Ceramic Manufactory of the Grand Duchy of Hesse. A participant and medalist between 1900 and 1910 at world's fairs and other expositions, he contributed designs on a freelance basis to Wächtersbach and other potteries. He taught classes in Nuremberg, while, at the same time, instructor and, afterward, professor of metalwork at the State Vocational Workshops in Stuttgart (Baden-Württemberg).

In 1938, for two years, he was appointed director of the State Arts and Crafts School of Württemberg in Stuttgart.

GUSTAV HEINKEL (1907–1945) was apprenticed between 1923 and 1925 as a ceramic decorator at the Majolica Manufactory in Karlsruhe. In 1926–1928, he assisted in the studio of Ludwig König there, learning modeling, painting, and glazing techniques for ceramics. He, later, studied painting in Karlsruhe at the Baden State Art School and sculpture in Munich. Active, independently, in the production of art pottery, he also, through 1944, collaborated in the design and execution of architectural ceramics and artistic tiles at the Majolica Manufactory in Karlsruhe. In 1941, for three years, he was appointed instructor at the Master School for Handicraft in (at that time) Strassburg.

OSWIN HEMPEL (1876–1965) studied art in Dresden and Munich, as well as in Italy, before commencing his active career as an architect, designer (of furniture, etc.), and teacher. From 1904, he taught at the Technical High School in Dresden, before being appointed, in 1907, professor of drawing, interior design, and ornamental and figural design and additionally, in 1929, director of the department of garden design there. A successful architect and designer throughout his life, he was a sometime consultant to the Meissen Stove and Porcelain Factory.

JOSEF HILLERBRAND (1892–1981) was an architect, painter, craftsman, teacher, and designer of furniture and decorative objects, who, after studying in Munich, was hired, in 1922, as professor at the School of Arts and Crafts in Munich, where his courses included classes in design and decorative art. Most of his designs were commissioned by the German Workshops, including those executed by the Nymphenburg Porcelain Manufactory, but, from c. 1920, he collaborated, sporadically, with the Majolica Manufactory in Karlsruhe, particularly through the 1930s and afterward, providing designs for decorative objects,

Illustration from "Deutsche Kunst und Dekoration" (Vol. 13, October 1903 – March 1904, p. 182) of a tiled frieze (approximately 36" x 12" / 91.44 x 30.48cm), composed of 12 Scharvogel tiles (designed as furniture decoration, c. 1903, by Paul Haustein).

as well as tile designs for stoves and fireplaces. One of his designs for a "dining-room stove" ("Speisezimmer - Ofen"), manufactured at Karlsruhe, was featured prominently in *Deutsche Kunst und Dekoration*.[173]

JOSEF FRANZ MARIA HOFFMANN (1870–1956), Moravian-born architect, designer, craftsman, and teacher, studied at the Academy of Fine Arts in Vienna in 1892–1895, after which he was active in Otto Wagner's studio in the city. He was a co-founder of the Vienna Secession in 1897 and a member through 1905. From 1898, he was an instructor and, in 1899–1941, professor at the School of Arts and Crafts in Vienna. In 1903, with Koloman Moser and industrialist Fritz Wärndorfer, he established the Vienna Workshops, of which he remained director through 1931/1932. He was a co-founder of the German Work Federation in 1907 and the Austrian Work Federation in 1912, heading the latter organization through 1920. Of his work in all branches of applied art – working alone or in collaboration with other artists and craftsmen – his ceramic designs were executed by companies in Vienna, Gmundn, and Berlin. His major Vienna Workshops commissions, including installations of wall and floor tiles, showed his endless inventiveness as an artist/ craftsman and his influential and forward-looking design aesthetic. He brought a new level of elegance and simplicity to the domestic and public environment.

LUDWIG HOHLWEIN (1874–1949), after his studies in Munich and Dresden, was celebrated as an architect, painter, craftsman, and, particularly – from 1898 – poster artist. From 1906, he was active in Munich.

In 1910, he designed a set of not less than twenty-one 4.88" square tiles – featuring mainly animals and fish in an impressionist manner – that was produced by Villeroy & Boch Schramberg; one set was used in the decoration of a Munich restaurant, Weinhaus Schneider.

Other ceramics/tiles work around that time included designs for the Majolica Manufactory of the Grand Duchy of Baden, as well as Utzschneider and the Westerwald stoneware industry.

By 1925, Hohlwein had designed three thousand different commercial posters.

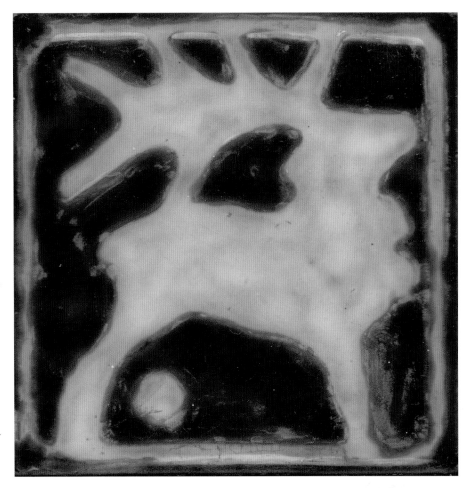

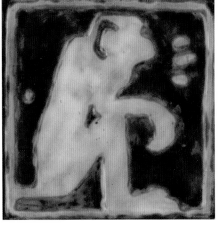 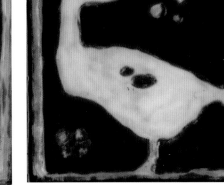

V & B S tiles, designed by Ludwig Hohlwein: each approximately 5" (12.7cm) square.

PAL HORTI (1865–1907), a Hungarian-born and Vienna-trained architect and designer, is reputed to have produced a design(s), around 1905/1906, used by the Wessel company of Bonn, though, in ceramics circles, he is more readily recognized for his collaboration with Zsolnay in Pecs.

KARL HUBER (1872–1952) studied in Munich and, later, worked there and in Nuremberg and, briefly, Berlin, as an architect, sculptor, and designer. From around 1908/1909, in collaboration with Jakob Julius Scharvogel at the Ceramic Manufactory of the Grand Duchy of Hesse in Darmstadt, he produced designs for ornamental vessels in terra cotta, sculptural items in stoneware, and, possibly, also tiles. As a designer of such work for the Ceramic Manufactory, he was awarded a gold medal at the Exposition in Brussels in 1910. He was later hired to teach at the

Arts and Crafts School in Offenbach-on-the-Main (Hesse).

FRIEDRICH HUDLER (1889–1982), who, around 1920, studied at the Technical School for Ceramics in Landshut was a graphic artist, sculptor, and ceramist with an interest in glaze chemistry. Active in ceramics, from the early 1920s, at leased premises, he worked, from 1926, at his own studio in Diessen (Bavaria).

At some period during his career – probably earlier rather than later – Hudler acquired blanks for decoration from tile manufacturers such as V & B Dänischburg.[174]

HEINRICH JOBST (1874–1943), a sculptor, designer, and teacher, having studied in 1896–1898 at the Munich Academy of Fine Arts, was appointed instructor in 1901 at the Arts and Crafts School in Munich. As a member of the Mathildenhöhe Artists' Colony in Darmstadt from 1907 through 1914, he also collaborated with Jakob Julius Scharvogel at the Ceramic Manufactory of the Grand Duchy of Hesse there. Also, during that time, he taught at the Grand Duchy of Hesse Atelier for Applied Arts in Darmstadt in 1909–1911.

GERTRUD KILZ of Berlin-Friedenau was a designer and painter of landscapes and still-life subjects (especially in gouache technique), active by 1900 in Berlin and, later (by c. 1905), also in Dresden. In 1898, she received an Honorable Mention for a tile design "Yellow and Green" (of conventionalized, orange-colored blossoms and green leaves on curvilinear stems) in a competition organized by – and announced in the October edition of the magazine – *Deutsche Kunst und Dekoration*. This tile was later put into production by the Saxony Stove and Chamotte Wares Factory, formerly Ernst Teichert Meissen (S. O. F.)[175] In the following year, she was awarded a third prize in the magazine's wallpaper-design competition announced in its November issue.

ARMIN KLEIN studied at the School of Arts and Crafts in Vienna prior to embarking on a long career from 1878 as a designer and modeler at Zsolnay in Pecs.

GERTRUD KLEINHEMPEL (1875–1948), an artist, craftsman, teacher, and designer of furniture, toys, and textiles,

Unidentified tiles/plaques, designed/decorated by Friedrich Hudler (possibly using blanks produced by V & B Dänischburg): (top and middle) each approximately 5" (12.7cm) square, (bottom) approximately 6" square.

after completing her studies in Dresden and Munich, directed her own private arts and crafts school from 1900 through 1907 in Dresden, together with her brothers Fritz and Erich Kleinhempel. In the period 1907–1938, she taught, first, as instructor and, later, professor, at the School for Handicraft Workers and the Arts and

Crafts School, in Bielefeld (North Rhine-Westphalia). She was a sometime contributor of designs to the Meissen Stove and Porcelain Factory.

ANTON KLING (1881–1963), an Austrian-born painter, designer, craftsman, and teacher, studied under Josef Hoffmann in Vienna, before taking up an appointment to teach, from 1908, at the Arts and Crafts School in Hamburg. From 1923, he was director of the Arts and Crafts School in Pforzheim (Baden-Württemberg) and, in 1927–1930, taught at the State Technical College in Karlsruhe. At one time associated with the Vienna Workshops in Austria, he engaged in collaborative work with several ceramics companies in Germany, including the State Majolica Manufactory in Karlsruhe, for which he produced designs for vessels, figures, and artistic tiles from 1935 for about seven years.

LUDWIG KÖNIG (1891–1974), after studying in Dresden, enrolled for classes under Richard Riemerschmid at the Arts and Crafts School in Munich. On Riemerschmid's recommendation, he joined the Majolica Manufactory in Karlsruhe, where, in his master's studio, he collaborated on the production of figures, functional wares, decorative ceramics, and tiled stoves between 1922 and 1929. A ceramist and designer, he also taught from 1925 at the Baden State Art School and, from 1929, held the positions of professor and director of the ceramics department there. He, later, taught in Cologne, Bunzlau, and, after 1945, Landshut.

WILHELM KREIS (1873–1955) studied in Munich, Karlsruhe, Berlin, and Braunschweig (Lower Saxony). An architect, designer, and co-founder of the German Work Federation, he was, in 1902–1907, professor of interior design at the Arts and Crafts School in Dresden; in 1908–1920, director of the Arts and Crafts School in Dusseldorf; and, in 1926–1941, professor of architecture at the Dresden Art Academy. Around 1920, he performed design work for the Majolica Manufactory of the Grand Duchy of Baden in Karlsruhe.

ALFRED KUSCHE (1884–1984), a graphic artist, craftsman (silversmithing and goldsmithing), industrial designer, teacher, and, from 1912, member of the German Work Federation, studied in Pforzheim and at the Arts and Crafts School in Karlsruhe and taught at the State Technical College in 1909 in Karlsruhe. He supplied designs to a number of ceramics companies, including, in 1908–1921/1922, the Majolica Manufactory of the Grand Duchy of Hesse and, from 1911, the United Schmider Ceramics Factories in Zell, as well as the Reinhold Merkelbach Stoneware Factory in Grenzhausen (Hesse).

MAX LÄUGER (1864–1952) studied painting and interior design, in the period 1881–1884, at the Arts and Crafts School in Karlsruhe and, later, painting and sculpture in Paris. At the School in Karlsruhe, he was an instructor from 1884 and professor later (through 1898). Also, in 1894, in Karlsruhe, he was responsible for classes in interior and garden design at the Technical High School, where, from 1898 through 1933/1934, he was professor. First introduced to ceramic work around 1885 in Kandern and Karlsruhe, he directed the artistic production of the Kandern

Clayworks at his own art pottery studio there from around 1895 through 1913/1914. "During the time he was active ... (there) ... he created 738 designs for vessels and 320 for architectural ceramics,"[176] (presumably) including tiles and plaques.

Notable examples of Läuger's early Art Nouveau / Jugendstil work (in addition to his pottery vases, bowls, tiles, etc., and his designs in hammered sheet-iron and other metals for such products as fireplace equipment, fire hoods, screens, and fenders, decorative doors for stoves, and radiator grilles) include:

i).   a tiled "Bacchus" wall fountain made for a house in Karlsruhe;[177] and

ii).   two gas-fire chimney pieces, one with four rows of five approximately 6" square tiles (decorated with an interesting, artistic glaze) surmounted by a row of three approximately 9" (22.86 cm) square tiles (decorated with a cluster of tall-stemmed tulips), and the other all-metal.

iii). two large fireplaces (together with accompanying vessels and unique tiles/plaques) exhibited (along with, possibly, other scenic fireplace surrounds) at the Exposition Universelle in 1900 in Paris.
a). One of them had a tile picture (surrounded by rectangular border tiles), composed of fifty-nine approximately 6" square tiles, portraying a young white deer in a darkly colorful, treed landscape.
b). The other featured a tall surround of plain, approximately 6" square tiles that enclosed a picture panel of twenty-four decorative tiles of the same size, composing a fantastic, evocative scene with a female figure, snake, and trees, all beneath a high, carved, wooden mantelshelf and between slender, square, carved wooden, supporting columns, surmounted by pottery vessels and metal sculptures on the mantelshelf.[178]

Illustration from "Die Kunst," 1900-1901 ("Max Läuger - Karlsruhe," by Fr. Walther Rauschenberg, p. 236) of a fireplace, designed by Max Läuger and installed at the Exposition Universelle in 1900 in Paris.

Max Läuger tile/plaque, made at Kandern: 7.88" (20.02cm) square.

However, from even before the turn of the century, much of Läuger's design and production work – particularly his unique tiles/plaques for the decoration of domestic interiors – has little to do with strictly Art Nouveau/Jugendstil ornamentation but, instead, displays the first signs of a highly personal signature within ceramic tradition.

After receiving awards at several World's Fairs (Gold Medals in Paris and St. Louis) at the beginning of the twentieth century, co-founding the German Work Federation, and subsequent travels and studies, he opened a studio in 1916 at the former premises of the Majolica Manufactory in Karlsruhe. Afterward, in the period 1921–1929, under the auspices of the manufactory, he both produced models there for execution by the manufactory and decorated specially commissioned orders, as well as creating unique work with underglaze painting at his own master's studio. In 1919–1922, he also taught ceramics at the Baden State Art School. From 1929/1930, he maintained a home studio in Lörrach (Baden-Württemberg).

As one of the most significant innovators in German ceramics, Läuger produced handmade tiles and vessels – many with leaf and flower motifs – noteworthy, first, at Kandern and, later, Karlsruhe, for the painterly quality of the colored ornament under a transparent glaze, as well as for his distinctive use of the labor-intensive, tube-lining technique in the decoration of a red stoneware body. While at Karlsruhe – together with work of the kind he had produced earlier – he also created tile pictures and plaques, for a few years, with impressionistic, figural representation and, at times, the additional artistic feature of craquelé surfaces that required unique treatment (emphasizing further his opposition to the manufactory's increasing interest in series-production work).

A few of Läuger's designs are reported to have been freely adapted for similar production by both Villeroy & Boch in Dresden and Wessel in Bonn.

PAUL LESCHHORN was active in Strassburg, where he furnished designs for border and other tiles to Villeroy & Boch Mettlach.

BERTHOLD LÖFFLER (1874–1960), a craftsman, graphic artist, designer, and teacher, studied in Reichenberg, in Bohemia, and at the School of Arts and Crafts in Vienna. Between 1904 and 1909, he taught at the School of Artistic Embroidery, also in Vienna. In 1905, with Michael Powolny, he founded Vienna Ceramics and later assisted, there, in providing tiles for the Fledermaus Cabaret and other Vienna Workshops commissions. In 1913, he and Powolny parted ways when Powolny merged Vienna Ceramics with Franz and Emilie Schleiss's Gmundn Cermaics

In the period 1909–1935, he was an instructor and, later, professor at the School of Arts and Crafts, Vienna.

CARL SIGMUND LUBER (1868–1934), after studying painting at the Munich Arts and Crafts School and sculpture at the Munich Art Academy, was hired in 1896 as artistic director at the J. von Schwarz Majolica and Terra Cotta Factory in Nuremberg through 1906.

There, in his own studio, he designed vessels, plaques, and artistic tiles to be executed in a faience body that included steatite, including picture panels for wall-hanging and tiles for furniture inlay or metal-mounting as trays and trivets, etc., that were completed by a staff of skilled assistants. These he had trained in the cuenca, pressed-relief technique of decoration – a less difficult and labor-

Max Läuger plaque, made at Karlsruhe: 7.5" (19cm) square; housed in a bronzed metal frame 7.75" (19.69cm) square and marked on the reverse "Ihren / Freunden u. Gönnern / Weihnachten 1928 / Staatl. / Majolika-Manufaktur."

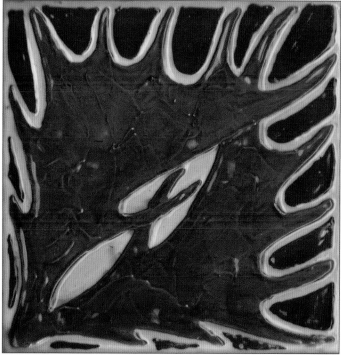

Max Läuger tile/plaque, made at Karlsruhe: 7.88" (20.02cm) square.

Von Schwarz tray, designed by Carl Sigmund Luber: 13.25" x 10" (33.66 x 25.4cm).

Von Schwarz plaque, designed by Carl Sigmund Luber: 6.5" x 11" (16.51 x 27.94cm).

Von Schwarz plaque, designed by Carl Sigmund Luber: 2.75" x 3.75" (6.99 x 9.53cm)..

process, result in ceramic surfaces incorporating the contours of the design. After pressing, the raised outlines produced by this technique separated the different, colored glazes that the painting assistants applied, according to the requirements of Luber's decorative scheme, in an Art Nouveau manner of floral or figural imagery or landscape scenery, etc.

Luber's employment in this field ended in 1906, when the J. von Schwarz company decided to discontinue the production of decorative ceramics and concentrate on the technical/industrial aspect of their business. He, later, for a short time, joined the design staff of the Nuremberg Metal and Lacquer Wares Factory, formerly Bing Brothers, that manufactured metalwares, other household wares, and toys.

From the summer of 1908, Luber was hired to head the Drawing Office (later, Department of Arts and Crafts) at the

intensive and, therefore, less expensive procedure than underglaze painting or tube lining – that would, by the use of specially prepared dies in the pressing

Upper Bavarian Chamber of Small Business's Institute for the Advancement of the Crafts that had been established that year in Munich. There, he was mainly concerned with completing Arts & Crafts design commissions for manufacturers (including furniture companies) and planning, teaching, and directing the institute's courses on painting, graphic design, and crafts (including woodworking, metalwork, leatherwork, etc.). He was also, through the time of his retirement in 1933, responsible for consulting with and advising clients on interior design matters and architectural decoration projects, as well as supervising the design of public and private sculpture, commemorative awards, and ceremonial items.

LAJOS MACK (1876–1963) studied at the Vienna Academy of Fine Art. A Hungarian-born artist, sculptor, and designer, he worked at Zsolnay in the period 1899–1916 and also, from 1909, was the instructor of ceramic art at the Zsolnay factory school.

EMANUEL JOSEF MARGOLD (1888–1962) was a Viennese-born architect, craftsman, and designer of furniture, carpets, porcelain, glassware, and jewelry, who had studied in Königsberg, Mainz, and, under Josef Hoffmann, in Vienna. He produced designs for the Vienna Workshops, Josef Bock Porcelain Manufactory, and other pottery/ porcelain manufacturers in Austria and Germany. In 1911, he was summoned to Darmstadt to join the Artists' Colony there. Later, around 1920, his collaborative work with the Majolica Manufactory in Karlsruhe included designs for tiled stoves and fireplaces. From about 1929, he was active in Berlin.

JOHN MARTENS, a sculptor and designer, was chief architect in the important, large Berlin architectural firm of Bruno Möhring (a founding member of the German Work Federation) for a number of years in the first decade of the twentieth century. He led a team of eleven architects and sculptors in designing the exhibit of the Velten Clay-Industry Association at the 1910 Exhibition of the Clay, Cement and Chalk Industry in Berlin. Represented there were thirteen Velten companies – including the Richard Blumenfeld firm and the "Adler" Stove and Claywares Factory, for which, at one time or another, Martens acted as design consultant. He was renowned for his development of an architectural ceramic material that met with great success, as well as for his tiled-stove design.

SIEGFRIED MEINHOLD studied in Munich and Paris at different times between 1889 and 1896. A painter, sculptor, ceramist, and designer, he founded the Meinhold Brothers Art Pottery in Schweinsburg (near Crimmitschau), in Saxony, around 1889 and, by 1903, produced decorative ceramic wares and wall tiles (mainly with molded images) there, designed by himself and other artists.

From 1905, he was active in Dresden.

SIEGFRIED MÖLLER was a creator of faience artwares, decorative wall tiles, and ceramic jewelry, who, in the period 1911–1915, studied at the Arts and Crafts School in Hamburg. In the early 1920s, he was active as a sculptor in that city. From 1923 through 1934, he was artistic director, then manager, of various C. E. Carstens businesses and other stoneware factories in Germany. In 1935, he founded his own workshop/studio in Kupfermühle (Schleswig-Holstein), which was later absorbed into an art and handicraft high school in Bremen, where he directed ceramics classes. He also engaged in collaborative work in design for the Majolica Manufactory in Karlsruhe and the Fürstenberg Porcelain Factory in Fürstenberg-on-the-Weser (Lower Saxony).

RICHARD MUTZ (1872–1931), a ceramist and designer with a special interest in high-fire and other artistic glazes, was apprenticed at his father's pottery in Altona (near Hamburg) and, later, studied at the Arts and Crafts School and the Museum of Arts and Crafts in Hamburg. From 1893 for about ten years, he directed his father's company Hermann Mutz Pottery Workshops. Later he founded his own Ceramic Art Workshops – first, in Berlin-Wilmersdorf and, from 1906/1907 through 1914/1915, with a partner, at Richard Mutz & Rother Workshops for Ceramic Art in Liegnitz, Silesia. There he manufactured small decorative pottery items, architectural ceramics, and wall tiles produced to his own design, as well as with the cooperation of other artists. In 1915, he was appointed director of the Majolica Manufactory in Karlsruhe. Afterward, in 1920–1922, he worked at his own Richard Mutz Ceramic Works, Stove and Claywares Factory in Velten and, between 1923 and 1929, at the R. Mutz Ceramic Workshop in Gildenhall.

CHRISTIAN NEUREUTHER (1868–1921) – from 1912, a member of the German Work Federation – was apprenticed as a decorator at the Wächtersbach Earthenware Factory in Schlierbach (Hesse) in 1882, prior to studying drawing, painting, and modeling under Professor Hutschenreuther and Max Rösler in Lichte, near Wallendorf (Thueringia). After further activity at Wächtersbach between 1888 and 1891/1892 and before returning there in 1893, he studied at the Munich Arts and Crafts School. Establishing his own ceramic studio in 1900/1901 in Schlierbach – with the support of his former Wächtersbach employers – he assisted in the execution of designs by Olbrich and Christiansen on a commission that Wächtersbach had received from the Artists' Colony in Darmstadt.

Two years later, Neureuther's studio was affiliated with the Wächtersbach factory as a "special" department of art. In 1904, he exhibited tiles with high-fired glazes at the St. Louis World's Fair and, by that time, was already beginning to be recognized for his tiles, wall plates, trivets, serving trays, etc., with brilliantly colored decoration in a style of geometric abstraction. Also from around that time, he continued his association and collaborative work with Albin Müller and various other Darmstadt artists.

In 1928 – after his death – the studio he had organized in Schlierbach closed.

ADELBERT NIEMEYER (1867–1932), who studied painting in Dusseldorf, Munich, and Paris, was active in Munich as a craftsman, architect, and designer of furniture, carpets, textiles, wallpaper, lighting, and small decorative items, including ceramics. In 1892, he was co-founder of the Munich Secession. With his own studio at the Nymphenburg Royal Bavarian Porcelain Manufactory from 1906, he was responsible for many form and decoration designs executed there, as also later pottery and porcelain designs for the Porcelain Manufactories of Berlin and Meissen, the Hutschenreuther company, Villeroy & Boch, the Majolica

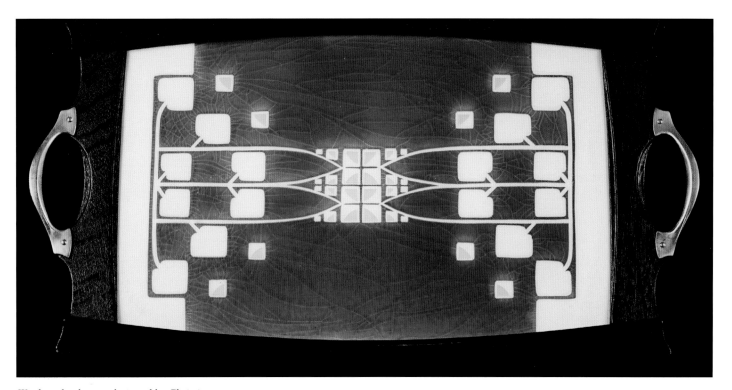

Wächtersbach tray, designed by Christian Neureuther: 14.63" max. x 8.38" max. (37.16 x 21.29cm).

Manufactory of the Grand Duchy of Baden, and many other companies. From 1907, when he co-founded the German Work Federation, he was a professor at the Munich Arts and Crafts School.

GEZA NIKELSZKY (1877–1966) was an artist, designer, teacher, curator (of the Zsolnay collection), and writer – with a strong interest in Hungarian folk art – who, in 1892–1897, studied decorative art and design at the Royal Hungarian School of Applied Arts in Budapest, before undertaking a further year's study in Munich. In 1899, he was hired by Miklos Zsolnay as a designer of vessels, tiles, stoves, fireplaces, etc., producing unique objects and tiles/plaques, as well as designs for serial production by the Zsolnay factory, through 1951.

HERMANN OBRIST (1862–1927), an influential and innovative, Swiss-born sculptor, craftsman, theorist, teacher, and designer of tapestries, furniture, ceramics, metalwares, monuments, and fountains, rejected tired rehashings of worn-out styles. Also rebelling against the relentless, realistic pursuit of nature, he promoted the importance, in design, of dynamic conventionalization and,

later, abstraction. In 1892, with Berthe Ruchet, he opened an embroidery and tapestry workshop in Florence, Italy, which they moved to Munich two years later. In 1902, he was co-founder of the Debschitz School's Training and Experimental Studios for Applied and Fine Art in Munich.

ROBERT OBSIEGER (1884–1958), Moravian-born sculptor, ceramist, designer, and teacher, studied at the Technical School for Ceramics in Znaim and, under Michael Powolny and Berthold Löffler, at the School of Arts and Crafts in Vienna. He was later an assistant instructor at the Vienna school in the period 1913–1918, after gaining practical experience as an apprentice at the Rudolf Sommerhuber Stove Factory in Steyr. He also taught in 1918–1919 at the Technical School for the Ceramic Industry in Znaim; in 1921–1932, as director at the Ceramic Workshops School of the Wienerberg Tile Factory and Building Company in Vienna; and from 1932, as departmental supervisor (from 1939, director) of the Ceramic Workshops at the School of Arts and Crafts in Vienna. He produced designs for the Wienerberg, Sommerhuber and Goldscheider companies.

JOSEPH MARIA OLBRICH (b. 1867 in Troppau, Austrian Silesia; d. 1908 in Germany), who had studied in Vienna and worked there later as an architect and highly influential designer of interiors, furniture, lighting, silverware, jewelry, and textiles, was a co-founder of the Vienna Secession. From 1894, he engaged in collaborative work with his former teacher and mentor Otto Wagner, prior to being summoned to Darmstadt in 1899 to be the leading organizer, architect, and designer at the Artists' Colony there. In 1899/1900, he took out citizenship in Hesse. In the year before his untimely death, he co-founded the German Work Federation. He received commissions for wall-tile designs from Villeroy & Boch,[179] in addition to other commissions from manufacturers of ceramics, glasswares, and metalwares in Germany, including the Royal Porcelain Manufactory at Meissen and Wächtersbach Earthenware Factory.

BRUNO PAUL (1874–1968) was a painter, architect, teacher, and designer of furniture and crafts. After studying in 1886–96 in Dresden and Munich, he was a regular contributor to the magazine *Jugend* and, in 1898, co-founder of the United Workshops for Art in Handicraft

Illustration from "Die Kunst" (Vol 12, 1905, p. 489) of the music room – incorporating the use of Scharvogel tiles – designed by Bruno Paul and exhibited at the 1905 exhibition of the Association for Applied Art in Munich.

in Munich. In 1905, for the Munich exhibition of the Association of Applied Art, he designed a music room that incorporated the use of Scharvogel tiles. From 1906/1907, he was director of instruction at the Arts and Crafts School in Berlin and, in 1907, co-founder of the German Work Federation. Discouraging unrestrained, creative flair, he was respected both for the functional quality of his design, with its minimal decoration, as well as his support for the rationalization of pattern work coupled with standardization.

In 1924 through 1933, he occupied the position of director of the State Schools for Decorative and Applied Art and the High School of Fine and Applied Art in Berlin. He also taught privately. He was an occasional consultant and collaborator of the State Majolica Manufactory in Karlsruhe and the State (formerly Royal) Porcelain Manufactory (KPM) in Berlin and contributed designs to the Richard Blumenfeld factories in Velten and the Rosenthal company in Selb (Bavaria).

HANS POELZIG (1869–1936), an architect, designer, and teacher, by 1911 and for a number of years, directed the Arts and Crafts School in Breslau, soon to be renamed during his tenure the Academy for Art and Arts and Crafts. For the Majolica Manufactory in Karlsruhe, he produced designs for architectural façades c. 1920–1923 and, possibly, tile designs for the stove industry in Velten, as well as designs for other projects.

MICHAEL POWOLNY (1871–1954) was a sculptor, ceramist, designer, teacher, and founding member of the Vienna Secession, who studied ceramics at the Technical School for the Ceramic Industry in Znaim and ceramics and sculpture at the School of Arts and Crafts in Vienna. He served an apprenticeship at the Rudolf Sommerhuber Stove Factory in Steyr. From 1909, for twenty-seven years, he taught at the Vienna school, from 1912 as professor. In 1913, he merged Vienna Ceramics – founded, eight years earlier, with Berthold Löffler – with Franz Schleiss's firm to form the United Vienna and Gmundn Ceramics and Claywares Factory in Gmundn (known, also, from 1916, as Gmundn Ceramics and, from around 1923, Gmundn Ceramic Workshops). He produced tiles for Josef Hoff-mann's Vienna Workshops commissions, including the Palais Stoclet and, with Löffler, the Fledermaus Cabaret. He was also an artistic collaborator with the Wienerberg Brick and Building Company, the Rudolf Sommerhuber Stove Factory and Art Pottery, and other pottery and porcelain – as well as glass – companies in Austria.

MAX PRUGGER (1876–1960) was a designer and modeler who collaborated with the Reinhold Merkelbach stoneware company in Westerwald. Design(s) by him are thought to have been executed by the Dusseldorf Claywares Factory (possibly in exact reproduction though more probably in free adaptation).

ANTON PRUSKA (1846–1930), a sculptor, designer, and teacher, first studied in Prague and Munich. In the period 1895–1914, he taught at the Arts and Crafts School in Munich, during which time – c. 1905 – he designed large-scale, terra cotta reliefs that were executed by the Nymphenburg Porcelain Manufactory.

RICHARD RIEMERSCHMID (1868–1957) studied painting, architecture, and applied arts in the late 1880s and early 1890s in Munich and was, later, director, there, of the United Workshops for Art in Handicraft, which he co-founded in 1898. An important architect, craftsman, and designer, with modernist taste – despite his use of modified, traditional forms and techniques – he taught at the Arts and Crafts School in Nuremberg in 1902–1905, prior to co-founding the German Work Federation two years later. He directed the Arts and Crafts School in Munich in the period 1912/1913–1924 and the Technical School in Cologne from around 1927 through 1931. Collaborating, occasionally, with the Majolica Manufactory in Karlsruhe in the 1920s, his work included designs for tiled stoves that were produced there. His other designs for industry by that time, including designs for porcelain, stoneware, and tile for such manufacturers as Villeroy & Boch, reveal his extreme economy of form and decoration, which evolved from the organic stringency of his earlier work. Beginning around the turn of the century, function, long-term use, and simple, universal appeal together with construction were, more

and more, determining factors in his design of household goods and furnishings.

JOSZEF RIPPL-RONAI (1861–1927), the celebrated Hungarian painter, graphic designer, and craftsman, collaborated on the design of articles and plaques produced by the Zsolnay factory in Budapest in the last years of the nineteenth century.

HUGO RUF, around 1935, engaged in collaborative work – mainly the design of relief tiles and plaques – with the State Majolica Manufactory in Karlsruhe.[180]

JAKOB JULIUS SCHARVOGEL (1854–1938), a ceramist, designer, and technician with a special interest in glaze chemistry, studied science, mathematics, and other subjects in Mainz (Rhineland-Palatinate), Darmstadt, Munich, and Zurich and, later, ceramic art and technology in England and France. In the early 1880s, he first became interested in design and handicraft, particularly, high-fired, decorative stoneware. After working from 1883 for a number of years, first, as a technician and, later, supervisor for the production of architectural ceramics and floor tiles at Villeroy & Boch in Mettlach, he moved to Dresden, then Leipzig, to develop projects for the company's pro-

duction of architectural ceramics. These involved promoting the use of terra cotta and other ceramic bodies with thick, water-resistant, opaque glazes – including floor tiles – in architecture and interior design.

After this training and experience, he joined the United Workshops for Art in Handicraft, after opening his own art pottery workshop – the Art Pottery for Decorative Vessels and Stoneware Articles – that he directed from 1897 through 1905/1906 in Obersendlin, near Munich. Pottery designs and tile designs (for several purposes, including chimneypiece decoration, furniture inlay, etc.) were contributed by Paul Haustein, Karl Soffel, and other artists.

In 1904, Scharvogel was summoned to Darmstadt for consultation on the organization and management of the Ceramic Manufactory of the Grand Duchy of Hesse that he directed from 1906 for Grand Duke Ernst Ludwig.

In 1905, he was also instrumental in the establishment of the Royal Technical School for Ceramics and Stove Construction in Landshut and, in 1907, he was a founding member of the German Work Federation.

Following on the Grand Duke's disappointment at the manufactory's lack of economic success, Scharvogel left Darmstadt in 1913. Around 1916, having already

Karlsruhe plaque, designed in 1927, by Hugo Ruf: 11.5" x 9.5" (29.21 x 24.13cm).

been appointed lecturer on architectural ceramics at the Technical High School in Munich (through 1925), he opened a studio for architectural and other ceramics in Munich, where he continued his experimentation in artistic glazes to produce unusual effects in the manufacture of vessels, tiles, and other wares.[181]

From 1925, he served as advisor/consultant to the Turkish ceramics industry.

EMILIE SCHLEISS-SIMANDL (1880–1962) studied at the Technical School for the Ceramic Industry in Znaim and, under Koloman Moser and Michael Powolny, at the School of Arts and Crafts in Vienna. In 1909, she married Franz Schleiss and, as a sculptor, ceramist, designer, and teacher, co-founded the F. and E. Schleiss Ceramic Workshop in 1911 and the Schleiss Ceramic School in 1917 in Gmundn.

FRANZ SCHLEISS (1884–1968), a sculptor, ceramist, designer, and teacher, studied ceramics at the Technical School for Ceramics and Associated Applied Arts at Teplitz-Schönau after apprenticing at his father's Gmundn Claywares Factory. Afterward, while directing his father's art pottery, he continued his studies in 1905–1909 under Michael Powolny and Berthold Löffler at the School of Arts and Crafts in Vienna.

In 1911, he co-founded the F. and E. Schleiss Ceramic Workshop in Gmundn with his wife Emilie and, two years later, merged their company with Michael Powolny's Vienna Ceramics as the United Vienna and Gmundn Ceramics and Claywares Factory – also known, from 1916, as Gmundn Ceramics and, from around 1923 (still in association with Powolny), Gmundn Ceramic Workshops. Included in the production at Gmundn, were tiles executed on commission for independent designers (for various purposes) and architectural ceramics for architects.

In 1917, he and Emilie founded the Schleiss Ceramic School in Gmundn and, in 1930 – during the period 1926 to c. 1932, when he was artistic director of the Munich Workshops – he established the Schleiss School Studio for Ceramics in Munich.

Franz Schleiss also collaborated on designs for the Rudolf Sommerhuber Stove Factory in Steyr.

ELISABETH SCHMIDT-PECHT (1857–1940), a painter, ceramist, and designer, engaged in freelance, collaborative work between 1894 and 1914 with Georg Schmider's ceramics factory in Zell, contributing tile designs and other designs for the decoration – and, later, also forms – of other wares.

In the period 1895–1906, she produced tiles, etc., at various other established potteries and, from 1907, at her own studio, the Schmidt-Pecht Art Pottery, in Konstanz (Baden-Württemberg). Around 1898/1899, she supplied pottery for the United Workshops for Art in Handicraft in Munich. In the 1900 and 1904 World's Fairs in Paris and St. Louis, her exhibits received Honorable Mention.

KARL SCRIBA (1845–1919) was a designer, who, by 1900, was employed in the Servais-Ehrang drawing office, completing designs for floor and wall tiles, etc.

ANTON JOHANN NEPOMUK SEDER (1850–1916) was a man of many parts – painter, craftsman, sculptor, decorative artist, interior designer, critic, publisher, and teacher. He studied at the Academy of Fine Arts in Munich and, for many years, taught at the Arts & Crafts School in Strassburg (Imperial Territory Alsace-Lorraine). In 1878–1882, he directed the Arts & Crafts School in Winterthur. In 1890, he was appointed director of the Strassburg School. There, in 1892/1893, he designed ornamentation for the School's new premises. For the façade, he chose monumental, richly colored tile panels representing allegories of Science, Painting, Sculpture, Architecture, Archeology, and Geometry, surrounded by botanical, historical and mythological motifs in a style, which combined elements of Historicism, Arts & Crafts design, and naturalistic Art Nouveau/Jugendstil. As interior decoration, he conceived tile schemes for walls and doorways. These and other panels depicting the decorative arts in an early Jugendstil manner were executed – in Süfflenheim (then, in the Imperial Territory) – by Seder's former pupil Léon Elchinger, son of the owner of Elchinger and Sons there. Some designs as well as colorful mosaic tiled floors in the school – also designed by Seder, again possibly, with the assistance of Léon Elchinger – were produced by Villeroy & Boch.

TADE SIKORSKI (1852–1940), a Polish-born architect, designer, and ceramist, married to Julia Zsolnay, was hired by the Zsolnay factory in 1883 for many years to direct design and construction projects there, advancing the use of the company's architectural ceramics as an alternative to expensive and time-consuming stone-carving in and around Budapest.

KARL SOFFEL (1877–1948) was a painter, designer, and zoologist, who studied in Munich. He collaborated, briefly, c. 1903 with Scharvogel to produce a number of tile designs, including some for tile pictures featuring single animal, fish, or bird motifs.

PAUL SPECK (1896–1966) studied in Munich. A painter, sculptor, ceramist, designer, and teacher, he operated his own pottery workshop in Munich in 1919–1924, prior to taking up a position in 1925–1933 teaching at the Baden State Art School in Karlsruhe (from 1929, as professor of sculpture). Afterward – and after directing, and producing designs for, the architectural ceramics department of the State Majolica Manufactory in Karlsruhe during the period 1924–1933 – he was active from 1934 as a sculptor in Zurich.

ERWIN SPULER (1904–1964), a painter, designer, and teacher, who had studied in Stuttgart and Karlsruhe, collaborated from 1931 on designs for architectural ceramics with the State Majolica Manufactory in Karlsruhe for thirty-three years. From 1944, he also taught at the Technical High School there.

WILHELM SÜS (1861–1933), as a painter, graphic artist, and designer, having studied in Dusseldorf and Dresden, was introduced to ceramics activity c. 1893/1894. By 1898, he was co-director of the Kronberg Ceramic Studios at Kronberg until 1901, when his studio was removed to Karlsruhe on his becoming artistic/technical director of the Majolica Manufactory of the Grand Duchy of Baden. There, he designed picture plaques, wall plates, and decorative vessels. In 1914–1917, he also taught at the Arts and Crafts School in Karlsruhe. From 1917, he was director of the Grand Duchy of Baden Gallery in Mannheim (Baden-Württemberg).

HANS THOMA (1839–1924) first became involved in ceramic work in the late 1970s in Oberusel-in-Taunus and, later, developed his interest through his association with the nearby ceramics studio directed by Wilhelm Süs. A painter, graphic artist, craftsman, and designer, who had studied in Basle (Switzerland) and Karlsruhe, he was appointed director of the Art Gallery of the Grand Duchy of Baden in 1899 in Karlsruhe, also heading a master studio at the Art Academy there at the same time. Two years later, he was instrumental in organizing the Majolica Manufactory of the Grand Duchy of Baden at Karlsruhe, where he maintained a studio through 1908. During that period – and also in 1921 – he collaborated with the Manufactory on the design and execution of wall plates, picture plaques, and decorative vessels, as unique pieces or for serial production. In 1913, he was appointed professor at the Karlsruhe Academy.

HENRY CLEMENS VAN DE VELDE (1863–1957), the Belgian-born painter, architect, craftsman, and designer, who, throughout his career, was of decisive importance in the improvement of German design, studied in Antwerp (Belgium), Paris, and Brussels. In 1892/1893, he transferred his interest from painting to interior design and the design and manufacture of furniture, lighting, other household goods, and jewelry.

The early influence of Franco/Belgian Art Nouveau in his work is evident in his initial use of organic intertwining lines to create stylized interpretations of floral imagery and in the furnishings he designed for Siegfried Bing's "L'Art Nouveau" gallery/store in Paris. But, even then in the mid-1890s, the English Arts and Crafts Movement had begun to exercise a strong influence on his aesthetic sensibility, as a result of which he began to redirect his efforts as a designer, commentator, and promoter of design in craft and industry. Interior design of his was represented in 1897 at the international Dresden Art Exhibition and, thus, two years later – already recognized in Germany for his seminal achievements in France and Belgium – he moved to Berlin.

From 1901, he designed for Westerwald stoneware manufacturers and began to produce ceramic designs for other German firms. From 1902, he was artistic adviser to the Grand Duke Wilhelm Ernst of Saxony-Weimar and, in 1906, began teaching at the Arts and Crafts School of the Grand Duchy of Saxony in Weimar. The following year, he was instrumental in the founding of the German Work Federation.

After moving to Switzerland in 1917 – but continuing his creative and educational work in Germany, Belgium, and Holland – he established the Institut Supérieur d'Architecture et des Arts Décoratifs in 1925 in Brussels. For the World's Fairs of 1937 and 1939/1940, he designed the Belgian Pavilions.

Van de Velde's influence on the German ceramics industry in the first two decades of the twentieth century was far-reaching and is especially noticeable in designs introduced by such pottery and tile makers as Villeroy & Boch.

Around 1905/1906, he designed a bank building in Augsburg, for which he commissioned floor tiles from the Ransbach Floor Tile Factory in Ransbach.

LUDWIG VIERTHALER (1875–1967), a sculptor, ceramist, and designer of crafts, who was associated with Tiffany & Co., c. 1894/1895, in New York City, engaged in cooperative work with Bruno Paul in 1908–1910 in Berlin. He, later, taught in the Instructional and Experimental Studio for Fine and Applied Art at the Debschitz School in Munich, and was active in ceramic work there. A member of the German Work Federation from 1912, his work included ceramic designs from 1914 for vessels and stove tiles produced by the Ernst Teichert company in Meissen and for tiled stoves for the Richard Blumenfeld company in Velten, as well as, from 1915, occasional collaborative projects with the Majolica Manufactory of the Grand Duchy of Baden in Karlsruhe. In the period 1915–1937 in Hanover, he taught sculpture and ceramics at the Arts and Crafts School and, from 1922, architecture, sculpture, and modeling at the Technical High School there.

JOSEF VINECKY (1882–1949) – trained by the master – was an assistant to Henry Van de Velde. He taught and, from c. 1907, directed the ceramics workshop at the Grand Ducal Arts and Crafts School in Weimar. Also a sculptor and designer of furniture, metalwares, glasswares, and fabrics, he founded his own ceramics workshop in 1910 (through 1914) in Sinn, near Herborn (Hesse), where – in his production of artistic tiles – he continued his interest in crystalline and flowing glazes, first developed with Max Pfeiffer at the Schwarzburg Workshops for Porcelain Art. In 1913, he designed tiles for the Town Baths in Wiesbaden (Hesse). He later worked in that city and taught there from 1919 for eight years, prior to moving to Silesia, to accept a teaching appointment at the Breslau Academy for Art and Arts and Crafts. In 1932–1936, he was active in Berlin and, in 1937, was appointed professor for two years at the School of Arts and Crafts in Pressburg.

HERMANN VOLLMER (1898–1972), after studying in Karlsruhe in 1918–1921 at the School of Arts and Crafts and the Baden State Art School, continued his training with Max Läuger in 1921–1925 at the Majolica Manufactory.

From 1926, he maintained his own studio there and collaborated with the Majolica Manufactory on the design and production of small ceramic items, large picture plaques (after historical models), and architectural ceramics. In 1934, he was appointed director of the newly formed faience department at the Manufactory.

After teaching in 1941–1944 at the Art Academy in Strassburg (Administrative Division Upper Rhine), he returned again – by 1947 – to his own studio in Karlsruhe.

MARIANNA (EDLE) VON ALLESCH (1886–1972) studied at the Royal Academy in Berlin and with Bruno Paul. A craftsman, designer, and artist, she founded her studio – the Blue House – in Berlin, where she designed and created artistic products in a variety of media. Many of her designs

Karlsruhe plaque, designed by Hermann Vollmer: 5.88" (14.94cm) square.

were executed by specialist craftsmen, among them those of stylized human and animal figures in glass by the glass artist Hugo Gerlach in Lausche (Thuringia), some of which were purchased by the Metropolitan Museum of Art in New York.

In 1927, at the Third International Exhibition of Decorative Arts in Monza, Italy, along with Paul and other major German artists, she displayed work in glass and pottery, including murals.

Having, two years earlier, divorced her husband of six years, Gustav Johannes von Allesch (Austrian-born psychologist), she traveled alone to New York in 1928, becoming a naturalized American citizen in 1930. In New York City, for many years, she continued her career as a ceramist and designer of functional and decorative pottery, lighting, furniture, and interiors.

The Cubist influence seen in some of her later products in Germany was gradually superseded by her espousal of the American Modernist aesthetic through the 1950s.

MARGARETHE VON BRAUCHITSCH (1865–1957) was not only a painter but also a designer of embroideries and other textiles, as well as stained glass, wallpaper, carpets, tiles, and women's and children's clothing. After studying in Leipzig and Vienna, she moved to Munich in 1898, where she was a founding member of the United Workshops for Art in Handicraft.

In the twelfth competition organized under the auspices of *Deutsche Kunst und Dekoration* – as reported in the magazine's October 1898 issue – she won an Honorary Mention for a tile design, illustrated in the magazine in the January 1899 issue, that was executed, later, by the Saxony Stove and Chamotte Wares Factory, formerly Ernst Teichert Meissen (S. O. F.)

She, later, exhibited embroidery designs at the Paris (1900) and Brussels (1910) Expositions. A member of the German Work Federation, she directed her own studio in Munich, supervising sixteen assistants employed in the execution of machine-made embroideries of her design.

EMANUEL VON SEIDL (1856–1919), who was later an acclaimed architect/ designer (exterior/interior), first studied at the Technical High School, under Professor Gottfried von Neureuther, and the Atelier for Interior Decoration in Munich. From 1893, he commissioned work by the Nymphenburg Porcelain Manufactory in the city for various projects, where he collaborated, especially with Josef Wackerle, on designs for wall decorations, etc.

GABRIEL VON SEIDL (1848–1913), like his younger brother Emanuel, was a celebrated architect/designer (exterior/ interior) after completing his training at the Technical High School in Munich and gaining experience in the architectural offices of Professor Gottfried von Neureuther. From around 1901, he also produced collaborative design work for the Nymphenburg Porcelain Manufactory, most notably, c. 1912, majolica reliefs and fountain decoration with Josef Wackerle.

JOSEF WACKERLE (1880–1959) studied, first, in Partenkirchen then, in 1896–1899, at the Munich School of Arts and Crafts (under Anton Pruska) and, in 1900–1904, at the Munich Academy. A sculptor, painter, craftsman, designer, and teacher, he was hired in 1909 (for eight years) to teach at the School of the Berlin Arts and Crafts Museum. In 1917–23, he

Plaque, possibly late 1920s, by Marianna von Allesch: 10.75" x 8.75" (27.3 x 22.2cm).

S. O. F. half-tiles, adapted from a design by Margarethe Von Brauchitsch.

was instructor at the Arts and Crafts School in Munich and, from 1923 through 1950, professor at the Munich Academy. From 1905/1906, in a long career with the Nymphenburg Porcelain Manufactory – at first, as director then, later, as collaborator – he designed and produced exceptional ceramic sculpture, including unique and original creations, as well as serial production items, along with tiles and reliefs (for walls, columns, fountains, etc.) and other architectural elements. He also collaborated in design with KPM in Berlin, and the Grand Ducal, later State, Majolica Manufactory in Karlsruhe.

VALERIE (VALLY) WIESELTHIER (1895–1945), a potter, ceramic sculptor, and designer, began her studies in 1914, under Koloman Moser, Josef Hoffmann, and Michael Powolny, at the Arts and Crafts School in Vienna. From 1917, she worked at the Vienna Workshops creating unique items – as well as series ceramics – and, later, she worked on commissions for a number of Austrian companies at her own studio. In 1927, she returned to the Vienna Workshops to direct the ceramic workshop there. She moved, permanently, to the United States in 1932, where she continued to work independently and on commissions for American companies through the time of her early death in 1945.

For a number of Vienna Workshops patrons, including the Viennese firm of Paul Senkowitz,[182] she designed stoves clad in colorfully decorated tiles.

JULIA ZSOLNAY (1856–1950) was the well-traveled daughter of Vilmos Zsolnay and, from 1883, wife of Tade Sikorski. From about 1874, she designed and decorated vessels, wall plates, plaques, etc., at the Zsolnay factory for many years until after the First World War. Around the mid-1890s, she interrupted her work to study painting in Budapest and Vienna.

TEREZ ZSOLNAY (1854–1944) – later Mattyasovszky – the elder daughter of Vilmos Zsolnay, was engaged in design and decoration at the Zsolnay factory in Budapest from about 1874 for many years.

Among **OTHER DESIGNERS**, architects, painters, and/or sculptors, who commissioned or designed wall/floor/stove tiles and architectural ceramics between the 1890s and 1935 are included: Josef Feller, Alfred Grenander, Otto Friedrich Gussmann, Fritz Höger, Max Hans Kühne, Erich Mendelsohn, Bruno Möhring, Georg Müller (sometimes referred to as Georg Müller-Breslau), Fritz Schumacher, Bruno Taut, and Max Taut.

COMPARATIVE CONSIDERATION OF ENGLISH, FRENCH, BELGIAN, AND DUTCH TILE PRODUCTION

During the Period of Jugendstil and Secessionist Activity in Germany and Central Europe

During the nineteenth century, the giant of tile production in the Western world was Great Britain, with English tile manufacturers supplying demand not only in the British Empire but also in much of Continental Europe and the United States of America. The mass production of plain and decorated tiles in ENGLAND since the time of the Industrial Revolution was indeed large and the variety of design and technique was no less so, particularly of its decorative wall-tile product and especially in the later years of the Victorian era.

In the last thirty years of Victoria's reign, the influence of the Arts and Crafts Movement on British design was strong, though aspects of the earlier Neo-Classicist, Neo-Renaissance, and Romantic styles, as well as Gothic Revival, continued alongside the interest in Japanese art and vestiges of influence from the Aesthetic Movement and Medieval and Pre-Raphaelite art.

By the beginning of the twentieth century, decorative tiles with Arts & Crafts ornamentation – designed by in-house personnel or freelance artists – were used extensively for a variety of purposes throughout Britain. By the time of the outbreak of the First World War, "hardly a house, in or out of town, terraced or detached, was complete without a tiled porch"[183] or fireplace.

With transfer, low-relief, or, even, tube-lined decoration under translucent, colored glazes, many of these tiles were initially ornamented with naturalistic, floral, and plant-inspired images filling the tile surface. Later, others in a more abstract vein bore decoration that was centrally and symmetrically arranged, surrounded by vacant space. However, since these kinds of tile decoration date from before the mid-1890s in England, it has been posited that, from that time into the twentieth century, they signified, to some degree, a "mere segment in a continuous pattern of change ... and the development of a past tradition,"[184] rather than a prefiguration or manifestation of a new style. Nevertheless, a great number of tiles of the Arts and Crafts Movement period undoubtedly have an undeniable Art Nouveau appeal, no matter how the origination of their ornamentation is construed, what stylistic influence was most evident in their background, or in which category they are considered to be.

Elsewhere in Europe in the 1890s, many architects, artists, and designers – like their British counterparts – were eager to divest themselves of the His-toricism and eclecticism represented by the continuation or revival of earlier styles. Since, by that time, the Arts and Crafts Movement had already heralded in Britain a different and more modern design ethos, soon, decorative artists in Continental Europe emulated aspects of the English style.

Similarly, at the same time, in France and Belgium – with the first stirrings of Art Nouveau – decoration was becoming predominantly naturalistic, but, by the mid-to-late 1890s, a more abstract design began to appear there. Interest in the "new art" grew rapidly, leading to the apogee of the 1900 Exposition Universelle in Paris. At the fair, both aspects of Art Nouveau style were apparent in most media and the influence of Franco/Belgian Art Nouveau was seen to be spreading to other countries in Europe and to the United States, fostering a number of variants.

In FRANCE, large ceramic tile panels and "special" mosaics for commercial architecture along with sculptural and, sometimes, monumental, ceramic, decorative detail, usually in stoneware, were designed by artists and architects. However, without a similar emphasis on the use of tilework in domestic interior decoration up to the First World War – due, perhaps, to a longtime preference for ornate "boiserie" and decorative wainscoting – the mass production of Art Nouveau wall tiles in France for apartment buildings, villas, and other private homes, though undoubtedly significant, was, possibly, not as large as in England, Belgium, and Germany in the first decades of the twentieth century.

In BELGIUM, the large-scale production of wall and floor tiles dates only from the last part of the nineteenth century. From c. 1895, a number of later-significant factories were founded, as well as smaller workshops specializing in custom orders for tile panels for

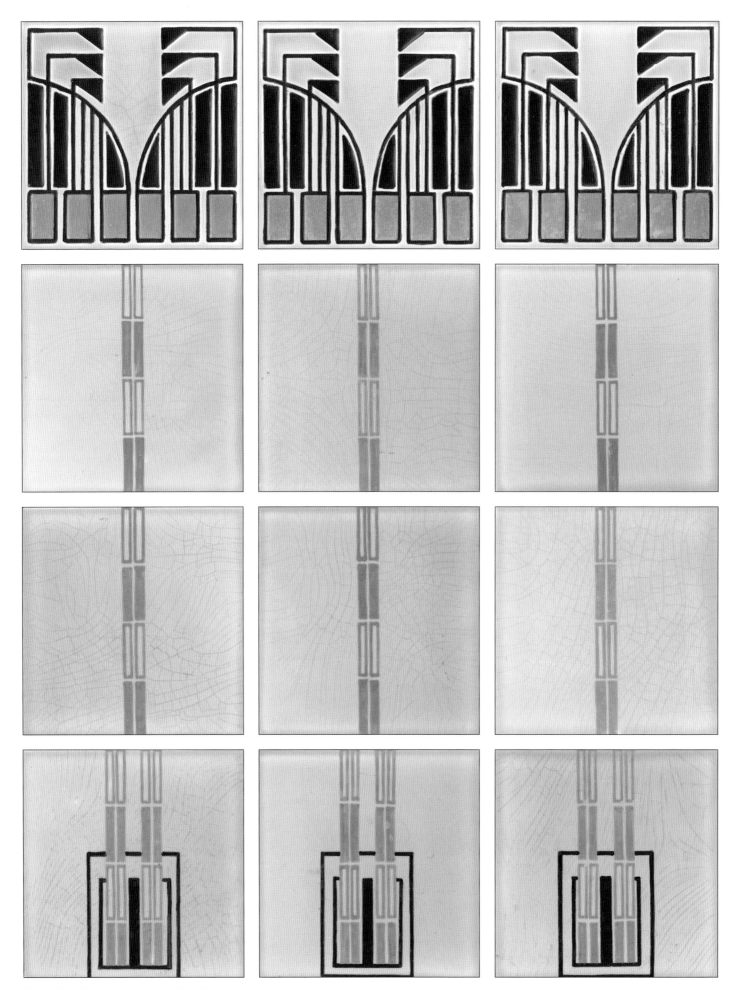

V & B M wall-tile panel, designed by Peter Behrens

architectural installation. This resulted, soon, in the country joining England and Germany as a leading manufacturing center of decorative wall tiles in Europe. Locally, in the late 1890s, architects' eagerness to use color in exterior façades – as in France – and designers' interest in interior, Art Nouveau-inspired, wall-tile installations – as fashionable, particularly, in England and Germany – connected with additional design influences from England, Scotland, Austria, and Germany, to increase to around twenty-five, by 1910, the number of factories successfully producing wall tiles with translucent, colorful glazes and/or encaustic floor tiles.

Into the 1920s – with regard to wall tiles bearing conventionalized and more abstracted decoration of flowers, foliage, figures, female faces, birds, animals, and pictorial scenes (landscape and ocean shore) – the Belgian output remained of similar size and variety as those of England and Germany.

In the NETHERLANDS, a small, industrial manufacture of decorative tiles began toward the end of the nineteenth century that differed greatly from the production of the popular, Dutch blue-and-white Delftware using traditional craft techniques. Many of these were artistic tiles for framing and other purposes, with an emphasis on flat-surface decoration by handpainting, stenciling, and printing.

Scenes from rural life and Batik-type patterning were preferred. Arising from an awareness of stylistic practice in England, France, and Belgium, a semi-abstract and spare representation of natural forms joined a growing interest in the two-dimensional, geometric design of Nieuwe Kunst. For a brief time, makers produced labor-intensive tile panels and dados for architectural commissions. In addition, wall tiles with ornamentation could be imported into Holland from Belgium and England along with tile blanks for local decoration.

NOTES

1. *Reports on the Vienna Universal Exhibition of 1873*: "Professor Archer on Pottery and Porcelain," p. 122.
2. In this text referring to the period from the 1890s to the 1900s.
3. Items pressed/cast, decorated, and glazed – by the techniques/methods employed in tile production for architectural or stove use – that serve other purposes, including articles with surface addition/adaptation after pressing.
4. To facilitate comparison with the contemporaneous tile industries of England, France, Belgium, and the Netherlands, tiles from those countries are discussed peripherally.
5. Coincidentally, decorative roof tiles, too, have embellished both public and private construction for centuries, particularly in Eastern Asia, and also at times in the Western world – as evidenced, for instance, in the use of 230,000 colorful tiles to form ornate patterns in the repair of the roof of St. Stephen's Cathedral, in Vienna, after the Second World War. These patterns include mosaics of the coats of arms of Vienna and the Republic of Austria as well as the double-headed Habsburg eagle symbolic of the Austro-Hungarian Empire.
6. The word "Fliesen" is most often used in a generic sense to simply signify "tiles," including ceramic wall tiles and ceramic or cement floor tiles, as well as "artistic" tiles and some others put to other uses.
7. It is to be understood that German words in parentheses throughout this text are:
   i). appropriate terms used, at some time, in the German tile/ceramic industry,

   or
   ii). recognized names of organizations, associations, companies, etc., or,
   iii). if in quotation marks, actual words used in direct quotation from source material.
8. Except where otherwise indicated, all square floor tiles illustrated are in the approximately 6.75" (17 cm) square format.
9. When Herbert Minton acquired the sole right to Samuel Wright's patent for tile manufacture that allowed this inlaying of colored decoration, by mechanical means, as a constituent part of the polychrome tile formed of plastic, wet clay.
10. In this text and photograph captions, reference to tile companies (by brand name or other recognized abbreviation, etc.) is as listed in Chapter Four: The Manufacturers, Locations, Identifying Marks / Brand Names – Germany, Austria, Hungary, Bohemia, Moravia (Czechoslovakia). Reference to companies can also be found in the Register of Companies in Section 4 under the English wording (followed by names, titles, etc., in German). Reference to schools, associations, and organizations, etc., as well as some official or industrial designations, is to be found in the General Index, in Section 4, also under the English wording (followed by names, titles, etc., in German).
11. *Journal of the Franklyn Institute*, Vol. 145, p. 200.
12. British Patent No. 2176, of September 3, 1863, completed March 3, 1864.
13. Designed in 1864–1887 by architect August Ritter von Essenwein, Director (1866–1892) of the German

    National Museum in Karlsruhe, assisted by artist Fritz Geiger (who, after Essenwein's death in 1892, was charged with executing Essenwein's designs for the choir, etc., through 1899).
14. Today, almost all of the tiled floor can be publicly viewed. Only the section in the Crossing cannot be seen at present (and since 1956), as it is covered by the carpeting surrounding the altar/communion table. In Gothic church architecture, the Crossing is the area in front of the Chancel, where the transept intersects with the nave along the main axis of the church.
15. Between 1812 and 1814, the manufacturer of architectural ceramic products Tobias Christoph Feilner produced a white enamel glaze, which, used with tiles made of Velten-area clay, was the starting point of his development with architect and painter Karl Friedrich Schinkel, in Berlin, of the white-tiled stove – styled in the Classically strict tradition – which was commonly used throughout Germany, for at least the next fifty years.
16. This catalog is 6" x 11" x 1.13" (15.2 x 27.9 x 2.9 cm) when closed, approximately 33" (84 cm) long, when open. The seventy-five sample tiles, each measuring 1.4" x 1.6" (3.5 x 4 cm), are attached to the five "pages" of this "book."
17. The Stove and Ceramics Museum – opened in 1905 in Velten and exhibiting both tiled and iron stoves made in Germany, Austria, and Switzerland from the sixteenth century through the beginning of the twentieth century (along with decorative ceramics, household

china, and other claywares made by local companies) – is, today, located in the building occupied by the still-operational Schmidt Lehmann Stove Factory that was founded in 1872 in Velten.

18. Special-use tiles for furniture installation were usually in the same square format of 6" and – though rarely required – other sizes as wall tiles; also for use as trivets, with the added availability of round shapes of approximately 6" and 4" diameter; and coasters, generally circular and in a diameter of 3.25" (8.26 cm).

19. In the case of mounted trays, trivets, coasters, etc., as well as framed tiles and plaques, all measurements pertain to the visible ceramic area.

20. Unless specified otherwise as floor, stove, special-use, or artistic tiles/plaques, all references in captions are to wall tiles of varying sizes.

21. British Patent No. 8548 issued to Richard Prosser.

22. In Germany, the wet-clay process continued in regular use for the production of wall tiles, at several firms, up to the turn of the century.

23. Or about 0.25" (6 mm) in the case of the North German Earthenware Factory's production after 1899 in Grohn; or about 0.17" (4 mm) for the white wall tiles manufactured by the end of the 1930s by the Villeroy & Boch branch factory in Dänischburg.

24. Unless otherwise indicated, it is to be understood that all square wall tiles pictured are in the approximately 6" (15 cm) format; rectangular half-tiles (horizontal/vertical) in the approximately 6" x 3" (15 x 7.5 cm) format.

25. However, in many instances, for today's collector/enthusiast, even supposedly individualized tile backs can add confusion and frustration in an attempt at identification, since close variations – and, even, identical versions – of such reverse patternings were, in fact, frequently shared by a number of German and other European makers. For this reason, the author has chosen to omit a discussion of this subject from his text and, instead, prefers to refer the reader to other more specialized publications on European tiles, where such information might prove helpful – such as *Jugendstilfliesen*,

by Michael Weisser, and *Jugendstil-Fliesen* (a collection catalog of the Baden State Museum, Karlsruhe), edited by René Simmermacher – prior to the possible introduction, at some time in the future, of a fully researched and computerized system of "forensic" identification.

26. *Jugendstilfliesen*, by Michael Weisser, p. 36.

27. See: p. 54 (Zsolnay tile of Persian inspiration.)

28. In addition to wall tiles, these techniques apply also to the decoration of other categories of ceramic tile including stove tiles, special-use tiles, and artistic tiles.

29. Tube-lining was used by the Roman Britons – and the Chinese – to attain decorative graphic effects. From the 1890s, it was a standard, decorative feature of British art pottery; a number of potteries in the United States also employed the device from around 1900 (along with the use of slip-painting as a medium for the decoration of flat or relief surface areas, a technique already popular, there, since the 1880s); around the early 1900s, tube-lining was practiced by a few German ceramists, studios, and companies.

30. After Herbert Minton's adaptation, for tile making, of Richard Prosser's dry-compression patent.

31. William Boulton's British Patent No. 2176.

32. *Collecting Victorian Tiles*, by Terence A. Lockett, p. 25.

33. The Aesthetic Movement flourished in England, particularly in the 1870s and 1880s, with Oscar Wilde and James Whistler as disciples.

34. The Pre-Raphaelite Brotherhood, founded c. 1848, was highly influential in British art and design circles for a number of years from about 1860.

35. *The Art Nouveau Style,* by Stephan Tschudi-Madsen, p. 283.

36. *Art Nouveau, 1890–1914*, edited by Paul Greenhalgh; Part IV: "The Metropolis and the Designer," 21: "Glasgow: The Dark Daughter of the North," by Juliet Kinchin, p. 320.

37. A term implying a striving for unity, cohesion, and harmony in art and life and embracing/defining:

i. a synthesis of the arts, including theater, music, architecture, and

applied art; or

ii. more specifically, in this study, a total work of art: for instance, an environment – building, home, room, etc. – with architectural design, interior decoration, and multi-media completely and aesthetically integrated into a homogeneous whole; and

iii. art for everyday life, available to all, with the cohesive and stylistically coordinated effect of furniture, wall and floor coverings, lamps, doors, and other ornamental fixtures and fittings, and everyday practical household goods, all harmoniously installed.

38. Early in his career – in the late 1890s – Van de Velde designed a small number of wall tiles for the French ceramist Alexandre Bigot – as reported by Mario Baeck in a doctoral thesis "The Flourishing of Belgian Ornamental Tile Panels in the Art Nouveau Period."

39. *Art Nouveau, 1890–1914*, edited by Paul Greenhalgh, Part II: "The Creation of Meaning," 2. "Alternative Histories," by Paul Greenhalgh, pp. 40-41.

40. *The Collected Writings of Hermann August Seger*, Vol. II, C. III: "Reports from the Paris Exposition 1878," pp. 897-898.

41. "Founders' Period" – also sometimes referred to as the "Wilhelmian Golden Age."

42. The German term "Kunstgewerbeschule" is often translated as School of Arts and Crafts or, sometimes, School of Applied Arts. In the German-speaking areas of the German and Austrian Empires, instruction was offered at such advanced schools in ceramics and ceramics-related subjects possibly sometimes, with classes, also, in associated applied arts, including glass, metalsmithing, and graphic art. After renaming as the Arts and Crafts School in Nuremberg in 1833 (downgraded that year, under that name, on the order of Bavarian King Ludwig I, from the previously named, long-existing Academy of Fine Arts) and after subsequent re-structuring in 1853, the example of this school was followed by the founding, in 1868, of the Imperial/Royal School of the Museum of Arts and Crafts in Berlin and the School of Arts and Crafts in

Munich, also, in 1869, the opening of the School of Arts and Crafts in Kassel.

"Fachschulen" (Technical Schools) and "Werkschulen" (Works Schools) – terms already used in the nineteenth century – were similar schools for professional/vocational/technical training in ceramics and/or associated applied arts and craft.

Prior to the end of the First World War, some of the major schools of these kinds in Germany, Austria, Hungary, Bohemia, Moravia, and Silesia bore the titles "Imperial" and/or "Royal" – "Imperial/Royal" indicated, in German, by the initials "K. K." After the end of the First World War, previously so-named "arts and crafts schools" were also referred to, most often, as "Fachschulen," "Meisterschulen," or "Werkschulen." Later, in the second half of the twentieth century, schools under these names in Germany were mostly merged with – or converted or incorporated into – local or regional universities, academies, or high schools of the arts / applied arts.

43. First used in Germany in the 1840s.

44. By the end of the nineteenth century, a generic term used in Germany to designate industrially produced, architectural floor tiles, including those manufactured by Villeroy & Boch and Villeroy & Boch's competitors.

45. The English exhibitors competed with magnificent fireplace mantels in bronze, polished steel, and expensively painted, porcelain tiles.

46. The wet process continued to be used by some makers up to the turn of the century particularly for the production of relief designs with colored glaze.

47. Other tile installations on the liner included the swimming pool with marine-themed tiles supplied by Pilkingtons Tile & Pottery Co. Ltd., of Manchester.

48. Bohemia and Moravia – together with Czech Silesia (most of the area of the Duchy of Upper and Lower Silesia, also known, before 1918, as Austrian Silesia and, between 1938 and 1945, as Sudeten Silesia, a German territory) – were the names of provinces in the Habsburg's Austrian Empire that belonged historically to the traditional Czech lands in Central Europe, with the largest, Bohemia, having occupied the western two-thirds of that region. In 1742, most of Silesia – annexed by Austria along with Bohemia and Moravia in 1526 – was seized by Prussia and, in 1871/1872, was part of the German Empire.

49. Wikipedia.

50. Architects Adolf Loos and Jan Kotera were both born in the Moravian capital city Brünn and artist Alfons Mucha, born elsewhere in Moravia, was educated there.

51. Through the time of the Second World War, Bohemia, Moravia, and Silesia were inhabited by Slavic people, mainly of Czech ethnicity, along with a large minority of ethnic Germans. After the Second World War, most of German-occupied Silesia was eventually returned to Poland and German residents were expelled; Germany retained a small area to the east of Leipzig, which is now part of the federal state of Saxony.

52. *Arts & Crafts in Britain and America*, by Isabelle Anscombe and Charlotte Gere: "Introduction," p. 7.

53. *Beauty in Common Things: American Arts and Crafts Pottery from the Two Red Roses Foundation*, by Jonathan Clancy and Martin Eidelberg, p. 33.

54. *The Arts and Crafts Movement in America 1876–1916*, edited by Robert Judson Clark; 5: "Art Pottery," by Martin Eidelberg, p. 150.

55. *Collecting Victorian Tiles*, by Terence A. Lockett, p. 35.

56. *Art Nouveau, 1890–1914*, edited by Paul Greenhalgh, Part II, "The Creation of Meaning," 2: "Alternative Histories," by Paul Greenhalgh, p. 49.

57. These concepts concerned official, public support for – and protection of – the physical and cultural environment and national architecture and art in Germany, as well as interest in the improvement and promotion of local handicraft and design there.

58. Art Nouveau is both the name of the specific style, which came to prominence in France and Belgium c. 1895, as it was practiced in those two countries, and a term, used adjectivally, to describe facets of that style employed around the world and in any period in architecture, decoration, and ornament.

59. *Art Nouveau, 1890–1914*, edited by Paul Greenhalgh, Part I, "Introduction," 1: "The Style and the Age," by Paul Greenhalgh, p. 26.

60. *Ibid*, Part IV, "The Metropolis and the Designer," 19: "Munich: Secession and Jugendstil," by Gillian Naylor, p. 290.

61. Alfons Mucha's first poster featuring Sarah Bernhardt appeared in 1894, a year before Siegfried Bing opened his celebrated store L'Art Nouveau in Paris.

62. *Art Nouveau, 1890–1914*, edited by Paul Greenhalgh, Part II, "The Creation of Meaning," 3: "The Cult of Nature," by Paul Greenhalgh, pp. 65-68.

63. *Ibid*, Part II, "The Creation of Meaning," 2: "Alternative Histories," by Paul Greenhalgh, p. 44.

64. *Art Nouveau Tiles*, by Hans van Lemmen and Bart Verbrugge, p. 9.

65. Especially influential were:

i. Arthur Heygate Mackmurdo and the preoccupation with movement evident in his revolutionary design of the Century Guild dining chair (c. 1882/1883) and his book cover for *Wren's Churches* (published in 1883);

ii. Aubrey Vincent Beardsley and the disturbing personal imagery, curvilinear design, and Japanese abstraction exhibited in his drawings and illustrations (in the 1890s), also his cover designs and illustrations for *The Yellow Book* (which he edited in 1894–1895);

iii. Charles Frances Annesley Voysey and his innovative designs (of the mid-1890s) for furniture wallpaper, and textiles;

iv. Arthur Lasenby Liberty and the growing popularity of the progressive-looking fabrics, objects, and jewelry sold by him (in the 1890s);

v. George Frampton and Alfred Gilbert and their continued ventures in the "New Sculpture" (also Frampton's jewelry designs), in spite of their self-professed ambivalence towards Art Nouveau;

vi. Charles Robert Ashbee and his search

for a new decorative design; and

vii. the artist potter William de Morgan and his experimentation in Persian colors and the innovative luster glazes and firing techniques he achieved.

66. Quotations from Symposium I/ III: "L'Art Nouveau: What is It and What is Thought of It?" reported in *The Magazine of Art*, Vol. 2, 1904, pp. 209-213 and 324-327.

67. Quotation from the article "L'Art Nouveau," by L. F. Day, concerning the Exposition Universelle in Paris, in *The Art Journal*, Vol. 62, 1900, pp. 293-297.

68. *Art Nouveau, 1890–1914*, edited by Paul Greenhalgh, Part IV, "The Metropolis and the Designer," 28: "Louis Comfort Tiffany and New York," by Alice Cooney Frelinghuysen, p. 401.

69. In France and Belgium, names other than Art Nouveau included "Style Moderne," "Style Guimard," "Style Coup de Fouet," "Style Mucha," "Style Jules Verne," "Art Belle Époque," "Art Fin-de-Siècle," "Style Métro," and "Yachting Style;" elsewhere, "Wave Style," "Lily Style," "Eel Style," and "NoodleStyle."

70. *Art Nouveau in Munich*, "Introduction," by Kathryn Bloom Hiesinger, p. 23.

71. *Art Nouveau, 1890–1914*, edited by Paul Greenhalgh, Part I, "Introduction," 1: "The Style and the Age," by Paul Greenhalgh, p. 26.

72. *Art Nouveau, International and National Styles in Europe*, by Jeremy Howard, p. 17.

73. As with Art Nouveau, the term Jugendstil can be – and is – used in two distinct ways; firstly, as the name of the specific style, peculiar to Germany, as discussed in German art history, and, secondly, with adjectival implication, in general reference to the characteristics of the German style in descriptions of decoration/ornament in the various Art Nouveau variant movements in Central Europe and elsewhere.

74. August Endell (1871–1925), in addition to being a student of aesthetics, philosophy, and psychology, with strong opinions on the role of perception and its impact on feelings, was a self-taught artist and architect, theoretician, writer, and teacher. At first, under the influence of Obrist, he was an enthusiastic participant and influential designer in the expressive mode of Jugendstil in Munich through the turn of the century. Afterward, with a developing interest in the objective study of form in art, he founded and directed a school for design in Berlin in 1904–1914, during which time, his architecture and other design projects began to show an advancing concern with simplicity and utility. Between 1918 and the time of his death, he directed the Breslau Academy for Art and Craft.

75. Published in his essay "Was ich will" in 1901 in the magazine *Die Zeit* in Vienna.

76. Published in 1907 in Leipzig.

77. In 1899, the Grand Duke Ernst Ludwig of Hesse, grandson of Queen Victoria – supporting the revival of applied art as a major feature of life uniting artists and craftsmen – summoned seven artists – Peter Behrens, Rudolf Bosselt, Paul Bürck, Hans Christiansen, Ludwig Habich, and Patriz Huber – to Darmstadt to form an Artists' Colony (Künstlerkolonie), at the Mathildenhöhe, under the leadership of Joseph Maria Olbrich. There, Olbrich established a new architectonic phase of design, superseding the old order of style and ornament, in order to awaken a sense of modern design in Hesse. His aim was the eventual realization of freedom of expression as the goal of art and the recognition of mankind's right to beauty as a universal attribute of social achievement.

Through the time of his early death, his work urged his colleagues – and later artists at the Colony (on 3-year contracts, through 1914) – to seek a new, artistic future arising from a concern with aesthetic principles. The program was to represent art for all people based on beauty and simplicity and to mark a new direction that had little to do with Franco/Belgian Art Nouveau. For the colony's 1900 exhibition, rather than representing a single, consolidated, German style, each artist created his own conception of a unified model environment. A later exhibition of applied art in 1908 had a social, as well as an artistic, aim in presenting designs for workers' houses furnished with functional, tasteful, and affordable objects.

78. In 1898, after the end of his studies under Wagner at the Academy of Fine Arts in Vienna, Moravian-born Aloys Ludwig (1872–1969) joined Wagner's office as an architect and assistant to Wagner, becoming head of the studio after Joseph Maria Olbrich left for Darmstadt the following year. He went on to enjoy a long and brilliant, independent career in Austria.

79. *Art Nouveau, 1890–1914*, edited by Paul Greenhalgh, Part IV, "The Metropolis and the Designer," 20: "Secession in Vienna," by Gillian Naylor, p. 301.

80. *Art Nouveau, International and National Styles in Europe*, by Jeremy Howard, p. 66.

81. The Zsolnay tile celebrating the Millenium reproduces an etching/ illustration that the Finnish artist Axel Gallen produced in 1895 – for the magazine *Pan* – of Paul Scheerbart's *The King's Song*. The painting/illustration/tile depicts "a naked couple on a celestial throne and in a swirling astral dance." Jeremy Howard goes on to comment on the image's "dynamic unity" fusing Symbolist philosophy and Art Nouveau design, achieved through the "cloisonnist outline, black and white contrasts, flattening of elements on the … surface ... (and the inclusion of) three pairs of hands rising ... to hold aloft glasses and apples amidst floating membrane forms" (quoted from *Art Nouveau, International and National Styles in Europe*, by Jeremy Howard, p. 163).

82. *Art Nouveau, International and National Styles in Europe*, by Jeremy Howard, page 84.

83. *Art Nouveau, 1890–1914*, edited by Paul Greenhalgh, Part IV, "The Metropolis and the Designer, 25: "The New Art in Prague," by Milena Lamarova, p. 369.

84. *Ibid*, p. 371.

85. *The Decorative Arts in France*, by Yvonne Brunhammer and Suzanne Tise – quoted in *Art Nouveau, 1890–1914*, edited by Paul Greenhalgh, Part IV, "The Metropolis and the Designer," 19: "Munich: Secession

and Jugendstil," by Gillian Naylor, p. 297.

86.   Other third prizes were won by Adolf Eckhardt (a teacher at the Hamburg Arts and Crafts School) for *Diamond* (*Carreau*) and Nikolaus Dauber (a painter in Marburg-on-the-Lahn) for *Red* (*Roth*), whilst Gertrud Kilz for *Yellow and Green* (*Gelb und Grün*), Paul Bürck, Ludwig Paffendorf (an architect in Cologne), Hans Schlicht (an architect in Dresden), and Margarethe von Brauchitsch received Honorable Mention, as did also Eckhardt for *Life* (*Leben*).

87.   *Deutsche Kunst und Dekoration*, Volume 3, October 1898 – March 1899, pp. 187–190.

88.   *Art Nouveau in Munich*, edited by Kathryn Bloom Hiesinger: "August Endell," Exhibit # 34: Chest, 1899, described by Dr. Hans Ottomeyer, p. 58.

89.   Illustrated in *Dekorative Vorbilder*, Vol. 17, 1906, plate 5, top row, center.

90.   See: p. 148.

91.   In *Jugendstil-Fliesen aus den Sammlungen Husmann, Bahte, Actiengesellschaft Norddeutsche Steingutfabrik*.

92.   In *Kacheln & Fliesen im Jugendstil*.

93.   Clinker is a high-fired, partially vitrified form of brick, often with an enameled or glazed surface. The use of enameled brick, in particular, dates from between two- and three-thousand years ago and, in modern times, it seems to have become fashionable, for some time from the late nineteenth century on, as an alternative aesthetic to regular brickwork, popular with architects and designers. Fireproof, moisture-resistant, sanitary, and light-reflecting, it is an excellent material for facing walls, both interior and exterior, in courtyards, open passageways, stairwells, lobbies, etc., and can be produced in any color (most effectively, white, blue, red, and brown).

94.   The German business-designation term "GmbH" (Gesellschaft mit beschränkter Haftung), also "mbH," indicates a form of limited liability company in Germany, Austria, and some other Central European countries; the German "AG" (Aktiengesellschaft) refers to a stock corporation in Germany and Austria, etc., owned by shareholders (with liability limited by their shareholding); the German "KG" (Kommanditgesellschaft) refers to a limited liability partnership, established in Germany, Austria, etc., by general partners (with unlimited liability) and limited partners (whose liability is restricted to the amounts of their fixed contributions to the partnership); the German "GmbH & Co. KG" refers to a limited partnership in Germany, Austria, etc., in which the sole general partner is a limited liability company. The French terms "SARL" and "SA" are used, in France, Belgium, etc., to designate two forms of limited liability company, the latter for a, probably, larger, alternative, corporate form. The abbreviation "NV" denotes a Dutch (or, possibly, Belgian) public limited liability company owned by shareholders (but whose shares may be traded on a public stock market).

95.   Chamotte – or schamotte – as used in the titles of many companies listed here, is defined as a refractory, ceramic, raw material, also known as grog, which is ground-up and, often, pulverized, fired clay, consisting of a high percentage of silica and alumina, resistant to heating shock, and reducing shrinkage, preventing warping and cracking, aiding in even drying, and adding structural strength.

96.   See also: MARIENBERG.

97.   See also: SCHARVOGEL.

98.   Possibly, in this context, a variety of stoneware, containing a high proportion of chamotte.

99.   For further information, see: *Die Kunst*, 1904/1905, pp. 393 and 396-397.

100.   See: OSTERATH/OSTARA.

101.   See also: NSTG.

102.   After leaving his Kandern studio in 1913, and before opening his Karlsruhe studio in 1916, Läuger marked much of his work with an "LM" monogram, incised.

103.   "Majolica" is a historical term originally applied to wares covered with an opaque tin glaze, thought to have originated in Majorca. The word was used in the nineteenth century to indicate ceramic ware with a colored glaze. In the tile industry, the majolica glaze was superseded, in the later nineteenth century, by the translucent color glazes that are such an important feature of Art Nouveau tiles.

Further confusion might stem from the fact that, in the nineteenth and early twentieth centuries, in the German tile industry, the glazed, single-colored, plain, square tile, used extensively in wall installations, was often referred to as a "majolica tile" (Majolikafliese).

104.   Plates (Teller) or wall-plates (Wandteller) – so described in the "Small Art Register" ("Serienverzeichnis der Kleinkunst, 1901–2001"), pp. 82-85, published in *Karlsruher Majolika 1901 bis 2001*, edited by Monika Bachmayer and Peter Schmitt – refer to circular plaques, in most instances (supposedly) with foot rings, intended for hanging as wall decorations. For the years 1901 through 1904, not less than forty-three of these – primarily by Thoma, Süs, Haas, with a few by Karl Würtenberger and Hans von Volkmann – are listed in the "Register," along with fifteen tiles/reliefs (Fliesen/Relieffliesen) and twenty-nine decorative, tray-like panels (Platten) of one kind or another.

105.   See: DESIGNERS, Greiner.

106.   See: DESIGNERS, Ruf.

107.   See: DESIGNERS, Vollmer.

108.   After leaving the Manufactory in 1929 and opening a home studio in Lörrach (Baden-Württemberg), Läuger usually marked his work with his initials "M.L.," incised.

109.   See: MEISSEN.

110.   See also: BROITZEM.

111.   Having survived the Second World War attack on Dresden, the installation remains, today, one of the major sightseeing venues in the city.

112.   *Reports on the Vienna Universal Exhibition of 1873*: Professor Archer on "Pottery and Porcelain," published 1874, in London, by the Great Britain Royal Commission for the Vienna Universal Exhibition.

113.   See: POLKO.

114.   See: TEICHERT (ERNST TEICHERT MEISSEN), SAXONIA, S. O. F., and SOMAG.

115. "VEB" indicated a nationalized, state-owned enterprise.

116. Richard Mutz, along with Max Läuger and Jakob Julius Scharvogel, is considered to have been among the very finest of German ceramists of the early twentieth century.

117. The long history of industrialized ceramic-pipe and chimney-pot manufacture in Germany began in 1863 at the Polko factory.

118. See also: DARMSTADT.

119. In 1897/1898 – to negate import restrictions – another Servais branch was opened near Radom in the Ruthenian (Rusyn) area of eastern Poland.

120. It is supposed that, for a brief time – presumably, in the first decade of the twentieth century – the Sinzig factory was engaged in a very limited wall-tile production.

121. See also POLKO.

122. Marks already used from the first year of production in 1872.

123. See: SOMAG.

124. The ninth edition of the *Register of Ceramic Manufacturers* in 1906 lists the Saxony Stove and Chamotte Wares Factory under the S. O. F. name (on p. 423) with "Saxony Stove Factory in Meissen AG" as its telegram address. In the twelfth edition in 1913, it is still listed under that name, though with "SOMAG" as its telegram address and showing "SOMAG" as the company's mark, and its manufacture described as "earthenware wall tiles of all kinds, weather-proof tiles, architectural ceramics, tiled stoves, chimneys, and heater covers." However, through 1913, no listing is included in editions of the *Register* for the Saxony Stove and Wall Tile Factory. Also, in the twelfth edition of the *Clay Industry Newspaper* in 1914 – Part I, p. 574 – the company is referred to by its original name.

125. In the absence of definitive evidence, it might be hypothesized that wall tiles produced in the early years of the Saxony Stove and Chamotte Wares / Wall Tile Company (S. O. F. / SOMAG) bore "SOF" markings, as would indeed many later pressings of those designs. Tiles from designs of a later date, presumably, bore the "SOMAG" mark; it might indeed be argued that these, probably, would not have been so identified as Saxony Stove and Wall Tile Factory production until (or even after) the time of the branch-works addition, in 1910, for the expansion of wall-tile manufacture.

126. See: M.O.&P.F.

127. See: S. O. F.

128. See: M.O.&P.F., SOMAG, S. O. F., and SAXONIA.

129. After the defeat of France in 1940, the area, then known as Alsace and Moselle, was not officially annexed again by Germany through 1945, though, as Administrative Divisions West March / Upper Rhine (Reichsgau Westmark/Oberrhein), it was administered from Berlin during that time.

130. See: p. 27.

131. See: p. 27.

132. As restored.

133. First used in Germany in the 1840s.

134. By 1900, manufacture at the Merzig factory included the production, in single colors, of 4-, 6-, and 8-sided floor and pavement tiles.

135. Tiles bearing a mark "VILLEROY & BOCH METTLACH DT. LISSA" are known.

136. Interestingly, it is reported:
    i. in the *Register of Ceramics Manufacturers*, Ninth Edition, 1906, p. 256, that, by 1906, the Schramberg location of Villeroy & Boch was under the management of a Dr. Lindhorst; and
    ii. in the *Marken Lexikon, Porzellan und Keramik Report, 1885–1935*, by Dieter Zuehlsdorff, Vol. 1, p. 606: "3-1152," that, in 1912, Lindhorst was still manager and director at the time the Schramberg factory closed. See also: VON SCHWARZ.

137. In the the first edition of the *Register of Ceramics Manufacturers* of 1883, the J. von Schwarz Majolica and Terracotta Factory announced/advertised "wall tiles" ("Wandplatten") among its list of products at that time, and – through at least the date of the later, ninth edition of 1906 – its advertisements continued to refer to "furniture inlays and wall tiles" ("Möbeleinlagen und Wandfliesen"). However, no other references have been located, in previous literature or source material, regarding the industrial production of tiles for wall-*installation* in the firm's history. A notice in the advertising section of *Innendekoration*, No. 12, of 1901, mentions the company's tiles for "wall-*decoration*" ("Fliesen für Wanddecoration"), presumably referring to Luber's wall-hung, artistic tile pictures. It is possible that the earlier reference might, also, have been in regard to such decorative *plaques* – though, of course, pre-Luber – intended for wall-hanging; it is likely – or, at least, possible – that these items of the early to mid-1880s would, therefore, have been of the same genre as the "wall-plates" ("Wandteller / Teller") produced, for instance, by the Majolica Manufactory of the Grand Duchy of Baden at Karlsruhe and so-named in the "Small Art Register," pp. 82-85, published in *Karlsruher Majolika 1901 bis 2001*. No examples of von Schwarz tiles – manufactured for wall-installation – are known to exist.

138. See: V & B SCHRAMBERG, p. 186.

139. For example, tile #627, rectangular shape, pictured in *Carl Sigmund Lube*r, by Wolfgang Koenig and Rudolf Weichselbaum, p. 81, with authors' Register # 90/91.

140. For example, tile #1010, of irregular shape, pictured *Ibid*, p. 106, with authors' Register #221.

141. Achieved, at other locations, through collaboration with pewter and similar metal manufacturers and other appropriate, corresponding specialist firms, likewise sharing the Luber / Von Schwarz goal of high-quality, industrial art.

142. For example, small tray #507, pictured Ibid, p. 135, with authors' Register #26.

143. For example, tray #1618, pictured Ibid, p. 142, with authors' Register #240.

144. *Ibid*, p. 49.

145. *Jugendstilfliesen*, by Michael Weisser, p. 12.

146. See: KAUFFMANN.

1471. See: SERVAIS ii). Servais & Cie. Witterschlick Clayworks.

148. See: NSTG.

149. See: DESIGNERS: BOSSE.

150. The company is now – from 1997/1978 – a subsidiary of Lafarge SA.

151. Vol. 51, October 1922 - March 1923, pp. 59-61: "Tiled Stoves ("Kachelöfen").

152. The word "Ziegel" in the company's German name is usually translated as "roof tile" or, otherwise, indicates a variety of brick used in wall construction.

153. *The Collected Writings of Hermann August Seger*, Vol. II, C. II: "Reports from the Vienna Exposition 1873," p. 851.

154. See: HUNGARIAN SECESSIONIST TILES.

155. The Hardtmuth company of Budweis and Vienna was probably most famous for its research into lead-free glazes as well as its production of pencils.

156. *Commercial Relations of the United States with Foreign Countries during the years 1882 and 1883*, Vol. 1, published, in 1884, at the Government Printing Office, in Washington, by the United States Bureau of Foreign and Domestic Commerce.

157. *The Artist: An Illustrated Monthly Record of Arts and Crafts and Industries*, Vol. 26, October 1899 – January 1900, page 108.

158. *Adressbuch der keramischen Industrie*, Ninth Edition, 1906, p. 601.

159. By 1905/1906, the Unter-Themenau Claywares Factory, established in1876, employed seven hundred workers.

160. Principally to Germany, Austria, and neighboring countries in Central Europe.

161. See: pages 94 and 201.

162. The number of wall- and floor-tile designs documented as being by Behrens is not as large as sometimes assumed by some collectors/dealers. However, there are several designs with Behrens-type ornamentation, which, in commercial advertising and negotiation today, are sometimes (perhaps, more and more) "loosely" attributed to the master. Where documentary evidence is not available proving that designs originated with Behrens himself (or other designers such as Van de Velde), descriptions should cautiously suggest merely that they are of his (or their) inspiration.

163. See also: page 8.

164. *Die Kunst / Dekorative Kunst*, 1904/1905, pp. 402-403; these and other illustrations accompany the article "Peter Behrens – Düsseldorf," by Julius Meier-Graefe, pp. 381-390, 393, and 396-397. See also: *Peter Behrens und Nürnberg*, edited by Peter-Klaus Schuster, p. 265, #9.

165. *Die Kunst / Dekorative Kunst*, 1904/1905, pp. 396-397.

166. *Illustrated in Journal of Design History*, Vol.7, No. 1, 1994: "The Werkbund in Delmenhorst: A Forgotten Episode in German Design History," by Matthew Jeffries, p. 15; also (along with historical designs for fabrics and textiles), in *Die Kunst / Dekorative Kunst*, 1904/1905, pp. 418-422 and 425-426.

167. See also: p. 144

168. Full name: School of the Imperial/ Royal Museum for Arts and Crafts, Berlin.

169. See: p. 139.

170. See: p. 164.

171. Full name: Imperial/Royal Technical School for Ceramics and Stove Construction, Landshut.

172. *The Artist: An Illustrated Monthly Record of Arts and Crafts and Industries*, Vol. 26, October 1899 – January 1900, p. 108.

173. Vol. 51, October 1922 - March 1923, pp. 105 and 109.

174. See also: pp. 26 and 27.

175. See: p. 106.

176. *Jugendstil*, by Irmela Franzke.

177. Illustrated, *Ibid*, p. 235.

178. Illustrated in *The Artist, An Illustrated Monthly Record of Arts, Crafts and Industries*, November 1900: "Glass and Ceramic Industry at the Paris Exhibition, II. – Ceramic," by W. Fred, p. 131.

179. See pp. 140 & 141.

180. See: pp. 25 and 164.

181. See also: GERMAN TILE MANUFACTURERS … DARMSTADT/SCHARVOGEL.

182. *Deutsche Kunst und Dekoration*, Vol. 51, October 1922 – March 1923, p. 236.

183. *Collecting Victorian Tiles*, by Terence A. Lockett, p. 221.

184. *Ibid*.

SECTION 3: BIBLIOGRAPHY

Adressbuch der keramischen Industrie, First and Ninth Editions. Coburg, Germany: Verlag Müller & Schmidt, 1883/1906.

Anscombe, Isabelle, and Charlotte Gere. *Arts & Crafts in Britain and America*. New York, NY: Rizzoli International Publications, Inc., 1978.

Archer, Professor. "Professor Archer on Pottery and Porcelain." *Reports on the Vienna Universal Exhibition of 1873*. London, England: Great Britain Royal Commission for the Vienna Universal Exhibition, n.d.

Bachmayer, Monika, and Peter Schmitt (editors). *Karlsruher Majolika 1901 bis 2001*. Karlsruhe, Germany: G. Braun Verlag, 2001.

Baeck, Mario, and Ulrich Hamburg, Johan Kamermans (ed.), Hans van Lemmen (ed.), Thomas Rabenau, and Bart Verbrugge. *Industrial Tiles, 1840–1940*. Otterlo, Netherlands: "published as part of a travelling exhibition" with catalog produced by Nederlands Tegelmuseum, Otterlo, 2004.

Bott, Gerhard (editor). *Kunsthandwerk um 1900, Jugendstil*. Darmstadt, Germany: Hessisches Landesmuseum, 1973.

Bott, Gerhard (editor). *Ziele und Geschichte der Ausstellungen der Darmstädter Künstlerkolonie: "Ein Dokument Deutscher Kunst"* (1901 exhibition of architecture, painting, sculpture and handicraft). Darmstadt, Germany: Hessisches Landesmuseum, 1973.

Brunhammer, Yvonne, and Suzanne Tise. *The Decorative Arts in France*. New York, NY: Rizzoli, 1992.

Clancy, Jonathan, and Martin Eidelberg. *Beauty in Common Things: American Arts and Crafts Pottery from the Two Red Roses Foundation*. Palm Harbor, Florida: Two Red Roses Foundation, 2008.

Csenkey, Eva, and Agota Steinert and Piroska Acs (editors/curators). *Hungarian Ceramics from the Zsolnay Manufactory, 1853–2001*, published in conjunction with the exhibition held at the Bard Graduate Center for Studies in the Decorative Arts, Design and Culture, New York, New York. New Haven / New York: Yale University Press, 2002.

Day, L. F. "L'Art Nouveau." *The Art Journal*, Vol. 62, 1900 (article concerning the Exposition Universelle, in Paris). London, England: H. Virtue & Co. Ltd., 1900.

Dekorative Vorbilder, Volume 17, 1906. Stuttgart, Germany: Julius Hoffmann, 1906.

Deutsche Kunst und Dekoration, Vol. 13, October 1903 – March 1904, also Vol. 51, October 1922 – March 1923. Darmstadt, Germany: Alexander Koch, 1904/1923.

Die Kunst/Dekorative Kunst, various volumes, 1904/1905 and other years. Munich, Germany: Verlagsanstalt F. Bruckmann AG., 1905 and other years.

Eidelberg, Martin. "5: Art Pottery." *The Arts and Crafts Movement in America 1876–1916*, Robert Judson Clark (editor). Princeton, New Jersey: Princeton University Press, 1972.

Erlebach, Jürgen, and Jürgen Schimanski (editors). *Westerwälder Steinzeug, die neue Ära, 1900–1930, Jugendstil und Werkbund*. Dusseldorf, Germany: Contur Verlag, 1987.

Franzke, Irmela. *Jugendstil*. Munich, Germany: Battenberg Verlag, 1987.

Gaethke, Birte, and Manuela Junghölter. *Wo Mauerblumen blühen*. Husum, Germany: Husum Druck- und Verlagsgesellschaft mbH u. Co. KG, 2004.

Gebauer, Heinrich. *Die Volkswissenschaft im Königreiche Sachsen*, Vol. II. Dresden, Germany: Wilhelm Bänsch Königliche Sächsische Hofverlagsbuchhandlung, 1893.

Forrer, Dr. Robert. *Geschichte der europäischen Fliesen-Keramik vom Mittelalter bis zum Jahre 1900*. Strassburg, now, France: Verlag von Schlesier u. Schweikhardt, 1901.

Greenhalgh, Paul. "Part I, Introduction, 1: The Style and the Age." *Art Nouveau, 1890–1914*, Paul Greenhalgh (editor). London, England: V & A Publications, 2000.

Greenhalgh, Paul. "Part II, The Creation of Meaning, 2: Alternative Histories." *Art Nouveau, 1890–1914*, Paul Greenhalgh (editor). London, England: V & A Publications, 2000.

Greenhalgh, Paul. "Part V, Conclusion, 30: A Strange Death." *Art Nouveau, 1890–1914*, Paul Greenhalgh (editor). London, England: V & A Publications, 2000.

Hamburg, Ulrich. "Abstraktion des Ornaments." *Trödler u. Sammeln Journal*, April 2001. Reichertshausen, Germany: Gemi-Verlags GmbH, 2001.

Hamburg, Ulrich. "Boizenburger Wandplatten." *Trödler u. Sammeln Journal,* June 2003. Reichertshausen, Germany: Gemi-Verlags GmbH, 2003.

Hars, Eva. *Zsolnay Ceramics Factory Pecs*. Bulgaria/Hungary: Helikon Editions Ltd., 1997.

Hecht, Dr. Hermann, and Eduard Cramer. *The Collected Writings of Hermann August Seger, prepared from the records of the Royal Porcelain Factory at Berlin and translated by members of the American Ceramic Society*, edited by Albert V. Bleininger, Ohio State University. Easton, Pennsylvania: American Ceramic Society and the Chemical Publishing Company, 1902; copyright 1903 by Edward Hart.

Howard, Jeremy. *Art Nouveau, International and National Styles in Europe*. Manchester, England: Manchester University Press, 1996.

Jackson, Lesley. *Twentieth Century Pattern Design*. London, England: Octopus Publishing Group, 2002.

Jeffries, Matthew. "The Werkbund in Delmenhorst: A Forgotten Episode in German Design History." *Journal of*

Design History, Vol.7, No. 1. Oxford, England: Oxford University Press, 1994.

Journal of the Franklyn Institute. Philadelphia, Pennsylvania: 1918.

Keramische Monatshefte, Illustrierte Monatsschrift für die Gesamte Kunst- & Bau- Keramik, Vol. 3, 1906 (and other issues). Halle, Germany: Wilhelm Knapp, 1906 and other years.

Kinchin, Juliet. "Part IV, The Metropolis and the Designer, 21: Glasgow: The Dark Daughter of the North." *Art Nouveau, 1890–1914,* Paul Greenhalgh (editor). London, England: V & A Publications, 2000.

Knekties, Ines. "Flora & Fauna satt." *KeramikMagazin,* Nr. 3, June/July 2005. Frechen, Germany: Ritterbach Verlag, GmbH, 2005.

König, Wolfgang, and Rudolf Weichselbaum. *Carl Sigmund Luber.* Einbeck, Germany: König-Weichselbaum Verlag, 2006.

Lamarova, Milena. "Part IV, The Metropolis and the Designer, 25: The New Art in Prague." *Art Nouveau, 1890–1914,* Paul Greenhalgh (editor). London, England: V & A Publications, 2000.

Lockett, Terence A. *Collecting Victorian Tiles.* Woodbridge, Suffolk, England: Antique Collectors' Club, 1979.

Magazin Sammeln, Nr. 53, June/July 2005: "Industrielle Fliesen." Schaffhausen, Germany: Sammeln AG, 2005.

Naylor, Gillian. "Part IV, The Metropolis and the Designer, 19: Munich: Secession and Jugendstil." *Art Nouveau, 1890–1914,* Paul Greenhalgh (editor). London, England: V & A Publications, 2000.

Naylor, Gillian. "Part IV, The Metropolis and the Designer, 20: Secession in Vienna." *Art Nouveau, 1890–1914,* Paul Greenhalgh (editor). London, England:

V & A Publications, 2000.

Roggmann, Bettina (curator). *Jugendstil-Fliesen aus den Sammlungen Husmann, Bahte, Actiengesellschaft Norddeutsche Steingutfabrik,* catalog of exhibition at Museum Kellinghusen, 3.27 – 6.19.1988. Kellinghusen, Germany: Museum Kellinghusen, 1988.

Schuster, Peter-Klaus (editor). *Peter Behrens und Nürnberg.* Munich, Germany: Prestel, 1980.

Simmermacher, René (editor). *Jugendstil-Fliesen,* collection catalog of the Baden State Museum, Karlsruhe. Karlsruhe, Germany: Verlag dtp-Realisation, 2000.

The Artist, An Illustrated Monthly Record of Arts, Crafts, and Industries, various issues in 1899 and 1900. New York, New York: Truslove, Hanson, & Comba. 1899/1900.

The Magazine of Art, #28: "L'Art Nouveau: What is It and What is Thought of It?" (Symposium I/III), January 1904, No. 257. London, England, and New York, NY: Cassell, Petter, Galpin & Co., 1904.

Thieme, Ulrich, and Fred C. Willis (editors). *Allgemeines Lexikon der Bildenen Künstler,* various volumes, 1921 and other years. Leipzig, Germany: Verlag E. A. Seemann, 1921 and other years.

Tschudi-Madsen, Stephan. *The Art Nouveau Style.* Mineola, NY: Dover Publications, Inc., 2002 – unabridged republication of Sources of Art Nouveau, originally published in 1956 by H. Aschehoug, Oslo, Norway.

Van Lemmen, Hans, and Bart Verbrugge. *Art Nouveau Tiles.* New York, NY: Rizzoli International Publications Inc., 1999.

Van Lemmen, Hans, and John Malam (editors). *Fired Earth.* Shepton Beauchamp,

Somerset, England: Richard Dennis Publications, 1991.

Vitochova, Marie, and Jindrich Kejr and Jiri Vsetocka. *Prague and Art Nouveau.* Prague, Czech Republic: V. Raji Publishing House, 1995.

Weisser, Michael. *Jugendstilfliesen.* Frankfurt-am-Main, Germany: Verlag Dieter Fricke, 1983/1989.

Weisser, Michael. *Kacheln & Fliesen im Jugendstil, Keramische Ornamentträger zwischen Handwerkskunst und Kunstindustrie.* Münster, Germany: F. Coppenrath Verlag, 1980.

Weisser, Michael. *Wessel's Wandplatten-Fabrik Bonn.* Cologne, Germany: Rheinland-Verlag GmbH on commission from Rudolf Habelt-Verlag GmbH, Bonn, Germany, 1975.

Zühlsdorff, Dieter. *Marken Lexikon, Porzellan und Keramik Report, 1885–1935,* Vol. 1. Stuttgart, Germany: Arnoldsche Verlagsanstalt GmbH, 1988.

SECTION 4: APPENDICES

Appendix A: Register of Names

Albert, Ernst (1835–1908): 166, 171
Albert, Heinz: 166
Amberg, Adolf (1878–1913): 166
Apati-Abt, Sandor (1870–1916): 195, 201
Ashbee, Charles Robert (1863–1942): 72, 80, see Note 64, p. 224-225
Baillie Scott, Mackay Hugh (1865–1945): 72, 77, 80
Baarmann, Arthur: 174
Balsanek, Antonin (1865–1921): 154-155
Bankel, Christof: 157
Bankel, Georg (1851–1926): 157
Bankel, Georg, Jr.: 157
Basch, Oskar: 200
Baudoux, Henri Clément: 60
Beardsley, Aubrey Vincent (1872–1898): see Note 65, p. 224
Becking, Eduard (1861–1934): 176, 201
Beck, Jean (1862–1938): 134, 137, 186, 201
Behrens, Peter (1868–1940): 8, 10-11, 33, 75, 77-79, 81, 134, 136, 140-141, 144, 161, 167, 182, 186, 201-203
Belz, Johann (1873–1957): 202
Benedikt, Jaroslav: 155
Benes, Jan: 155
Bicheroux, Max: 158
Bigot, Alexandre (1862–1927): 62, see also Note 38, p. 223
Bing, Siegfried (1838–1905): 216, see also Note 61, p. 224
Bloch, Bernard (1836–1909): 197
Bloch, Oskar (d. 1927): 197
Bloch, Arthur: 197
Bloch, Otto: 197
Blumenfeld, Richard (1863–1943): 182, 211
Boch, Edmond (1845–1931): 185
Boch, Eugen (1809–1898): 62, 184-185
Boch, Jean François (1782–1858): 62, 184
Boch, Pierre Joseph (1737–1818): 184
Boch / von Boch-Galhau, René (1843–1908): 63, 182, 185
Bosse, Walter (1904–1979): 152, 192, 202
Bosselt, Rudolph (1871–1938): 202-203
Boulenger, Hippolyte (1836–1892): 61
Boulton, William: 8
Bourdet, Eugène François (1874–1954): 62
Bradley, Will (1868–1962): 75

Breuhaus, Fritz August (1883–1960): 165, 203
Brouwer, Dirk ten Cate (1885–1962): 158
Bucher, Herta (1898–1960): 15, 152-153, 192-193, 203
Bürck, Paul Wilhelm (1878–1947): 138-139, 203
Büttner, Hermann: 158
Bugatti, Carlo (1856–1940): 73
Chambers, John (1869–1945): 72
Chéret, Jules (1836–1932): 62
Christiansen, Hans (1866–1945): 75-76, 107, 138, 144, 148, 183, 186, 189, 203, 211
Cizek, Franz (1865–1946): 203
Clayton, John Richard (1860–1913): 74
Coleman, William Stephen (1829–1904): 72
Collinot, Eugène (d. 1892): 61
Colonna, Édouard (1862–1948): 75
Crane, Walter (1845–1910): 72, 74, 86
Darilek, Henrik (b. mid-to-late 1870s): 196, 203
Day, Lewis Foreman (1845–1910): 72, 74, 86
Deck, Théodore (1823–1891): 61
De Geiger, Baron Alexandre (1803–1891): 181
De Geiger, Paul (1837–1915): 181
De Morgan, William (1839–1917): 72, see also Note 65, pp. 224-225
Ditmar, Karl Rudolf (1818–1895): 197
Dresser, Christopher (1834–1904): 72, 86
Duensing, Hans: 158
Eckmann, Otto (1865–1902): 33, 75-76, 134, 137, 186, 203
Elchinger, Léon (1871–1942): 160-161, 203, 215
Elchinger, Wendelin (1809–1895): 160-161
Elmslie, George Grant (1869–1952): 75
Essenwein, August Ritter von (1831–1892): see Note 13, p. 222
Endell, Ernst Moritz August (1871–1925): 75, 147, see also Note 74, p. 225
Fahrenkamp, Emil (1885–1966): 165, 203
Feilner Tobias Christoph (1773–1839): see Note 15, p. 222
Feller, Josef: 15, 167, 218
Feuerriegel, Kurt (1880–1961): 161

Foster, Herbert Wilson (1848–1929): 72
Frampton, George (1860–1928): see Note 65, pp. 224-225
Gasteiger, Anna Sophie (1877–1954): 106, 178, 203-204
Gaudi, Antoni (1852–1926): 73
Gentil, Alphonse (1872–1933): 62
Geiger, Fritz: see Note 13, p. 222
Gies, Ludwig (1887–1966): 171, 182, 203
Gilbert, Alfred (1854–1934): 74, see also Note 65, pp. 224-225
Gillig, Joseph: 169
Godwin, Edward William (1833–1886): 58, 72
Goldscheider, Friedrich (1845–1897): 192
Gradl, Eugen: 138-139, 204
Gradl, Hermann (1869–1934): 186
Grand Duke Ernst Ludwig of Hesse and by Rhine (1868–1937): 159, 214, see also Note 77, p. 225
Grand Duke Friedrich I of Baden (1826–1907): 163
Grand Duke Wilhelm Ernst of Saxony-Weimar (1876–1923): 216
Grathes, Matthias: 62, 161, 171
Greber, Charles (1853–1935): 62
Greiner, Daniel (1872–1943): 161, 164, 204
Grenander, Alfred (1863–1931): 15, 182, 218
Gropius, Walter (1883–1969): 182
Gross, Karl (1869–1934): 161, 167, 204
Grossmann, Hans (1879–1949): 164, 204
Guimard, Hector (1867–1942): 62, 73
Gurschner, Gustav (1873–1970): 193
Gussmann, Otto Friedrich (1869–1926): 218
Haas, Hermann (1878–1935): 164, 205
Habich, Ludwig (1872–1949): 175
Hadasy, Sandor Pillo (b. 1886): 196
Hakenjos, Hermann, Sen. (1879–1961): 163
Hammel, Rudolf (1862–1937): 198, 205
Hartmann, Karl Otto (1861–1934): 205
Haustein, Paul (1880–1944): 160, 175, 189, 205, 214
Heinkel, Gustav (1907–1945): 164, 205
Hempel, Oswin (1876–1965): 167
Heytze, Johannes Cornelis (1873–1943): 59
Hildebrandt, Albrecht: 171

APPENDIX B

Register of Companies

APPENDIX C

General Index:

APPENDIX D

Location Names Past (German) and Present (with Relocation in the Czech Republic, except Where Otherwise Noted):

Bechin – Bechyne

Blanz – Blansko

Bodenbach (later, part of the city of Tetschen) – Podmokly (now, part of the city of Ducin)

Breslau – Wroclaw (Poland)

Brünn – Brno

Budweis – Budejovice

Bunzlau – Boleslawiec (Poland)

Cilli – Celje (Republic of Slovenia)

Eichwald – Dubi

Hohenstein – Uncin

Kasnau – Kasiiow

Königsaal – Sbrazlaw

Lemberg – Lviv (Ukraine)

Liegnitz – Legnica (Poland)

Liboje – Lipovec (Republic of Slovenia)

Obergrund (later, part of the city of Tetschen) – Horni Zleb (now, part of the city of Decin)

Ober Bris – Horni Briza

Olomuczan – Olomucany

Pardubitz – Pardubice

Podersam – Podborany

Pressburg – Bratislava (Slovakia)

Rakonitz – Rakovnik

Reichenberg – Liberec

Saargemünd (Imperial Territory Alsace-Lorraine / Administrative District West March) – Saarguemines (Moselle, Lorraine, France)

Schattau – Satov

Schönau – Sanov

Strassburg (Imperial Territory Alsace-Lorraine / Administrative District Upper Rhine) – Strasbourg (Bas-Rhin, Alsace, France)

Süfflenheim (Imperial Territory Alsace-Lorraine / Administrative District Upper Rhine) – Soufflenheim (Bas-Rhin, Alsace, France)

Teplitz – Teplice

Troppau (Austrian Silesia) – Opava

Turn – Trnovany

Unterthemenau – Postorna

Znaim – Znojmo

Other Schiffer Books by the Author:

Alternative American Ceramics, 1870-1955: The Other American Art Pottery. ISBN: 978-0-7643-3610-2, $59.99

Biographies in American Ceramic Art: 1870–1970. ISBN: 978-0-7643-3611-9

Other Schiffer Books on Related Subjects:

Art Nouveau Tiles: 1890–1914. Wendy Fowler & Sandy Harvey. ISBN: 978-0-7643-1441-4, $49.95

Designed by Molly Shields
Type set in Desdemona/Times New Roman

ISBN: 978-0-7643-4915-7
Printed in China

Published by Schiffer Publishing, Ltd.
4880 Lower Valley Road
Atglen, PA 19310
Phone: (610) 593-1777; Fax: (610) 593-2002
E-mail: Info@schifferbooks.com

For our complete selection of fine books on this and related subjects, please visit our website at www.schifferbooks.com. You may also write for a free catalog.

This book may be purchased from the publisher. Please try your bookstore first.

We are always looking for people to write books on new and related subjects. If you have an idea for a book, please contact us at proposals@schifferbooks.com.

Schiffer Publishing's titles are available at special discounts for bulk purchases for sales promotions or premiums. Special editions, including personalized covers, corporate imprints, and excerpts can be created in large quantities for special needs. For more information, contact the publisher.